Master and Disciple

Master
and
Disciple

The Cultural Foundations of
Moroccan Authoritarianism

Abdellah Hammoudi

The University of
Chicago Press
Chicago & London

ABDELLAH HAMMOUDI is professor of anthropology at Princeton University. He is the author of *The Victim and Its Masks: An Essay on Sacrifice and Masquerade in the Maghreb,* also published by the University of Chicago Press.

THE UNIVERSITY OF CHICAGO PRESS, CHICAGO 60637
THE UNIVERSITY OF CHICAGO PRESS, LTD., LONDON

© 1997 by The University of Chicago
All rights reserved. Published 1997

Printed in the United States of America

06 05 04 03 02 01 00 99 98 97   5 4 3 2 1

ISBN (cloth): 0-226-31527-4
ISBN (paper): 0-226-31528-2

Translated from the French manuscript, "Maître et disciple."

LIBRARY OF CONGRESS CATALOGING-IN-PUBLICATION DATA

Hammoudi, Abdellah.
    [Maître et disciple. English]
    Master and disciple : the cultural foundations of Moroccan authoritarianism / Abdellah Hammoudi.
        p.   cm.
    Includes bibliographical references (p.   ) and index.
    ISBN 0-226-31527-4. — ISBN 0-226-31528-2 (pbk.)
        1. Political culture—Morocco.   2. Authoritarianism—Morocco.
    3. Islam and politics—Morocco.   4. Morocco—Politics and
    government.   5. Islam and politics.   I. Title.
    JQ3949.A15H3613   1997   96-43270
    306.2′4′0964—dc20   CIP

C O N T E N T S

A Plea for Bounded Knowledge

Completing the present work took much longer than I expected. The first time I came close to formulating a coherent argument for it was in the spring of 1986 at the Wissenschaftskolleg, in Berlin, when I gave a paper on the subject of authoritarianism in Arab societies with an emphasis on Morocco. Since the publication of that paper (in the *Wissenschaftskolleg Jahrbuch* 1986), I could only sporadically pursue the research and the writing of what was to become *Master and Disciple*. Reasons for the long delay included duties of teaching, other publication deadlines, and the rather strenuous maturation of the project itself.

Writing about power relations in my own society, I found it difficult and exhausting to evade the multiple controls that impede and censor analysis. My very real sense of estrangement and daily maladjustment vis-à-vis the dominant structures of self and society was often paralyzing. That estrangement—which I could only partially unravel—informed the analytic process itself.

An ethnography of forms of domination and submission that play themselves out in important social sectors required a parallel work of introspection. Power relations, tactics, and strategies could not be written about without reaching a threshold where they made themselves manifest to, and unsettled, the investigator's sense of self. Although such introspection may not be explicit in these pages, it remains their underlying rebus, a counterpoint to the book's every statement. This personal introspection—one which recognizes the subject's ethical and political accountability even as it abdicates a transcendental subjectivity—becomes inseparable from the ethnographic inspection of human action and meaning.

My study of the cultural foundations of Moroccan authoritarianism shows how they were historically elaborated in struggles for the definition of the real. There is no philosophical foundationalism involved here, or any assumption of transhistorical "cultural frames" divorced from action and creation. Rather, building on Foucault's notion of *diagramme*, I describe how sets of emotional relations, such as master/disciple, evolved in mystic initiation, extended beyond Sufi circles, and attained a new credibility as the main operator of power relations. This unprecedented extension materialized in the precolonial diffusion of Sufi networks intimately connected with the state. But a thorough and systematic reordering of discourse and action occurred only under colonial and postcolonial rule. At this stage a "normalization"—under particular regimes of managing words in specific spheres of action—reached its full force. The emergent social frames imposed the "knower" (al-ʿārif) as the principle of knowledge. This in turn created a situation of generalized perils, pervaded by the sense of a radical reshaping of things and lives—a situation, that is, in which a new symbolic violence constructs a new "order of things."

Symbolic violence, as is well known, concerns, not domination per se, but the domination of the constructed image of the self. Defined in this way, it cannot be posed as separate from or beyond communication. "Power," then, is not an analytic alternative to "culture." Symbolic violence implies a communicative field in which fear, uncertainty, and the precariousness of one's own mastery of body affect the capacity cognitively to define the real and the self within that real. Such a field insinuates its web and dynamic snares by turning people into guarded individualities. The coercive apparatus generates terror through repressive measures, of course, but perhaps more durably through undermining the *corps propre*, and in extreme cases slowly eradicating it. Subjects become impotent at producing interpretive concepts to account for the oppressive milieu created; that milieu thus defeats the formation of discourses that can compete with those promoted by (and promoting) the authoritarian state.

Reflecting on this threshold of enunciability—i.e., a threshold at which enunciation is stimulated or discouraged—it became clear to me that the process of selection, rather than the epistemic conditions of selection, is, again, the crucial aspect of "rarefaction" of discourse. In other words, the work of selection does not simply take place at the level of discourse itself. Considering this process led me to another conclusion, which complements the first: in the work of the "disciplines" the power–knowledge connection itself remains obscure. While the control admittedly inherent in knowledge is unraveled, its power as knowledge is left analytically untouched. Here I want to stress the emotional energies invested in the process of knowing itself and in the consideration of the institutions involved in selection and repression (which is to say of any production) which give a concrete plausibility to discursive formations.

What authorizes discourse, or makes it possible for it to be authorized, does not seem to be contingent on epistemic structures as they are narrowly defined by Foucault. For, such an approach, despite vigorous contention to the contrary, still rests on the major assumption of structuralist thinking in the priority it gives to pure concepts and conceptual architectonics in the advent of discursive formations. Indeed, for Foucault, rarefaction, the principle he identifies as responsible for the authorization of the enunciated, is inseparable from power relations. However, what it proceeds from remains outside the scope of his analytics. As it appears in the case I examine here, rarefaction proceeds from the symbolic intimidation of utterance, from the repeated microdefeats of conceptualization. These microdefeats in the formation of concepts result from emotional inconsistencies generated by symbolic violence, a phenomenon comparable to motor disorders, verging on paralysis, that some particularly radical experience of fear can engender.

※

The brand of authoritarianism I describe in this book is one that produces conceptual impotence. It came into being in a historical moment filled with tensions and struggles. The issues in dispute were definitions of the postcolonial nation and state, prime movers and beneficiaries of this new configuration, and its future. The first chapter concerns arguments and risks taken by particular protagonists. Symbolic violence forced people back into the "politics of notables": leadership through patronage as the dominant mode of political association, which in this context works as a cultural form. Thus power does not supersede culture, nor does it turn into (mere!) ideology, as political scientists often assume. The same intimidation which centered allegiances around personal ties could not exhaust it. Networks among persons gave energy to an underground "sociality" rallying around food and warm conversation. This informal hospitality countered emotional impairment and impotence of conceptual formulation.

Indeed such informal "civil society" supported the writing of the present book in spite of the devastating effects and scars left by symbolic violence. Power—the empowerment to speak up—is here dependent on culture rather than the reverse.

This last point brings me to issues of ethnography and imagination. A post-orientalist anthropology as "cultural critique" has set its goals of mapping relationships between knowledge and power; deconstructing bounded units (tribe, village, town, nation, subject, book, master narrative, etc.); and freeing the imagination by straddling "borderlands." Theorists today strive to perform as a ubiquitous eye (or is it a body?) in a ceaseless movement along transnational lines of the chaotic circulation of commodities. Paradoxically, the rhetoric of this critical anthropology often leaves me perplexed; its proponents have thus far failed to engage issues that raise some passion in the societies the ethnographer crosses or travels through. The sufferings under authoritarian rule and fervent debates about how to change the predicament of a postcolonial society and state join me to many people deeply engaged with Moroccan society and its plight. This connection makes my approach both bounded and unbounded. My knowledge was bounded by the very issues that monopolized my associates' attention. Their particularity derived from the ways in which we felt and discussed them, and from the forms they took in our discourse and action, notwithstanding the fact that other people in other places experienced plights comparable to ours. Unbounded was the very fact that I speak from a particular position, the definition of which is, of course, not exclusively local. The utopian imagination, nurtured by transnational experience, is the very engine of bounded knowledge as I tried to define it. Unbounded approach and bounded knowledge constitute the vantage point from which I speak—or speak up—to issues as an anthropologist, with the risks and responsibilities that enunciation entails. It is that particularity which makes critical anthropology, with its insistence on the unbound, the transnational, and the deconstruction of representation both pertinent to my enterprise and, in its realization, different from it, insofar as critical anthropology as it is practiced (at least by the majority of my colleagues here in the United States) does not seem to aim at bounded knowledge.

This book attempts to sketch certain limits within which what I call a *bounded knowledge* can be produced. In the trespassing of traditional limits (cultural, political, territorial, etc.) anthropology's commitment to "partial truths" sounds hollow when confronted with its accomplishments. Its discourse, on the contrary, tends toward ubiquity; refusing to proceed from its bounded character, it seems to push towards a vicious circle: partial truths which in fact universalize. It would be difficult to exhaust the great number of these universalizing partial truths; suffice it here to cite some of the current equations, dichotomies, and deconstructions on which the new anthropology bases its powers of persuasion: representation/domination, knowledge/power and vice versa, nation, gender, tribe, ideology, author, and work are all constructs; body/mind, private/public, discourse/action, signifier/signified are all to be deconstructed. Something like a recipe has been invented. And it seems likely that this type of deconstruction can generate an unlimited supply of universalizing partial truths!

꽃

How can we break out of this vicious circle? I want to make a move toward an answer to this question after a brief summary of what I take to be the matrix of the new critical anthropology since the late 1970s. The key word here is "representation." It articulates a rich bundle of dichotomies: center/periphery, subject/object, hegemony/subversion, construction/deconstruction. A critical anthropology takes as its task the undoing of those dichotomies or, in other words, the subversion of the common postulate of "the thing out there" to be represented by the unloaded and transparent consciousness of the observer, a postulate which runs through orientalism, colonialism, and positivism. Many a strategy has been implemented in order to unpack representations and blur these dichotomies, including dialogics of knowledge, analytics of power, and writing (to ward off a haunting ghost of metaphysics). Some of these strategies experiment with performance not only through the textual circulation of simulacra which produce a rhetorical effect of the real, but also through the displacement of the two terms of the dichotomies. Hence, for example, one (but who?) is encouraged to dwell on borders, but never for long, because one has to change borders (spatial, linguistic, political, gender-related, color-bound, etc.). In this strategy borderlands and stages become the virtual spaces sought after. Stage as liminal space and limit intensifies the border as rhetoric. Recourse to illusion techniques breaks out linearity and simultaneity (historicism and structuralism as narratives) and works at encoding political economy into the subversive illusions of magic, shamanism, and fetishism. The wild man rather than the mature Marx becomes the devastating unsettler of (late) circulation/consumption capitalism (rather than the old labor one).

Repositioning the anthropologist in the way I have delineated above is not to underestimate the value of some of the contributions of anthropology to the critique of representation. It invites their harnessing in the service of the partial. For, in speaking to a particular group of people concerned with particular issues, the anthropologist feels the new bond that binds his/her knowledge; thus the necessity of theoretical construction asserts itself, rather than a universal (shall I say empty?) criticism. Because the knowledge he/she strives to generate is partial and committed, it says something significant about how self-definitions impact on unbounded circulation (of peoples, goods, information, images, and the like).

Thus some forgotten topics may return as processes of self-definition. For example, kinship rules and practices, modes of livelihood and use of resources, generation and organization of knowledge, technologies and the structuring of their spread and usage, hierarchy, class, ritual, warfare, all come back under various considerations as constituted in discourse and practice, but the task of the anthropologist would not stop at that. If anything, this would merely be a first step; as indispensable as it may seem, it would bring us back to the old positivist circle if we do not proceed beyond. And proceeding beyond would seem to mean the investigation of the structure of each of these constructs as well as the order that unfolds from the study of their relationships. Short of this, all attempts at undoing narratives will result in other narratives beyond the scope of critique. Even the most uncanny strategies of the anthropologist breaking linearities in order to bring in uncharted events can be interpreted along the lines of a plot which ultimately positions the anthropologist him/herself as narrative. And an ethnography of corridor gossip at the American Anthropological Association meetings or of authorship could easily illustrate the centrality of the anthropologist as narrative.

Connecting those constructs as constructs by a sort of feedback helps us learn more about them. How much we learn about the particular shapes of life-in-society, how many previously invisible qualities, tones, colors of existence, how many paths of change, freedom and enslavement, how many previously invisible aspects become visible under an unexpected guise, all that would go into our debates about the struggle for the definition of reality. Power, writing, or the economy of communication as the new face of political economy—all those categories which help articulate a critique of practice and discourse—can be compared and weighed in terms of how rich a set of connections between constructs they help unravel. A new idealism of power or a new mystique of "the text" and "the letter" can only hinder such an effort by warding off attempts at speaking from particularities (which are not to be confused with exotica, boundedness, or some ineffable qualities). The production of universalizing partial truths could become a highly sought-after position for a new, universal intelligentsia that does not speak to any particular marginalized or dominated group because it pretends to profess on behalf of all of them.

There may be more than one way to break out of this new straitjacket. One of these is to strive toward a bounded knowledge of unbounded phenomena, such as how some peoples with whom the anthropologist happens to be related by interest (making a career), create a self-definition through the circumstances of their lives, and what consequences (economic, social, or political) that practice creates for them. Engaging with them binds this knowledge to their future. Instead of the study of bounded community, it is the bounding of the transnational, the constant process by which transnational circulation and the work of imagination are turned into concrete and vital issues for the people as well as the anthropologist engaged with them. Here, power relations are, of course, crucial. However, I want to stress that they play themselves out in the struggle for the construction of social forms and not simply within discursive constructions of social life. The construction of the social involves as well a struggle in the flesh. Foucault, philosopher and "martyr," knew that, and by his own life testified to the risks involved. Like Pierre Rivière, Raymond Roussel, Damiens, and Sade (his other hero), he engaged with people about the redefinition of French society to which he was related by sentiment and career. The strategy I thought I could derive from reading Foucault and others was to pursue a sort of meditation on their engagement with French forms of social life and to follow, in my own context, the close connection that engagement has with the construction of social forms within the "order of discourse."

🌿

Let me now summarize how this book approximates the strategy just outlined. My point of departure was simply a series of setbacks. My generation was in its teens when the independence of Morocco was wrested from the French by the nationalists. No doubt most of us thought and felt a new era was dawning: a millennial dream coming true. As we grew up, this dawn made of us an elite, and—through education—gave us magnificent opportunities. With those blessings, however, this new era also taught us the bitter lessons of unequal development within the country: the chasm between economic liberation for us and the servitude imposed by economic need on the majority, together with moral and political servitude for everybody. Finally, there was the nagging sense that whatever the brilliance of our accomplishments (personal careers, economic success, etc.) these were somehow borrowed, not ours. We were to fit the slot of the respected, learned, and privileged elite, but the disciplining of our minds and bodies was effected through that fit as well as through coercion and privilege itself.

How did that control prove to be so successful? Is there a way to speak about it, to speak to it, to talk back at it? Many militants in the political parties and the unions sacrificed their careers and lives to shake the shackles of that control. However, those admirable examples of sacrifice and self-denial stood isolated from global social and political dynamics. At that isolation the regime worked hard, helped along by a domesticated opposition. Discourses about authenticity, identity, relation to the past and national unanimity around one or the other "sacred causes" were rife and saturated the political spectrum. Finally, seen closely and independently of the courage and sincerity of individuals, those examples rose and fell within organizations and a moral climate fraught with symbolic violence. The latter was not the monopoly of the regime alone.

An ethnography of dispersed authoritarianism covers what happens in interaction (always communicative)—a process of unfolding social forms and a contest about their meaning and shape. I include here encounters in words—including my own words, as an anthropologist—and other gestures, objects, and composed motifs (in the arts proper, in the arts of practice, and in practices of knowledge). A semiotic development of the central idea in question here would go as follows: while there is no motivation that links signifier and signified in the linguistic sign, the arbitrariness of that relation cannot be assumed to be complete for all other categories of codes. The problem here is of course that what motivates the relation between code and referent in turn needs to be stated in linguistic signs. As far as anthropology is still practiced through the medium of the morphosyntactic ordering of linguistic signs, which is also an ordering of concepts, it remains differentiated from other enterprises like poetry, painting, photography, music, architecture, to take but a few examples. I believe in this differentiation, which requires a talent and a training different from those required by the above-cited trades, a differentiation that stems from the ordering of linguistic signs being better suited to the formulation of the desirability of possible reals (those most proper to formulate ethical justification and contestation).

What is it then that as an ethnographer I record and transmit? Only discourses that I think I understand. Statements on other statements in the narrow sense I distinguish from the ordering of things by other codes, statements about other ordered codes, or else I register other objects assumed to be intelligible but for which I have no statement except that "no one knows" (ruins or historical artifacts not interpreted by the people or by archaeologists and historians, for example). There are different ways in which all statements thus can be ordered according to universal categories (constructed by the mind of the anthropologist, which is supposed to work in the same way as the minds of his/her interlocutors, as Lévi-Strauss contended long ago); the meaning thus arrived at is the one deduced from identity of differences in the same way the meaning value of a sign can be formulated as the difference between signs. An alternative approach would assume that those statements can be related to a small number of propositions structured by a central assumption about the nature of the relation between "words" and "things." The assumption of that relation can entail different working postulates: that some substance is deposited in the word, thus hermeneutics is the proper method and knowledge consists in an ad infinitum *dépliage* of metonyms and metaphors; that the relation is one of representation, the signs registering a

stability out there in space/time classifications; or else that either allegory or representation are suspect of distortion due to desire, greed,
class interest, and amnesia turning the imposed into the natural.
However, a radical critique of representation would be one that
would do away with it altogether in favor of a concentration on the
link between power and discourse. Finally, the anthropologist can re-
pudiate the dichotomy word/thing or the other famous (but not the
same) signifier/signified dichotomy as ones that are responsible for
bringing back a metaphysical substance within critical discourse and
anthropology as critical discourse.

In order to advance toward a more precise characterization of my
own work I will take in succession the structuralist and the poststructuralist in the order in which I brought them in (leaving aside major
differences within the second argument). I will not repeat the many
critiques which have been leveled at the structuralist approach. I have
tried elsewhere to write an ethnography from a perspective that assumes that unless we show structuration at work in the very localized
conflicts in which they are utilized, the universal aporia their structuration helps unravel can exhaust only a limited space of their work
(see *The Victim and Its Masks*, 1993). We need not, for these struggles,
posit a project in the traditional phenomenological sense of this notion. However, something like unfolding configurations can be shown
to be constantly coming into existence through a dynamics of confrontation, efforts, disputes, compromises, and mere chance. Every
"sketch" of that configuration can only be described as such through
the logic of its potential closure, hence opening the debate about its
alternative ethnographic renderings. Hence also the recourse to an
ethnography of the processes of construction which dynamize statements and actions in tasks and places in which people come together
(sacrificing, masquerading, eating, dancing, working, fighting, etc.) or
commenting on these events. Those statements and actions are
configured, together with statements and actions performed by others
who are not directly involved in the accomplishment of those tasks,
especially anthropologists and other commentators and writers. Anthropologists are performers insofar as their presence elicits statements and actions that influence the accomplishment of these tasks; in
the sense also that they perform the configuration in writing. There is
no escape from this. At this point, it seems clear that the reconfigura-
tion they operate has to go beyond discursive critiques of representa-

tion in anthropology as a discourse. Such an approach has produced many a repetitive "unraveling" of discursive objectifications and dominations. Moreover, such an approach often loses sight of the discourses involved in the accomplishment of particular tasks, discourses at work in those tasks and their definitions and in the definition of a social life, the goodness of which they are supposed to embody (family, community, nation, use of resources, modes of interaction and procedures of communication, exchange of things, words or blows, etc.) That discourse which the ethnographer writes down, it is important to remember, is also a substantivist discourse. But that substantivism cannot escape ethnographic critique because the signified (the ideal objective to be accomplished) is disputed, and its many concrete realizations become signifiers of differences, that is, alternative meanings and constructions of social forms and relations.

The work of the anthropologist would be incomplete if human action, admittedly always simultaneously a representation cleaved by the work of the negative, is not approached within the works and the institutions carved by human beings with the negative as their very background, wrested, so to speak, from nothingness. Loss, incompletion, and absence can be shown to inhabit all these accomplishments; however, the latter are the outcomes and the very forms which bear and express social life itself, forms resulting from trial and error, confrontations, and mutual subversions of representations. In this mutual subversion process it is indeed impossible to separate the cognitive from the political. But this inseparability does not result in unqualified relativism, for the weight of the argued facts and what the dynamics of argument unravel as formulations make new questions about the same topic impossible to ignore. We cannot know what the object reality we are striving to discover is, but we can know which statements about it are more valid than others and those statements bring with them partial truths we did not know before, or partial truths which are more sustainable than others. Cultural forms base their coming into existence, their longevity, and their more or less long-term viability on these partial truths which sometimes remain more defendable than others. The defendability of cultural forms, including the forms that agreement takes, need not be imagined as obeying one type of rationality. We know from Weber not to fall into the trap of instrumental rationality. Trial and error and global analogy give solid rational bases for many institutions and many forms of

life, and degrees of instrumental success can be sacrificed to sentiment and utility of togetherness as well as to the emotion of aesthetic
communion.

卷

The type of authoritarianism I try to describe and account for in
this book appeared to me—as I am, a bounded participant-observer
—to be a mixture of coercion and a transfer of a powerful sentimental
motif of community to newly unfolded spheres of the political (constructed as a human association with limited space for argument).
There are two bases which make this statement the most sustainable
partial truth I could come up with. The first is that it has a rough edge
that cuts across the claims upon which the Moroccan power structure
founds its legitimacy and the plausibility of its power practices. The
second is that the same rough edge seemed to trim to the bone any
other inbuilt fears, sedimentation of privileges, and emotional sense
of community, to the point of threatening the economy of my own
personality. Therefore, I must confess, the famous philosophical trend
which insists that there is no "reality out there," outside of that language or discourse, has less stringent appeal for me than the pursuit
of the new partial truths and the near images of power embodied in
institutional constructions and the shaping of social forms, and power
tactics, and strategies which, until now, has seemed to elude structuralist and poststructuralist approaches.

My endeavor is inherently comparativist and historicist. Comparativist because of the extent to which limited argument and
bounded analysis can be compared across political and social systems;
this comparability helps identify types of authoritarian regimes by
marking them off from totalitarian regimes and realizing the differences between those and democratic ones. The same can be said
of differences in terms of sense and structure of community. In my
account, comparison is at work and the coming into existence of
the picture I present (in chapters 1, 2, and 6) is due to that com-
pari son. This comparativist approach is a historicist one as well in
the sense that discourses, together with the cognitive and social dia-
grams which constitute the principle of their production, are approached within the processes of their coming into existence at a particular time.

That historical shaping of social, cultural, and political life is studied in this book in order to arrive at a theory of what it is that gets connected with some regularity in what I call Moroccan authoritarianism. The master–disciple diagram, described in its historicity, its crucial colonial reelaboration, and its postcolonial transfer to many sites of social interaction, is one that connects every site with the other in a global form of association with limited argument (chapters 3, 4, and 5). I try to account for its working as it connects political domination to gift exchange, rites of passage and initiations, social ambivalences, and gender reversals, not only in what is usually called the seat of power, but within the society itself as a specific cultural formation. All these connections are fraught with aporias and carried through from one partial refiguration to the next movement of inexorable, if not always visible, change. Yet it is that work of connecting and reconnecting all of them that I see as the cultural foundation of authoritarianism in Moroccan society and probably elsewhere in the Arab world.

Pursuing those connections was the guide to the particular ethnography I have tried to practice in this book, one that is also a sort of cultural history. The discourse of the master–disciple relationship, which came to occupy such a central connecting function, I analyze as discourse as well as a practical and imaginary form of association, production, control, and creation (chapters 4 and 5), all visible and realized in the transient groups of men and women they bring together in times and spaces which survive the transience of the grouping itself. The ethnography of those forms as the imagined reals goes beyond a power/knowledge type of critique and the critique authorized by the inevitable cleavage of the word as writing. It restitutes an approach to concrete and historical forms that tend to disappear in favor of an approach to human affairs in terms of performance.

I hope this book will be read neither as a solipsistic exercise in political lucidity nor as a rejection of the mystic path toward spiritual self-fulfillment and salvation in communal or individual forms. It is, before all else, an effort toward collective liberation from cultural and historical constructions weighing on the present and future of all of us who live in Arab societies. In the following chapters I deal with those cultural and historical forms we encounter in our daily lives as the core of a "personality," the defense of which can only be arrived at by a specific form of authority and political domination. As such they pervade our life so much so that their very strangeness, spread at the surface of every action and institution, remains removed from scrutiny; thus we live as if we did belong to them and they did belong to us by a sort of natural consubstantiality. This book aims at introducing a disjunction between those sources and our current lives in such a way as to render more visible the political work responsible for their perception as ours, as our roots, as our authenticity, as our difference vis-à-vis others. The disjunction introduces the necessary distance and offers an analytical space within which those roots and forces appear for what they are: a remake of things traditional, one among other possible remakes of things traditional, themselves impossible to apprehend as substances and in an unmediated way. Other possible remakes may then become possible, together with some realization of the price to be paid for each. The price that until now we have been paying for this pseudo-immediate contact with the sources of authenticity has become insufferably high for many of my generation, including myself. The exorbitant price we have been paying is expressed, of course, in the number of victims of repression and violence (here one should include not only the dead but also the extremely poor and the morally impaired and depressed), but the accounting should also include heteronomy and disempowerment, the two anticlimactic factors working against creation in the spheres of knowledge and the arts and ultimately against the imagination of the future.

How this necessary disjunction can help position anew crucial problems such as the status of reason, intuition, imagination, emotion, worship, work, eroticism, play, laughter, etc., I can only briefly outline through my previous comment on mysticism. The problem of recapturing the past is, of course, a haunting leitmotif among the nationalists and the postcolonial intelligentsia, especially the one to which I belong, which happens to be part of the citizenry of a former protectorate. For some it is to be recaptured as patrimony and legacy, to be reread and processed by rationalism—rationalism itself being recaptured as part and parcel of that "Arab patrimony." For others there is no such recapture, but the resumption of Islam as a living and transhistorical creed which, as such, defies recapturing through any reinterpretation or new reading. Both of these approaches postulate a direct contact with something alive yet marginalized by the malign agency of political, social, and psychological "aberration" and "deviation." The first and widespread trend follows a dubious intellectualism and runs the usual risks of a blind rationalism by which all differences will be seen and condemned as irrational. This has a sinister precedent in Arab history when, under the spell of this hyperrationalism, a famous Abbasid Caliph mounted a witch hunt against those who believed in allegory and revelation. It is important to note that this blind rationalism of the past and the one of the present condemn vehemently the communal forms of the Sufi path. They do not realize and try not to realize that condemnation is the first sign of reordering knowledge and practice according to a power which has established or seeks to establish hegemony. This, to my test superficial, rationalism shares with the militants of a living and transhistorical Islam the abhorrence of the so-called extreme Sufi experimenters.

This book analyzes the transfer of mystic guidance in initiation to the realm of power relations and political institutions. I do not intend it as a campaign against Sufism in any of its forms. Hence I wish to be disassociated from these two movements and express my admiration for Sufism as a personal passion for God and as a revolution in many women's and men's lives that kept hegemonic conformisms (of religion and reason) in check. It seems to me that the rationalism of Ibn Rochd and Ibn Khaldun cannot be recaptured; but we can still aspire to the freedom of the mind and imagination that made them challenge the currents of their times and refrain from the power-loaded temptation of superficial hyperrationalism. Condemnation too often flows with dangerous ease into punitive legislation and violence. And from this point of view the virulence is the same, be it founded in reason or revelation.

Princeton, N.J.
22 February 1997

ACKNOWLEDGMENTS

Many people helped me with their critiques, remarks or encouragement. I owe a special debt of gratitude to M. Allaoui, C. Geertz, A. Kilito, and M. Naciri for their attentive reading of the text and their detailed comments on it. My colleagues J. Boon and L. Rosen gave me very helpful suggestions on the drafts for several chapters and worked with me on the preface. I wish to thank them for their very generous help. I wish to acknowledge the wonderful work J. Boon did with me, editing and finding useful formulations to fit the ideas expressed in the preface. I want to give my thanks to P. Brown for the inspiration and guidance I drew from several conversations with him. His insights proved invaluable to me, especially those regarding the lives of saints and their initiation. J. Waterbury, R. Leveau, and L. Valensi commented on chapters of the manuscript and gave me important remarks regarding the comparison of the Moroccan case with other Arab societies. I wish to thank them for the attention they gave to this work. Adonis's careful reading of the final version of this book and his encouragement were also very special to me.

I cannot include all those who in one way or another have stimulated my work and my thinking. I wish to thank especially J. Nettelbeck, W. Lepenies, E. Gellner, M. Bennouna, N. Bouderbala, H. Bienen, M. Gilsenan and A. Udovitch for their remarks and support.

M. Kenbib, A. M'hammedi, and O. Benmira were gracious enough to read my second chapter. I profited greatly from their historical expertise and their remarks. I want to thank them wholeheartedly for their help and encouragement.

N. Benabid translated sections of the introduction and the conclusion and was nice enough to help me edit them. I want to thank her very much for her help.

H. Allaoui, U. Zouiten Agoumi, T. Waterbury, and L. Dwyer gave me invaluable help in typing and editing the manuscript. I wish to extend to them my warmest thanks.

This work was started with a grant from the SSRC Committee on the Middle East. I wish to thank this institution and especially R. Owen and P. Von Sivers for their support. I pursued research on the subject during the academic year 1985–86 as a fellow of the Wissenschaftskolleg zu Berlin. I want to thank this institution for its generous support and for the good opportunities it gave me to advance my work and benefit from discussions with many colleagues. Finally, I wish to acknowledge the support I was given by the Center of International Studies, Princeton University, for the revision of the manuscript and the writing of the preface.

It goes without saying that I am solely responsible for the ideas expressed in this book.

The system of transliteration used in this book is a very simplified version of the one used by the *Encyclopaedia of Islam*.

This book was inspired by an issue that has haunted Arab intellectuals. It can be expressed in various ways, but the central question is constant: how can we account for the prevalence of authoritarian political systems in our societies, from the Atlantic to the Gulf? As a preliminary response—to be refined throughout the present analysis—one might characterize these regimes as follows: they refuse to deal with interests and conflicts through public negotiation and arbitration within the framework of institutions set up by civil society; rather, a single political entity determines the distribution of resources and the balance of powers.

The most commonly held hypothesis is that Arab regimes seek the support of the privileged classes, whose interests are linked to those of international capitalism in a process of accumulation at the "center" which impoverishes the "periphery."[1] In other words, it is assumed that the particular forms of government characteristic of postcolonial Arab nation-states are grounded, on the one hand, in inequalities within those societies and, on the other hand, in the dependency of their economies on the international market. Let us note, however, that authoritarianism has developed not only in societies with liberal economic systems, but also in societies in which the government has intervened precisely to limit economic disparities. Moreover, we would expect already to have witnessed numerous political upheavals if a decline in the standard of living of the masses ensured the demise of the existing systems.

Arab regimes are dependent. But one should not exaggerate the importance of foreign aid. Cooperation within the framework of political alliances undoubtedly contributes to easing domestic socioeconomic conflicts and thus reinforces the bureaucratic and repressive system of control, but the case of Iran shows that even a regime that successfully manipulates international cooperation is not assured of survival. In fact, the confrontation in Iran seems to have been fostered precisely by the contradiction between people's values and those which the Shah's regime sought to impose. While the conflict was undoubtedly stirred up by a decline in the standard of living of large urban masses, the revolutionary action was carried out in the name of Islamic ideals. Inversely, the cases of Morocco and Egypt prove that extreme economic disadvantage among such large masses may induce only temporary social outbursts which do not necessarily aim at political or social change.

If an authoritarian regime cannot be said to survive because of its dependency and if it cannot be weakened by economic bankruptcy, we must find other explanations for its persistence. Should we go along with those who claim there is a correlation between authoritarianism and accelerated modernization? Probably not, given the counterexamples of Morocco and Saudi Arabia, which prove that authoritarian structures can slow down the process of modernization and maintain ethnic, regional, and linguistic diversity in spite of the need for integration. Other factors have also been mentioned to account for Arab political authoritarianism: class structures and dependency, the patronage system and the elites' segmentary competition, and the conglomeration of stabilizing interests, to name just a few. But we still lack an interpretation of authoritarianism's characteristics and, more important, an explanation for the apparent acquiescence to it of much of the populace.

Previous authors have not failed to invoke theories of legitimacy, whether of the traditional kind, associated with monarchies, or of a revolutionary sort, for the republics. Nowhere, however, have they examined how concrete individuals perceive these theories; there has been no consideration, or at best only implicit consideration, of the exact ways in which these abstract principles of legitimation are vested with an emotional impact sufficient to foster action.

I will address these issues through the analysis of a single political system, namely that which exists in independent Morocco. While it is admittedly a particular case, one can extrapolate from it. I will first highlight the features of this regime and its foundations, which will result in a more precise definition of the modalities of the exercise of power and of their consequences. A preliminary picture of authoritarian systems will thus emerge. I will then—in light of the ideologists' and political scientists' failure to explain satisfactorily the stability of such systems—concentrate on discovering the essential features of power relations in the society itself, so as to identify their replication in the spheres of bureaucracy and institutionalized political action. This involves reconstructing the cultural models which account for the taken-for-granted nature of the kind of relations prevalent in social and political life.

This investigation will yield a description of a particular structuration of power relations. If we agree that such a structure operates in Arab societies at large, it would seem appropriate to evaluate their authoritarian regimes by referring to the characteristics uncovered in my analysis of the Moroccan system. It would also seem reasonable to try to account for the persistence of this system in terms of the affective impact of the ideas and images which anchor it at the individual level. Some readers may not approve of such generalizations because they appear to ignore particularities. But taking particularities into account should not prevent us from recognizing an amazing degree of consistency in the way power is exercised throughout the Arab world.

Let us now briefly elaborate on this last proposition. My point of departure is the relation of individuals to their chief—whether it be a political chief, their father, the masters who introduce them to the arts and knowledge, or their superiors in a bureaucratic setting. The same social actors may exhibit diametrically opposite attitudes in different situations, assuming an attitude of humble submission, which often borders on obsequiousness, when in a subordinate position, but expecting strict obedience when in a position of power, an attitude that takes precedence over any legal mediation. It seems that every individual has two coexisting personalities with features and comportments in one-to-one opposition and, most important, that the domineering personality is temporarily repressed and hidden by the display of submission while in fact preparing for its own sudden emergence. As a result the submission relation, which now can be seen as a waiting period and the price to be paid for access to power, is associated with a high degree of ambivalence, as might be expected.

When conflict erupts publicly between an individual and his chief the struggle is merciless. That neither protagonists nor spectators are surprised by this indicates beyond any doubt that such are the rules of the game which everyone accepts. But before rebelling and fighting for autonomy, one benefits from closeness to the chief and the prestige of a regular association with his most intimate circles, as well as from the exchange of gifts and services. The sacrifices this requires may go as far as a dramatized abdication of the signs of virility, despite their crucial role in the definition of male identity in Moroccan society.

These attitudes, which derive from a mostly unformalized and therefore powerful ethos, remain evident in daily political interaction, their staging reaching paroxysm in the etiquette and vocabulary of the royal palace. In fact there has been a definite return to such practices since Morocco regained its independence in 1956. This trend is associated with the clear restoration of the monarchical center after its temporary decline just before the protectorate and under the colonial regime.

These attitudes and the ethos which makes them acceptable or at least tolerable correspond to manners that have become stylized and have imposed themselves through historical development. As such, they lend themselves to a kind of archaeology. They are set in a theory of power and an official ritual that were reaffirmed in the nineteenth century and whose embodiment and last period of splendor under Hassan I—on the eve of colonial intervention—are still vivid in people's memories.

How can modern authoritarianism succeed in renewing archaic power relations, especially given the radical changes transforming Moroccan society and the firm grip of a nationwide bureaucratic system since the protectorate? It is my contention that all dominance and submission relations refer to a set of cultural schemata, reelaborated or reinvented under colonial rule, by which tensions are arbitrated. The contradiction in the present dialectic between these schemata and bureaucratic rationality is so pronounced that one is tempted to see it as the driving force behind attempted coups d'état and bursts of anger.

At any rate the continuous operation of networks of concepts and images defined by an implicit norm—which cancels out the meaning and liberating power of the legal-bureaucratic norm—is responsible for the serious malaise and extreme frustration which presently characterize daily life and conversation. However much individuals may resist this implicit norm, we can see that they are still guided by it. Most important, the rules governing people's attitudes in any type of dominance relation seem to function unhampered, as if in a sphere independent of will. These rules are not necessarily unconscious, but in the heat of action they seem always to prevent social actors from substituting other rules. They function as a sort of grammar which governs daily interaction and ensures the reproduction of existing authority and power relations in a human climate fraught with strong undercurrents of ambivalence. Indeed, every man in a situation of submission must not only give himself the illusion that he is accepting it; he must also painfully give up for a while the identity he wants to have: being the chief, the father, a virile and dominating man (in contrast with women), the master (in contrast with the disciple).

My basic hypotheses in this book are as follows: Inversion and ambivalence still constitute the cultural schema in terms of which access to any position of dominance is defined. Furthermore, this schema is grounded and sanctified by the concepts and procedures involved in the process of mystical initiation. In other words, the disciple's inversion imposes itself as the exemplary form for domination and submission. Signs of femininity—in the form of submission and service—are displayed in the relation of domination between father and son or superior and subordinate. But in no other sphere of life does this negation of virility become more extreme than in the process of mystical initiation, where the obligatory passage through a feminine role on the long path to masterhood, under a guide's authority, reaches an unequaled level of expression and stylization.

It is precisely my purpose in this book to describe the temporary inversion which every aspirant to spiritual masterhood must undergo. I begin my description of the process with one particularly illustrative case, so as to clearly identify the inversion model and its cultural schema before testing their scope and significance. I will indeed pursue the identification of such schemata not only in Sufi initiation, but also—and most significantly—at the center of ritual cycles which are still operating. My hypothesis will thus be tested not only through ethnographic observation, but also through the study of hagiography and cultural history.

The initiating guide is the principle of production of the initiate on his way to masterhood. The guide's action takes precedence over everything else. Only his miraculous intervention allows the initiate to reach the summit. Without it nothing can save the disciple: neither competence nor integrity nor fervor in prayer nor any other effort to reach godliness. This state of dependence while waiting for the charismatic climax, along with the attitudes it engenders, always informs the training methods and programs of political organizations that draw on some version of Islam. And the effect goes even further: in all political parties and trade unions, as well as public and private bureaucracies, processes of political interaction are dominated by the relationship to a chief, which is modeled on the exemplary master-disciple relationship. In each case a new master emerges through the display of attitudes which make him appear womanlike at the first stage but lead to a metamorphosis which, once he has severed his bonds with his initiators, turns him into a virile and absolute chief.

Having thus identified the model and the schema that legitimates the behavior needed for its application, how can we explain people's adherence to it? How can we account for the fact that the requirements of the master-disciple relationship are implemented and fulfilled as if taken for granted? This question calls for a complex answer. Let us first highlight the following general frame of reference. Only a saint—a man possessed of *baraka*, or charisma—can embody the constant miracle which manifests the reproducing principle of the society and its values. This monopoly forces the power holder (the sultan, the ruler) to boast of charismatic titles: a saint is always above a power holder, their respective standings grounded in the contrastive relationship between baraka and constraint through violence. The power holder thus attempts to present himself as the unique source of life by eliminating the representatives of creative revelation or keeping them in subordinate roles.

The dialectic of power and charisma in the saint-sultan relationship takes a particular form in Morocco. But all Arab societies share a view of the nation-state as a source of life, in the literal sense of distributing prestige and resources at the ruler's discretion. It can of course be pointed out that the authoritarian allocation of goods and powers is widespread throughout the third world and that the inversion model can be found in many societies. The counterargument I offer in this book sees the specificity of Arab societies in the extreme codification of the relation of domination between the sexes; this leads us to interpret the obligatory inversion in the power seeker as a way to obliterate the reproductive role of women. How could we expect this patriarchal society to accept the fact that women are responsible for the continuity of agnatic lines? The answer lies in the existence of the saint, which turns the master-disciple relationship into the exemplary one.

Some ambiguities may follow from the notion of a cultural schema. Indeed, investigating such schemata is hardly a matter of identifying notions and affects that could find their perfect expression in words. Cultural schemata as understood here are neither unchanging frames of interpretation, the configuration of which can be easily identified in daily life and quotidian language, nor givens derived from "classical texts" or the illusory assumption of a fit between texts and quotidian life. The chapter devoted to the colonial construction of authoritarianism and to the domestication of civil society after independence shows that the invoked model—that of the master-disciple relationship—has itself been refashioned and systematically transferred to a profoundly transformed political sphere. These phenomena have in fact coincided with the systematic extension of the state's control over religion in the aftermath of its newly established monopoly of violence and control over the civic and economic sphere.

The intent here is not the diagnosis of stable cultural features or of mentalities, that is to say, of a self-perpetuating "heritage" transferred from generation to generation regardless of historical upheavals. By highlighting the tentative, the novel, the disputed as well as the subtle mixture of persuasion, corruption, and coercion so characteristic of these authoritarianisms, this book wishes to avoid the dangers of essentialism and their familiar corollary—the antihistoricist usage of history. This double failing, which marks a number of orientalist works, has been the subject of a well-warranted critique. Such interpretations forego the task of reconstructing cultural references in relation to their circumstances, and they prod the idea of culture into the confines of a theory of race, emphasizing latent structures at the expense of human action. They are based on a peculiar type of culturalism which assumes the existence of some basic personality or the efficacy of particular traditions endowed with a transhistoric presence—for example, a Western tradition, traced to a Roman antecedent, that is supposed to have had a critical role in the elaboration of a "legal sphere," or the history of debates within the Catholic church concerning religious and political autonomy. The absence of these traditions in Islamic societies is then invoked to explain their "authoritarian state."

Explanation through absence cannot, however, substitute for the description of existing practices, and the concept of culture that such a method postulates suffers from a surplus of generalizations and idealism. Cultural models, as I understand them, are frames of reference and of quotidian interpretation; they are both public and practical. Their invocation by the actors, instead of lending them a character of pure ideality and immutability, plunges them into the precariousness of meaning. Men and women are consequently enabled to construct and reconstruct temporary consensus, to explore ambiguities and misunderstandings, or to shatter these frameworks—to the dismay, perhaps, of anthropologists who have grown attached to conveniently fixed meanings. All that happens occurs in a dialectic that draws its gravity from political dissent. Later in this work, we shall see that certain forms of submission are disputed even in instances where the exigencies of the master are extreme, and that the appearance of habitus may be quite deceptive. However, all the disputes and conflicting frames of interpretation seem to stop short of questioning the master-disciple relationship and the schema of inversion in the production of the new master. Hence the most diverse opinions and practices seem to proceed from it.

The master-disciple schema is neither a frame of interpretation nor an ideal type but the condition of production of both. As I shall show, it is more akin, both in ritual practice and in specific cultural history, to what Foucault calls a "diagram."[2] It is an abstract configuration which articulates the discourse of sainthood and of masterhood in general, as well as the visible arrangements (Sufi lodges and their networks, disciplined groups of initiates, fortresses, palaces, royal processions and progresses, etc.) within which they unfold and develop. This configuration also helps us map the shifting lines of power confrontations and the points of their intensification.

The diagram I describe in this book does not transcend historical developments. On the contrary, its emergence can itself be situated in the fifteenth century, within a history of debates and struggles over the question of moral authority and the definition of community. For over four centuries individuals and groups have mobilized, thought, and fought within the highly conflictual web they spun. This diagram, the master-disciple relationship, has been at the heart of the most potent metaphors of political community. Thus, powerfully embodied ideas and images have given shape to a specific system and provided it with deep affective efficacy at the individual level. Colonial and postcolonial rule have remolded it, both as a structure and as a "collective" memory. The result is a modern authoritarianism that remains entrenched in social and political life despite an unceasing struggle for change.

Foundations of Monarchical Authority and Forms of Exercise of Power: Toward a Redefinition of the Moroccan Political System

❧ What forms does the exercise of power take in the post-colonial Moroccan nation-state and what are the sources of its vitality and continuity since 1956? The description called for by the first, typological question will help us refine the terms of the second question. In other words, defining a type of power will lead to a better understanding of its foundations; a closer look at ways of governing will undoubtedly provide us with a better grasp of their internal mechanisms. One can account for the perpetuation of a form of exercise of power either in terms of values which are supposed to be held dear by those who submit to it, or in terms of factors which, unbeknownst to them, guide their will. Explanations based on economic interest belong to the second category, whereas explanations focusing on legitimacy fall into the first one.

Objectifying description is relevant not only for the so-called external factors, but also for the justifications that make certain forms of the exercise of power desirable or simply tolerable to the governed. Whether or not the actors are aware of their operation, these justifications serve as guidelines for individual and collective action. The daily experience of all who take part in an action is made up of attitudes, feelings, and gambles; judging by the endlessly varied comments any action may engender, transparent motivations are rare. Assuming that we agree on this last point, the so-called objective factors and their perception as expressed by the actors themselves can no longer be considered as belonging to different epistemological orders. We are then faced with the problem of deciding which factors to highlight in order to interpret action.

In the present case, namely postindependence Morocco, any consideration of material interest inevitably draws us into a sort of paradox: the assumption that the privileged classes support the regime for reasons of material interest leaves us uncertain as to why the majority, despite deprivation, is acquiescent. Inversely, it is questionable to attribute the popular attitude simply to repression, possibly combined with a system of ideas and beliefs that functions as an opiate. Aren't the elite and the popular majority alike on a constant quest for greater proximity to the center of distribution of wealth and power? If so, the impact of economic interest might account for the comportment of the underprivileged masses as well as that of the privileged classes. But it first undergoes a transformation which ties it to the source of its meaning, namely the mystique of the distributing center and its chief.

Is this a paradox? Not really; rather, the paradox lies in the patience of the underprivileged, who continue to hope for a miraculous improvement in their lot despite the regular frustration of their expectations. The persistence of such hopes does not, however, point to fatalism or fear of repression. The outbursts that periodically shake the cities, only to be harshly repressed, reveal an anger fueled by frustrations and unkept promises which alternates with faith in the capacity of the distributing center to save the most underprivileged.

My line of argumentation may help to resolve the apparent contradiction between growing inequality due to the regime's political and economic choices, on the one hand, and reference to "popular" legitimacy, on the other hand. The way both the underprivileged classes and the postcolonial elites perceive the system is related to the so-called objective factors involved in unequal development. The center which distributes favors to elites represents the only system known to the masses.

This link seems to have escaped the attention of both ideologists of the Moroccan political system and observers attempting to account for its considerable success. In this book, an examination of the ideologies of the present monarchical system will be followed by a reconsideration of the postcolonial political struggles as seen by political scientists. Both will contribute to a typological assessment. They will also enable me to outline the phenomena of perception and belief which give the variables of economic and sociological structure an orientation contrary to that usually attributed to them.

Allegiance, Charisma, and Royal Arbitration

Alawists posit the existence of a direct relationship, sanctioned by divine decree, between the sovereign and his subjects—thus establishing through a kind of structural confusion what constitutes legality in their eyes.[1] (I prefer in this context to use the notion of divine right, which is clearly distinct from the doctrine of general will in Hegel's sense of the terms; the divine right of kings, in a Hegelian perspective, would be regarded as a nonright.)[2] Those who hold such views assert that this primordial relationship is expressed in the solemn oath of allegiance (*bay'a*) presented by the community—as represented by the ulema, or doctors of Islamic law—to the candidate of its choice at the outset of each new reign. This oath of allegiance, renewed every year on the great Muslim feast days, constitutes an unbreakable bond between the people and the king. It also places the king above any cleavages which may divide the community.

Postindependence Morocco has had several constitutions, which have introduced a parliamentary system and the concept of a legislative assembly elected by the people, but the sovereign retains the initiative by divine law. The original nature of the situation stems from the fact that the constitution itself—especially the 1972 constitution— recognizes the sovereign's right to make decisions and legislate without regard to constitutional restraints. The allegiance of the Moroccan people—considered as a distinct Muslim community which at the same time is part of the worldwide Muslim community—establishes the monarch as "commander of the faithful." His power thus presents a doubly formidable obstacle for those who might think of vying for supreme command: attacking him would be both a crime and a sacrilege—inseparable notions in this logic—at once a violation of divine law and the desacralization of a figure of Islamic piety. Let us not forget that God ordains that the community never remain without a leader (imam) and indicates to everyone through the consent of the community which candidate is his elect. Herein lies the very first dissuasive argument against any act of rebellion.

A second argument follows naturally. The oath of allegiance is based on a consensus which now must be consolidated. The community transcends its divisions through obedience to this sacralized authority and, as a result, is in a position to triumph over both internal and external threats. Alawist monarchists forcefully claim that in the absence of a leader whose religious standing places him above civil society and its power struggles, divisions between townsfolk and country people, Arabs and Berbers, the bourgeoisie and the populace could break up the nation-state. Supporters of a monarchy of divine right use this argument, based on a particular interpretation of Islamic law and a particular form of allegiance, to underscore the eminent qualities of the ruling family as well as its accomplishments.[3] As a descendant of the Prophet, the monarch incarnates in the eyes of the people the miracle of his ancestor, namely the emergence of a community which restores the primordial Word and builds a new order. Consequently this lineage, which God's will has put above all others, is capable of transcending all differences. It has indeed always been able, historically speaking, to save the country—first in its fight against covetous Christian powers beginning in the sixteenth century, and more recently in the mid-twentieth-century campaign for independence, the "King's and People's Revolution." Even more important, Morocco has owed its existence as a political and cultural entity to the *chorfas* (descendants of the Prophet) since their founding of the first Muslim kingdom in the eighth century.[4]

This theory of allegiance, as presented by a segment of the cultured elites, does not inform the perception of legitimacy held by the rural and urban masses. The sharifian dimension, on the other hand, imposes itself in everyone's mind; no one ever forgets that the sharifs assumed leadership at crucial times in the community's struggle for survival. Charisma and sharifian action therefore override the theory of allegiance. We can reasonably assume that this has been the case throughout Morocco's modern history. An added dimension today is that the concrete expression of allegiance and the attending ceremony are regularly presented to everyone by the media. In terms of perception alone, the ritual of submission shown to general audiences puts the monarch above his society. The idea that sharifism is the foundation of the Moroccan nation and is responsible for its continuity since the eighth century is, however, a recent point of view, which may, incidentally, contradict the scholarly theory of allegiance.[5]

Whatever the case, neither sharifian charisma nor leadership in the community's struggles for survival can be regarded as a simple and transparent concept. It is not sufficient to inherit charisma, for it can only be validated by actions and success. As for leadership, it has to be negotiated. Let us note that these qualities, which according to the Alawist theory of monarchy foster a direct relationship between the king and his people—a relationship not mediated by civil institutions—turn out under examination to be highly problematic and open to interpretations imposed by power relations. This has been clearly demonstrated by a number of crucial events in Moroccan politics since the beginning of the century.

The relationship which once existed between the sultan and his subjects was profoundly modified during the period of the French protectorate, instituted in 1912. Resistance to foreign invasion, carried out in the name of Islam and local values, then coincided with the traditional power center's apparent collaboration with Christian invaders. Between 1894 and 1927 sharifian charisma gave way to other forces.[6] These took strikingly different forms: resistance by tribal chiefs assisted by religious leaders (not all of whom claimed sharifian descent), foundations directed by thaumaturges, wars between tribes that had regained their autonomy, nationalist struggle fueled by religious faith.[7] The so-called Rif War falls into this last category. As an organized movement with relatively clear objectives, the Rif struggle, under the leadership of Mohammed ben Abdelkrim al Khattabi, introduced modern reforms and founded a republic without any reference to sharifism.[8] Its popularity and the degree to which it inspired others in Morocco indicated a weakening of sharifian legitimacy.

In fact it was urban nationalism that pulled the monarchy and its symbols out of a long period of lethargy stretching from the death of Hassan I to the first decades of the twentieth century.[9] Historians usually consider that the beginning of this new nationalist movement coincided with the protest against the so-called Berber Dahir of May 1930.[10] When the sultan, Mohammed ben Youssef, refused to sign this law, which would have divided the country between Arabs and Berbers he was echoing popular feeling, but he was not then leading the movement. Nevertheless, as a result of his resistance the young sovereign—who had acceded to the throne in 1927—promptly became the leader of a movement activated by the urban elites, particularly the ulema; those who headed the protest against the Berber Dahir claimed him as the symbol of a nation threatened by colonial maneuvers and compliant centrifugal forces. These events drew the nation's attention to a monarchy which had been confined to the palace and reduced to figurehead status by the protectorate and its neo-sultanian administration. From these early stages of the struggle until the achievement of independence approximately a quarter of a century later, there was increasing collaboration and consultation between the Palace and the nationalists. It was the nationalist party that militated in favor of the monarchy's recovery of its lost prestige, promoting the idea, through constant campaigns and mass demonstrations, of the king as symbol of national unity. This designation was later clearly ratified in the triumphant reception of royal visits to the so-called imperial cities. The visits to Fez (1934) and Tangier (1947) are still vivid in many people's memories.[11] They had been preceded by the nationalists' Manifesto for Independence (1944), which made the preservation of monarchy and the nation a primary objective.

It seems almost impossible in this context to distinguish what stemmed from charisma and traditional legitimacy, on the one hand, and from the outcome of nationalist political strategies, on the other. The 1953 *coup de force*, which resulted in the deposition and exile of the king, changed the course of the struggle, which intensified and turned violent. Again the sultan's popularity was growing, as was that of Allal al-Fassi, the uncontested leader of the nationalist party Istiqlal. In the countryside the figure of Mohammed ben Youssef, the future Mohammed V, was invoked and legends circulated about the wonders that had occurred during his exile;[12] but there was also much reference to al-Fassi, the actual commander of the nationalists operating in the field, who was called *al-za'īm* (the leader).[13]

The sultan's recovered charisma therefore appears to have been due in great part to the efforts of the nationalist militants, but the single banner of the nationalist party covered divergences which soon came to the surface. A number of urban armed groups and the mountain-based Army of Liberation were so far beyond the control of the nationalist party that, after independence, the party joined efforts with the Palace to integrate them into the armed forces, the police, and the administration of the new state. In spite of the sultan's prestige and fervent support for the za'īm, repression was necessary to liquidate or integrate the independence fighters. The monarchy has in fact waged a continuous power struggle with various political organizations, trade unions, and other such forces, seeking to eliminate or at least weaken them so as to be able to claim unmediated legitimacy, as recognized by the people.[14] Thus, the celebrated direct link between the king and his subjects is in fact a recent slogan which has been transformed into an explanatory construct and a policy objective.

All observers agree that from the early days of independence to his death in 1961 King Mohammed V was the object of extreme veneration by his subjects. His appearance captivated the crowds and his presence unquestionably had spiritual power.[15] There was definitely a

direct relationship between him and the people. But should his popularity be attributed only to the sovereign's hereditary credentials?
Again I do not think so, for the Alawite genealogy contains names of
other sovereigns and pretenders who had become discredited or anon-
ymous by the time they died. Moreover, Mohammed V was able to
activate the charisma he inherited at the very moment when the nationalist movement was stripping his opponents of their legitimacy.
In the early stages of the protectorate some religious leaders—particularly the heads of Sufi brotherhoods—stopped resisting and allied
themselves with the colonial administration. The nationalist groups,
in organized demonstrations during the 1930s, fought the Sufi brotherhoods in the name of religious reform (*salafiya*), accusing them of
excessive ecstatism, anthropolatry, and collaboration with the occupying forces.

The fate of the Kettani *zāwiya* (religious brotherhood) and its
head are exemplary in this regard. During the troubled years in which
the occupation of Oujda (1907) was followed by the French troops'
landing in Casablanca, Mohammed ben Abdelkebir Kettani established himself as a champion of domestic reforms and of the struggle
against the invaders. It was in 1907 that the ruling sultan was over-
thrown in Marrakech, to the benefit of his brother who was brought
to the throne precisely on the basis of such a program. These events
led Kettani to initiate a movement in Fez which combined brotherhood Sufism and a reformist Islam of salafi inspiration; the objective
of this movement was to impose a representative constitutional regime while reactivating resistance against the Christian invaders. The
new sultan was offered conditional allegiance, and the spokesman for
the demands listed in the text of the *bay'a* was Kettani, who until his
death never stopped confronting the sultan on these issues.[16]

Observers have remarked that in addition to problems regarding
reform and jihad, there was a rivalry between Kettani—a man of non-
Alawite (Idrissid) sharifian lineage and the head of a powerful brotherhood—and the Alawite throne. Some contemporaries interpreted
Kettani's actions as a bid to be elected as a replacement for the deposed sultan.[17] Such a course would have meant standing in the way
of Moulay Abdelhafid, who had already been nominated in Marrakech to succeed his brother; at any rate, Kettani did not give up his
fight after the new sovereign assumed the throne.

The new and still fragile government realized early on that anger was mounting, as power relations between Morocco and foreign countries forced the sultan to make compromises. The coalition which brought Moulay Abdelhafid to power soon disintegrated due to his abandonment of jihad, a return to vilified fiscal practices, the introduction of new measures threatening traditional privileges, and diplomatic compromises with France as well as with some elites who had been temporarily kept out.[18] In 1909, as the sultan was preparing to leave Fez, where signs of mutiny were again appearing, Kettani, considered the main leader of the brewing rebellion and an advocate of limits on the sovereign's power, was apprehended and killed.[19]

Other powerful brotherhoods were also to face hostility from the Palace and the salafi groups. This undermining of the brotherhoods continued under the protectorate. The Kettaniya, like other important zāwiyas, supported French rule and led a relentless struggle against the governing dynasty. This drew the ire of the nationalists. Thus the monarchy and the nationalist party, which, during the interwar period, acted under the aegis of the royal house, coordinated their efforts to curtail the brotherhoods' influence.[20] The whole brotherhood system was now suspected of betraying the national cause. The campaign against religious orders, their ritual practices, morals, and yearly festivals (mousem), culminated in a 1940 sultanian decree prohibiting the creation of any new foundation without prior permission of the Palace.[21] Some important brotherhood centers, among them the powerful zāwiya in Ouezzane, were placed under the control of the royal bureaucracy, thus depriving them of their autonomy,[22] and from then on the sultan intervened in the selection of replacements for heads of brotherhoods who had died. The antibrotherhood movement intensified during the years of violent struggle for independence and until the liberation in 1956, becoming a particular priority in the press of the Istiqlal.[23]

The party's actions greatly benefited the monarch. In the first years of independence, following his return from exile, Mohammed V captivated the masses: he was in everyone's eyes the Prophet's descendant and the hero of independence. The simple juxtaposition of these features, however, is not sufficient to explain his popularity; it was the linking of the two that raised him to sanctity. His actions persuaded Moroccans that only he possessed the active and forceful prophetic charisma that was needed at that moment. In fact, Mohammed V's first nonordinary "action" in the view of the majority was to create consensus around himself, an achievement made possible by the nationalist movement: its struggle against the procolonial religious brotherhoods brought to a temporary halt the dispersion of popular veneration and focused it on the king alone.[24] It should be noted that the decline of the brotherhoods coincided with the creation and implantation of the Feast of the Throne rituals.

Supporters of the Alawite monarchy add the image of king as arbiter to the prestige he derives from his family's historical titles and the legitimacy bestowed on him by the process of allegiance. This image serves to reinforce the theory of a direct relationship between the king and his subjects; at the same time, the king's role as arbiter puts him above private interests and partisan squabbles. The ambiguous image of the king as arbiter is much more difficult to analyze than the other foundations of power invoked by Alawist ideologues. On the one hand it draws its significance from an old and well-established ideology; on the other hand it is verified to a certain degree in common practices, both old and new.

Let us first note that the history of Morocco contains instances in which the sultan preferred to arbitrate rather than impose decrees and that his intervention was solicited as a last recourse against all kinds of injustice.[25] Direct appeal to the sovereign has survived to this day in the form of special services—housed in the Palace—to which one can address grievances whose solutions require diverse competencies.[26] Since Morocco's independence it has become more common to have recourse to the king as arbiter. In the early days of independence such intervention was requested in unexpected ways. In some cases violence was used to push him to arbitrate disputes involving the prerogatives of the nationalist party (Istiqlal) and regional or local interests defended by the rural notables. Such was the case in the rural upheavals of 1958, for example, the rebellion in the eastern High Atlas headed by 'Addi ou-Bihi. The services of the Palace supported—without really showing it—the forces contesting the political hegemony of the Istiqlal. But their support was discreet; it simply consisted in favoring a counterbalance to the party's power.[27] The monarchy carefully avoided identifying with a political group, which can also be seen as part of its effort to maintain balance.

The monarchy is not necessarily averse to leaning on loyalist organizations at critical times. On the contrary, it instigated the creation of a political movement that was to give it support during the first parliamentary experiment of 1962. Later on, between 1972 and 1976, it encouraged the emergence of another party in elections which led to the establishment of a new parliament.[28] As we know, these two parliamentary experiments were separated by a long period of repression and a state of emergency.[29] In both 1962 and 1976 the newly established party was put in the hands of individuals close to the royal family and managed to make the population accept a constitution reaffirming sovereign powers limited only by Koranic precepts.[30] Both the referenda and the elections took place in a tense atmosphere and were marked by breaches of electoral laws as well as numerous instances of fraud. In 1962 the party supporting the monarchy—the Front for the Defense of Constitutional Institutions (FDIC)—was founded by A. Reda Guedira, a longtime friend and close advisor of the sovereign;[31] in 1976 the task was put in the hands of his brother-in-law, under top-level ideological supervision by a member of the Alawi lineage.[32] In both cases the royal house was careful not to identify openly with any specific group.[33] Within the logic of the system, such identification would have contradicted the notion of royal sovereignty as bestowed by divine grace upon the commander of the faithful. After each election the loyalists either disappeared or underwent scission and changes of orientation. It thus appeared as if the majority, like the opposition, could only be effective in division.

In the referendum for the adoption of the 1962 constitution and the legislative elections which followed in 1963, Hassan II, who succeeded his father in 1961, distanced himself from the partisan struggles by avoiding any action which could have been regarded as support for the FDIC. He went as far as declaring in a press conference that a king must definitely stay above political parties.[34] This attitude was not expressed as clearly in 1976. But it should be noted that the constitution of 1972 explicitly places the monarchy outside the debate of civil society, giving full force to a notion which was not yet clearly established ten years earlier—as evidenced by the fact that the ruler felt obliged to defend it himself.

The struggle for the Sahara and the success of the Green March—organized single-handedly by the monarch, who received all the credit for it—marked the beginning of a spectacular restoration of monarchic legitimacy after ten years of battles with opposition parties, characterized by repression and serious social and political upheavals.[35] As the guarantor of territorial integrity, with control over the timing of elections as well as the choice of strategies for recovery of the Sahara, the monarch skillfully rallied the opposition parties in a context in which the popularity of his actions could only diminish their influence. A new consensus emerged, which forced these parties to accept the number of seats allotted to them without regard for the results of the elections. The success of this new political game was proven in the 1976 and 1977 elections, which were to reactivate parliamentary life.[36]

Every election since the consensus achieved through the recovery of the Western Sahara has confirmed the perception of the king as arbiter, all the more so because the radical groups and the military putschists had been neutralized between 1970 and 1972. From then on the Moroccan parliament began to function as what has become the symbol of a monarchy above parties. This has made it easy for the monarch to accept some limitations on governmental action, and to grant the right of criticism and some freedom of opinion regarding issues that do not challenge the powers of the royal family.

The first legislature under the current constitution lasted from 1977 to 1983; the second was inaugurated in the fall of 1984 and a third one in 1993.[37] There is parliamentary debate, but the automatic reelection of the majority guarantees that the government can act without much worry about the influence of the opposition. In fact a new style of management has gradually emerged: ministers have increasing responsibility for daily affairs, while major decisions and fundamental choices are in the hands of the sovereign assisted by his advisors and a group of faithful who have access to him. Nevertheless, the legal opposition—represented mainly by the old nationalist party (Istiqlal), the more radical Socialist Union of Popular Forces (USFP), and Democratic Confederation of Labor (CDT)—must always be on the defensive. The USFP and the CDT were accused of instigating the serious riots of 1981, particularly in Casablanca. The USFP was also subjected to repression after questioning the handling of the Sahara issue; disagreeing was perceived as a challenge to royal power and a crime of lèse-majesté.[38] The accusations were repeated in the winter of 1990 when a general strike to protest increases in the cost of living and unemployment turned into riots which affected several large cities as well as the medium-size semirural centers.[39]

Nonetheless, the king's arbitrating role has not only survived but also expanded, as can be amply illustrated. Suffice it to mention three instances here. In 1978 an important national conference on the current and future situation of agriculture took place in Marrakech on the initiative of the head of state. The notorious priority given to the agricultural sector in postcolonial Morocco gave particular significance to this event, which was widely publicized and discussed in the national media at the time. It is important to mention briefly the context in which this colloquium took place. The last stage of recovery of colonization land by the government took place in 1973, marking the end of a long process by which a considerable amount of land fell into the hands of the postcolonial bureaucracy.[40] However, an important portion of the recovered land was acquired illegally by the new elites, leading to criticism of the government and some serious incidents.[41] Moreover, only a small portion was actually granted to the poor, contrary to what the impoverished rural masses expected from an agrarian reform which promised the redistribution of land to peasants. The rest was put in the hands of management firms supervised by the services of the royal cabinet. These measures were perceived as increasing inequality and favoring the privileged classes, who also benefited from the royal establishment's promotion of dam and irrigation projects and other large-scale development programs.[42] Some people voiced demands for a reduction of these socioeconomic disparities, which were also of concern to international circles.[43]

So the national congress made it its goal to achieve balanced development—which required royal mediation between the social classes in the countryside. The debate involved all political forces as well as the whole government, the chambers of agriculture, and high-ranking technicians and administrators. After serious in-depth discussion Hassan II, who met twice with the members of congress, was presented with recommendations stressing reforms in favor of small landowners and a reduction of inequalities. The king chose, on the contrary, to focus on an improvement of the agricultural credit network and access to modern technology. The reform of agrarian structures was not considered a priority. The arbitration process, which had been initiated by the sovereign, was accepted as valid by the various social actors, and its outcome has not been subjected to public criticism or challenge.

The king does not arbitrate only political conflicts. His intervention has also been solicited in labor disputes and technical controversies. In 1988, for example, there was a lengthy confrontation between the unions and the government about the scale of salary increases in the education sector. Protracted negotiations did not lead to any conciliatory formula acceptable to both parties. Again people automatically requested, and received, royal arbitration. As a result, wages were increased and career advancement procedures improved. That same year there was also a heated debate between engineers and top-level administrators regarding equipment and flood control around the Ouergha River (a tributary of the Sebou), which overflows dramatically and floods the large Gharb plain north of the town of Kenitra. There were two sharply contrasting opinions, one in favor of a set of small-scale projects to be completed gradually, the other in favor of a gigantic dam which would entail difficult and constraining financing. Once more a national conference requested royal arbitration. Without rejecting the first option, the king's decision was to start with the gigantic dam.[44]

These illustrations highlight the ambiguous nature of the notion of arbitration. The image of the king as arbiter, which was advanced as early as 1963, was temporarily compromised by actions of the royal house itself: up until the 1970s it had to take direct control of the administration and armed forces and contain the opposition through negotiations and harsh repression. The image regained legitimacy only through the success of the Green March. Alawist ideologues have long stressed that only the monarch could arbitrate between civilians and the military, Arabs and Berbers, urban and rural populations, rich and poor—only he could maintain cohesion across the fault lines which, in their opinion, would otherwise threaten the unity of the nation. But there has not always been consensus about such mediation.

Today, however, it seems that everyone wants to believe in it, even when the sovereign's decisions appear to be guided by the interests of the monarchy and the social categories closest to it. Is this arbitration? It is in the sense that it provides solutions which cannot be rejected by any political protagonists; it has the merit of closing debates and preserving a certain order. But if the main objective of arbitration is to maintain order, the process cannot also be above the political parties. So we are dealing with a fiction—but a fiction which is accepted by the political actors for a variety of reasons. Some of them see it as a guarantee that the military will not seize power—a strong motive for the majority as well as the opposition, despite the unrest engendered by growing inequalities. For others it complements the hope that a certain degree of economic development, as sustained through 1989, will eventually assure a minimum standard of living for everyone. The most important reason may lie in the efficiency and dissuasive power of the existing system of repression. Whatever the specific weight of each of these reasons, the consent of men and women to this form of exercise of power must be attributed to motives which operate on a deep, nonobjective level of awareness and guide their daily behavior. Political interaction reveals the efficacy, within the present Moroccan system, of political and social alliances the conditions of production of which still go unquestioned. To be sure, these alliances are today highly debated, but so far their basis has not been seriously challenged.

Observers—and above all political scientists—recognize the prestige the king derives from both his sharifian descent and the religious legitimation of his power through the procedure and rituals of *bay'a*. In 1961, after the death of Mohammed V, the ulema—the spiritual leaders of the Muslim community—took a solemn oath when the crown prince was brought to the throne, and the representatives of the people followed their example. These representatives are chosen by the administration, but it does not matter; so far nobody has challenged the representativeness of those who each year swear allegiance to the sovereign.

In practice, however, it is difficult to assess the relative significance of genealogical charisma and the oath of allegiance. They are assets, but of a vulnerable nature; descent from the Prophet does not conjure up norms but rather varying degrees of sympathy, as well as religious fear, for those who claim it. As for allegiance, it can be taken back, according to Sunni Islamic law (though only under certain conditions), if the recipient proves incompetent or is discredited. The 1972 constitution does designate the king as commander of the faithful, the supreme representative of the nation.[45] But by so doing, it maintains the sovereign's traditional, extraconstitutional legitimacy, giving him, moreover, legislative powers which far exceed those of the parliament. Enshrined in a constitution, however, this type of legitimacy becomes ambiguous.

In any case, in the absence of actual evidence of its efficacy, traditional legitimacy remains one kind of recourse among others. Strangely enough, it has a hold on the minds of people only at times when the monarch accomplishes exploits of a particularly striking nature.[46] Such was the case, for example, in 1971 and 1972 when he relied on his energy and talent to escape two attempted coups. But in periods of crisis, when disturbances occur, nobody seems to care about grace or religious titles. This is strikingly clear to anyone who witnessed the riots in Casablanca in 1965; those in the major cities in 1981; those which resulted in many casualties, particularly in Fez, in the winter of 1990; or the February 1991 demonstration in Rabat which openly challenged the king's stance in favor of the U.S.–led coalition during the Gulf crisis.[47]

We must therefore return to our examination of factors crucial to preserving the Moroccan political system other than religious prestige and allegiance, which in a sense remain merely formal foundations. All facts point to the elaboration of a structure based on three elements: an apparatus of coercion devoted to the monarch; a multifaceted struggle against the urban political forces that grew out of the struggle for independence (basically a petty and middle bourgeoisie supporting the ideal of reform and progress); and an alliance with the rural notables.

A Muzzled Civil Society

The period between Mohammed V's return from exile (November 1955) and Hassan II's declaration of a state of emergency on 7 June 1965 was marked by several events which led to a reinforcement of the apparatus of repression, a weakening of the opposition, and the establishment of a social coalition supporting the monarchy. During the following five years the exercise of power was supported mainly by the police and the armed forces. The king sought to win the support of rural notables and large landowners through the distribution of favors and a policy of vigorous agricultural development facilitated by foreign loans. But the ensuing corruption and the rural exodus engendered by these development policies created malaise—which led to new attempts at political overture and the activation of a second parliamentary experiment in 1970.

The fragile nature of this formula was demonstrated, however, by the abortive coups of 1971 and 1972. Unrest in the educational sector, renewed in 1971, continued until 1973; an overture attempted in September 1972, with the beginning of a dialogue between the Palace and the opposition parties, soon came to a deadlock due, on the one hand, to the opposition's internal divisions and demands and, on the other hand, to the sovereign's refusal to concede any power. A new wave of repression and a set of laws curtailing civil liberties completed the intimidation of the Istiqlal and Socialist Union of Popular Forces. The Sahara issue, which was vigorously reactivated by the Palace and the opposition parties, served as a catalyst for a rapprochement. Starting in 1975, a new consensus emerged. After a long period of repression the parties were overcome by the royal initiative, which engendered popular enthusiasm again. The taming of these two major political forces made possible the arbitrated elections already described.

Soon after independence Moulay Hassan (the crown prince who was to become Hassan II) succeeded in establishing his authority over the Ministry of Defense. An American author and former intelligence officer who was close to the head of the first independent Moroccan government remarks that despite the efforts of the national party (then at the peak of its popularity) the king wanted to preserve the tradition of a "royal army" and was able to give the task of organizing it to the crown prince. So the latter was the one who negotiated with France for the transfer to the new state of the law-and-order forces relinquished by the protectorate, as well as for the development of a professional army.[48] This undertaking involved the integration of the National Army of Liberation, a task accomplished as early as 1957 with the help of some of its own leaders.[49] The Istiqlal's hold over the administration, as well as the rise of the nationalist party's left wing under Mehdi Ben Barka's leadership, and with the support of the Moroccan Union of Labor, prompted the Palace to hasten the process of consolidating control over the armed forces—a task which was essentially completed by early 1960.[50]

The selection of officers was telling. Let us mention just a few names: Ameziane, Oufkir, Driss ben Omar, and a little later Medbuh, Bachir ben Bouhali, Oukacha, Hatimi, and Bennani. All came from families of rural or urban notables; they were sons of caids, pashas, and sometimes wealthy merchants. Most had attended the Meknes Academy, which specializes in military training of an elite of mostly rural origin. W. Zartman, who knew them well, makes the following remarks: "The nationalism of the officer corps was expressed in a firm, conservative loyalty to the king and a dislike for politics. They spoke French among themselves, and some had French wives; there was little turnover in their ranks. Because of these characteristics, they could perpetuate the established and successful relations between the French officer and his *goumiers*, based on loyalty and caste."[51]

The early transfer of Captain Mohammed Oufkir, then a famous young officer trained in the French army, from the intelligence services of the protectorate to the Palace amounted to a transfer of the police and the secret service. So the two machines, the police and the army, were now under the direct control of the royal house. The monarchy's rallying of officers who came from families of notables and who had had careers at the service of France amounted to promoting a force hostile to the urban bourgeoisie, which dominated the Istiqlal. These cadres despised politicians and considered themselves as technicians defending ideals which stood above partisan squabbles: God, the motherland, and the king. The army organized itself to maintain domestic order. Its first campaigns, in the fall of 1958, took it to the Rif and the Middle and High Atlas. Some disturbances had developed there, uprisings in which local "big men" contested the hold of the nationalist party over the administration—the monarchy was apparently allowing unrest to spread in order to create competition for the nationalists.[52] (It encouraged the establishment, as early as 1957, of the Popular Movement, which recruited from rural areas, particularly the High and Middle Atlas and the pre-Saharan regions.[53] The new party was legalized in February 1959, despite resistance from the Istiqlal.) The stationing of soldiers in Meknes, Kenitra, and Marrakech is revealing of the army's real function: it was in fact replacing the colonial troops, whose geographic distribution had been motivated by domestic security concerns rather than the defense of the territory. The army did intervene twice at the borders in the early days of independence—first within the framework of the Ecouvillon operation (1958) and again during the Sand War between Morocco and Algeria in 1963.[54] It should be noted, however, that the Ecouvillon operation amounted to a police operation, since the objective was to eliminate the remainder of the liberation army in the southern regions. Finally, the same tradition of defense of the monarchy accounts for the use of the army under the authority of the king and the leadership of officers handpicked by him. Among its leading officers was Oufkir, who as minister of the interior conducted the bloody repression of the Casablanca riots in March 1965. At that point, Oufkir became the strong man of the regime: the military institution was at the center of political life in the country. As chief of police, once

the Istiqlal party (and its left wing, which had assumed leadership between 1958 and 1960) was excluded from the government and as minister of the interior from 1964 until the summer of 1971.[55] And next to
Oufkir was General Medbuh, who after serving as governor and minister, became the head of the Royal Military Household in 1967.

The monarchy's monopoly over the police, the territorial administration, and the army is reflected in a number of facts. First, the Ministry of the Interior is always reserved for the Palace's close friends,
and second, the Ministry of Defense was, with one exception, in the
hands of the crown prince, later king Hassan II.[56] However, control
over the apparatus of repressing disturbances does not fully account
for the fact that the regime was put in place or for its perpetuation.
Rather, we need to think of reasons such as the reduction of the
sphere of political activity, the weakening of the parties, and finally
the economic prerogatives that favor a privileged class. Let us first examine the process itself. Later we will consider the cultural dimensions which assured its success.

Cleavages within the country were already being exploited in the
early days of independence—not only the cleavages between Arabs
and Berbers, which were used to limit the influence of the Istiqlal, but
also the rivalries between urban elites. Some key positions, for instance, were allocated to sons of Berber notables who had been educated at the College of Azrou,[57] and Hassan Louazzani activated a
small party hostile to the Istiqlal among the urban elites. Finally, it did
not take long for divisions to appear in the great nationalist party itself. The young leaders, who had received a modern education, opposed the old guard, which came from more traditional urban families and had been educated in the antiquated Islamic institutions of
learning.[58] Among the modernists, the Berbers educated at Azrou either rallied to the Palace or showed a leaning toward the party's left
wing—which particularly opposed the more conservative leaders on
the issues of agrarian reform and the reaffirmation of the inviolability
of private property. The powerful Moroccan Union of Labor (UMT)
supported the program of the Istiqlal's left wing, which formed the
Ibrahim cabinet in December 1958. Tensions increased and by January
1959 the Istiqlal split into two groups; approximately eight months
later the young radicals formed an autonomous party called the National Union of Popular Forces (UNFP).[59]

In the spring of 1960 the UNFP cabinet headed by Abdallah Ibrahim was dismissed and replaced by a new cabinet headed by the sovereign himself, which included a majority of so-called independent ministers.[60] By then the political scene in Morocco had taken on the features which were to characterize it until the 1970s and which have partially survived to this day: an aged nationalist party shaken by the scission and discredited by its temporary role in the government, divisions which keep part of the elite out of the center of the political arena, and numerous parties competing with one another—the Istiqlal, the Democratic Party of Independence, and the Popular Movement. The UMT, a powerful labor organization, claimed the loyalty of the working class. But it had competition from the General Union of Moroccan Workers, created by the Istiqlal after the scission. Finally, a plot against the crown prince ("discovered" in 1959, it motivated repression of UNFP militants and former members of the liberation army) and the strikes of 1960 were used to weaken the left and exclude it from the government.

At the center of this political world, atomized by competing interests and especially by the monarchy's action, was a king who had now recaptured most of the power and restored a vizierial style of government. Such was the situation when a number of political and union militants decided to collaborate with the monarchy, which they perceived as controlling the political game and the keys to social and political success. The structure then put in place was completed with King Hassan II's accession to the throne after Mohammed V's death on 26 February 1961.

This is the context in which the regime's economic decisions, particularly those favoring large landowners, must be understood. The 1960–1964 five-year plan, formulated under the influence of Abderrahim Bouabid, then minister of economy, stressed industrialization and agrarian reform, two priorities of the dismissed leftist cabinet. In practice, industrialization was soon abandoned and agrarian reform limited to the distribution of small amounts of land to poor peasants. The monarchy had earlier encouraged and publicly endorsed the creation, in July 1958, of the Moroccan Union of Agriculture (UMA), dominated by Mansour Nejjay, a large landowner who had been an engineer and a caid under the protectorate.[61] Nejjay remained loyal to the monarchy and was the first minister of agriculture in independent

Morocco. Under his direction the UMA advocated the use of large-scale farming (which in his opinion was the only way to integrate modern technology) and educational programs for farmers.

The UMA became the organizing center for the new landed class and maintained close contact with the Palace.[62] Another union affiliated with the UMT, the USA, which had seventy thousand members militating in favor of reform, was promptly eliminated. This cleared the stage for the UMA, which to this day functions as a powerful lobby.

Although the regime never overtly rejected the ideal of agrarian reform, it soon came to interpret it along the lines advocated by the UMA, namely as the adoption of modern technologies. Except for the distribution of land, which by 1965 had only affected eighteen thousand hectares,[63] all reform ideas were abandoned in favor of large-scale hydraulic projects and a program promoting cash crops such as sugar beets, sugarcane, and cotton. This led to the creation in September 1960 of the National Office of Irrigation, which was set up to equip and develop five large perimeters. The abandonment of agrarian reform resulted from the joint efforts of the UMA and the Palace, acting through the Ministry of the Interior.[64] The 1960 communal elections clearly established the dominant position of movements closely tied to the Palace, including the Popular Movement as well as a multitude of independent candidates; these independents were either defectors from the Istiqlal and the UNFP or rural notables who had often compromised themselves under the protectorate and were thus initiating a reversal of alliances. Disillusion in the rural areas after independence resulted in a vigorous comeback of traditionalist rural groups in local elections. In this context the UMA succeeded in attracting not only the large landowners but also the small farmers of the so-called traditional sector.

Reducing the influence of the Istiqlal in the countryside was accomplished by reactivating clientele networks and creating new political or union groups hostile to the UMT and the opposition parties. These actions allowed the notables to acquire former colonization land despite the fact that such transactions were prohibited.[65] The two objectives of blocking agrarian reforms and setting up rural communes for the reinsertion and consolidation of monarchic power at the local level were reached at practically the same time.[66] In this context the monarch's power was sufficiently entrenched to limit the distribution of land to peasants between 1959 and 1973 to only 185,000 hectares of the 750,000 arable hectares of recovered settler land.[67] The UMA fostered the transfer of part of these landholdings to its powerful adherents.

The 1960 municipal and communal elections were the last step in the administration's concerted action to reestablish relations with the rural notables, who for a while had sided with the colonial powers. This is the only way one can interpret a type of administrative organization in which both the sheikh, at the tribal level, and the *moqaddem*, at the village level, were chosen within the local groups and their prerogatives enhanced. It amounted to rebuilding a network through direct administrative channels. There was also indirect rebuilding through the communal and municipal elections held under tight supervision by the Ministry of the Interior in which voting procedures gave an advantage to new parties opposed to the old parties of the nationalist movement, the Istiqlal and UNFP.[68] The group the monarchy was to use as its support included people who had lost social positions acquired under the protectorate as well as large landowners who needed administrative access to protect property acquired illegally at the expense of the tribes.[69] Rural notables and urban large landowners thus coexisted in the social foundation the regime was patiently laying down. In the referendum for the adoption of the 1962 constitution as well as the 1963 elections which followed, they tried to win a majority in a parliament which, according to the organic law, had to be under the king's tutelage.[70] This attempt failed, however, and there was another period of repression. The rural notables, who were a counterweight to the urban entrepreneurs, consolidated their positions through the exchange of favors; the acquisition of colonial land and the traffic of influence at the top levels of administration illustrate the establishment of networks dominated by patrons who would capture resources and influence.

Another plot was discovered in 1963, and the UNFP was again subjected to repression. In this context, fraught with challenges and fear, the parliamentary debates about agriculture brought the government down in 1964. The riots that broke out in March 1965 were severely repressed by the army and a state of emergency imposed, which remained in effect until 1972. During those long years the monarchy based its exercise of power on the army and on governments consisting essentially of technocrats and nominally independent personalities.

The Patronage System and the Notables: Success through Personal Ties

The dissolution of parliament and recourse to a state of emergency put an end to the crucial first decade of political life in postcolonial Morocco. A relatively stable form of the exercise of power was gradually emerging—a formula in which royal power is still grounded, despite changes brought about since 1975 by the struggle for the Sahara and the election of a new parliament. J. Waterbury's and Rémy Leveau's descriptions and remarkable interpretations give us a good idea of the functioning of this power structure, revealing the social foundations on which the Moroccan political system is built and the types of action and organization by which it is perpetuated. In this section, I will discuss their ideas in some detail; this will give me a chance to identify other foundations which, although mentioned in their works, are not analyzed in depth.

The royal house (*makhzen*), which the nationalists had claimed and passionately defended against the protectorate regime, regained at the time of independence a degree of prestige it had not had since the late nineteenth century. It set up covert internal intelligence services, the network of which was dominated by an uncle of the king until 1988. The royal cabinet was consolidated and kept watch over every aspect of government. Finally the Royal Military Household, which appeared in the mid-1960s, seized control of the army, whose mission from the beginning had been to serve the monarchy. After declaring the state of emergency in 1965, the king governed with the help of the armed forces, and in 1967 he appointed General Medbuh as head of the Royal Military Household.

The military institution was at the center of the system. It maintained domestic order by repressing rural uprisings and urban riots. Some of its leaders also headed secret services and directed police forces; one of them was General Oufkir who, as minister of the interior from 1964 to 1971, led the forces that fired on the crowds in Casablanca in March 1965. The gradual weakening of political parties and unions—through repression of those seeking change and the co-opting of elites devoted to the system—is also characteristic of this postcolonial order. A civilian network emerged, alongside the makh-zen and the military network. The king acted in such a way as to maintain rivalry between the networks and to appear as both in-dispensable mediator and unique source of favors and prebends, which were bestowed as rewards for political service. The tacit grant-ing of recovered colonial land to notables and to officers, who were also given enterprises (particularly in the commercial sector), along with tolerance or even encouragement of large-scale corruption in the public sector and top-level administration, was indispensable to the system.[71]

The monarch thus assumed a role besides that of arbiter, becom-ing the central character in a patronage system, capable of restraining or putting at a disadvantage any political parties or unions that might challenge his power on the basis of class solidarities. This form of ex-ercise of power set up and reinforced networks centered on the king and the royal house, exploiting and refashioning regional and seg-mentary cleavages.[72] According to Waterbury, the choices made by the political actors under these circumstances are pragmatic rather than ideological; they are negotiated in a moral context in which social ideals and class objectives are usually given secondary importance.[73]

For such a patronage system to last, the patron must distribute resources sufficient to maintain the loyalty of the networks. Between 1956 and 1970—both before and during the state of emergency—this demand was met by, among other things, the sale of former colonial land, the development of the public sector, the total or partial Mo-roccanization of industrial enterprises, and finally the Moroccaniza-tion of the tertiary sector.[74] As these resources neared exhaustion, the structure was put in jeopardy; its precarious nature was made obvi-ous by the attempted coups d'état of 1971 and 1972.

There is no question that the mechanisms of balance and arbitra-tion between the networks are fundamental to this system; they may be the most crucial elements in a description of the political conduct of individuals facing concrete risks and dangerous choices. Royal ar-bitration—as an application of economic power and coercion—tends to keep at bay the urban working class and poor peasants, as well as that part of the urban bourgeoisie which makes up the business sec-tor, the professions, education, and public service. Individual con-duct, however, is necessarily shaped by its sociological context. Le-veau convincingly shows that the social forces pushing for structural reforms (the urban bourgeoisie) were from the beginning in competition with the groups which benefited from the colonial system, in particular regarding the acquisition of land.

Within this context the monarchy accomplished its reversal of alliances, essentially by using the 1963 elections and parliamentary experiment to build the foundation of rural notables which Leveau calls a "stability group."[75] The alliance of the royal house with the rural notables is definitely responsible for the weakening of ideology and its replacement by opportunism and the pursuit of favors; it extended to government institutions and to political activity the style and system of relationships which govern interaction between the local and rural elites, in which personal and family ties tend to reduce the importance of other ideals in motivating action.[76] Despite many changes, the alliance has become stronger and survives today.

This account shows that the instability of the Moroccan political system in the early 1970s cannot be fully attributed to the fact that available resources for co-opting elites were exhausted. In reality both the system's perpetuation and its instability were due to the blocking of reforms (especially in the countryside) which might have threatened the existing social foundation of the regime—hence the preferential treatment granted to large landowners and the preservation of the so-called traditional agricultural sector. However, rapid population growth (3 percent per year through the 1995 census) and increasing inequalities led to a massive migration of peasants to the cities—with consequent unemployment, social unrest, and instability. The aborted coups in 1971 and 1972 stemmed from this permanent contradiction. The 1972 constitution and the 1976 election constituted an overture to political organizations and unions which aimed at making room for the middle class and a bourgeoisie whose ranks had swollen thanks to the success of modern agriculture and the resumption of investments between 1970 and 1977 after a period of comparatively slower growth. The new dynamics generated by the struggle for the Sahara resulted in a new consensus, replacing the systematic recourse to repression which had operated until 1973. Since 1975 the weakened and even more divided opposition groups[77] have discredited themselves through their participation in elections manipulated by the administrative structure. The first and second legislatures confirmed the king's absolute power, tempered only by some procedural limits and timid initiatives by a parliament under control. Despite the country's economic accomplishments and the co-opting of new elites engendered by this development, the aspirations of civil society still clash with an archaic form of power, and the presence of a mass of unemployed educated youth constitutes a real challenge for the regime—as evidenced by the 1981 riots and the 1990 uprisings. These movements shook not only the major cities but also medium-size and small towns in which rural migration had created overcrowding. The political parties and unions which used to oppose the regime have tried to turn this discontent to their advantage, but neither these organizations nor the government seems to be able to control the youth; nor does their newly established collaboration in the face of radical Islamist threats seem likely to meet the expectations of the new urban masses.

How can we account for the apparent acceptance of the prevailing formula for the exercise of power on the part of the very same people who contest it? This passivity has been more and more obvious since the emergence of the new consensus in 1975. The foundations of a system such as this probably lie beyond the mechanics of the prebend and its competing networks. Leveau comments on the impact which culture and the style of culturally accepted relationships between notables have on national institutions as a whole, noting the significance of personal ties, generosity, family relationships, and brotherhood affiliation.[78] The co-opted elites accept the humiliation they must suffer in order to gain power or be favored by the makhzen, but they do so, it should be noted, with an ambivalence which oscillates between submission and rebellion, reverence and irritation vis-à-vis the system and its operators.

These are paradigms of action drawn from a reappropriated tradition. There has been, in a sense, a return to tradition in political life, which parallels an assertion of a refashioned tradition in daily life—the appearance, for example, in new forms, of certain wedding rituals or of antiquated family titles such as Moulay ("my lord"), which ordinary citizens must use when addressing the multitude of descendants of the Prophet. This tendency has also been visible in the reconstruction of tradition within the education system.[79]

A thorough analysis shows the theory of king as arbiter, transcending partisan struggles, to be a power construction. As such, it contributes to the cohesiveness of the social and political system. But as contradictions and inequalities increase, the fiction appears insufficient—which is what has happened at those crucial times when disturbances, uprisings, and coups have endangered the regime. On the other hand, if the arbiter's role is understood as a monopoly over the definition of segmentary interests from a position of power, arbitration by the Alawite sovereign is but one form of modern authoritarianism (following Juan Linz's definition).[80]

This form of authoritarianism can no longer be categorized as transitional semitraditional power or neopatrimonialism as suggested by Linz (after Hermassi)—all the more so since, in thirty years of practice, the authoritarian manipulation of segmentary interests (in a style of political behavior comparable to *caudillismo*) has matured and taken on relatively stable and observable dimensions.[81] The royal house also used these thirty years to increase its influence in all sectors of production. It should not surprise us: authoritarian arbitration is based on a monopoly over resources; thus there can be politically determined redistribution, and the new bourgeois can be kept in abeyance by the precarious nature of authoritarian favors.[82] If this is so, the alliance of the throne with the peasantry appears in a different light. The vulnerability of bourgeois fortunes and their dependency in relation to the distributing center clear the way for a treatment of the notables which is characteristic not only of the countryside, but also of urban centers.[83]

Leaving aside the position of the notables in the commercial and industrial sectors, I will devote the end of this chapter to the rural notables, since they are the ones who, so far, have been responsible for the stability of the regime. It should be clear that no particular notable will recognize himself in this list of traits I will sketch. But the picture will hopefully bear some resemblance to all of them and thus point to cultural schemata which are at the basis of the exercise of power—schemata which have too often been neglected by political scientists.

The rural notable differs from the new agricultural entrepreneur, in spite of some overlap between the two categories. The first category is made up of individuals with rural origins, whereas the second consists of individuals who invest commercial and industrial profits in agricultural operations. The rural notables often belong to families which exercised local power under the protectorate or collaborated with it due to their influence, religious or otherwise, on the peasants. The preeminence of these families sometimes goes back to the times before colonization and the advent of the new nation-state. Others are "new notables" who owe their improved condition to the mobility engendered by the colonial transformation, or the crucial period marking the end of colonialism and the consolidation of the postcolonial power center.

The rural notables live on their land and maintain an urban residence. Even when they are away from the village or the tribe, they keep strong ties with it. They play an active role in local political life and, since 1962, have been dominant in electoral consultations. Those who do not succeed in becoming members of communal or provincial assemblies take on local administrative positions (sheikh, moqaddem, commune delegate, customary judge, intermediary in dealings between the authorities and the population). The notables also control most of the regional and local branches and business offices of all political parties, whatever their ideological inspiration.

The notables are large landowners who do not work with their own hands. They mechanize work in the fields and adopt modern techniques once these innovations are widely accepted. Their management style is noncapitalistic, at least with regard to the use of profits—it may, however, be capitalistic at the operational level. In the first case the farm is managed as a family unit and domestic entity; in the second case the product derived from modernized and rationally calculated capitalist processes is spent in part on maintaining a clientele through generosity and the cycle of gifts and countergifts. Since the early 1970s he no longer worries about technological innovation: it has proven its worth and become a source of prestige. Social innovation, on the other hand, is approached in a very circumspect manner; the notable knows that he risks losing an asset if he modifies the relationships which condition his influence. One way or another, he must continue to associate with relatives, neighbors, acquaintances, and others who have always depended on these "old" bonds. Wages themselves do not eradicate the system which ties the notable to those whose subsistence and existence are dependent on him. In such a system even the position of wage earner is a favor granted by the notable.

We can now see the joint effects of an ecology and a kind of practical ideology. Being a notable requires freeing oneself from manual work so as to direct one's attention to social ties and their political consequences; this "social" work does require serious investment in energy, hospitality, and the distribution of favors. The resources applied toward these ends do not all come from the land; it is also important for a notable to obtain subsidies from outside (in this case from the government). These subsidies make up for the shortcomings of a still precarious agricultural production.

In places where urbanization and industry still have little influence, one can clearly see what might be called the notables' gradualism. They do not, for example, succumb to the temptation of living in modern houses. In a valley of the High Atlas near Marrakech, at the southern end of the Asni basin, a notable from a family of former sheikhs that had ties with the region's "great caid" under the protectorate, and who is himself a former House representative, still keeps a comfortable Berber house which looks like a *kasbah*—while also maintaining a modern villa in Marrakech. He makes fun of the nouveaux riches from the city who build European-looking residences below the village. Not far from there, in the N'fis, the former deputy is no other than a former friend of the family of Caid Goundafi, who married one of the daughters of the famous potentate; having thus inherited part of the lord's fortune, he shows obvious interest in maintaining an ancient-looking residence, but has also acquired a house in a fine neighborhood of Marrakech.

The same kind of behavior can be witnessed at the other end of rural Morocco; in the Innaouen, between Taza and Fez, the children of old makhzenian or brotherhood families are modernizing agricultural work while preserving the liege system and maintaining ancestral residences. In the basin of the Arich Oued, near Settat and Casablanca in the heart of the Chaouia, one of the new notables has acquired—through his studies in one of the *Madrasas*, Islamic institutions of learning, and his marriage into a wealthy family—a considerable amount of land, which brings profit thanks to the labor of his brothers and of workers recruited from the village. The tilling of the land is done with tractors and there are mechanical harvesters; however, shepherds under old-style "contracts" tend the flock, while a multitude of sharecroppers who receive payment in kind (*khammās*) take care of the crops and perform other tasks, including domestic services. While he supervises agricultural production, he also attends to the business of the rural commune to which he has been elected; for this he counts on the support of his in-laws, some of whom were local authorities under the protectorate and still own the land in a group of villages under their dominance. Its luxurious residence, refined cuisine, and large number of servants clearly indicate that this is a family of old notables.

The notables dislike innovation. But let us be clear about their attitude: in reality they feel that the group, the mass of faithful surrounding them, is observing them and even spying on them. Between 1975 and 1985 prolonged periods of drought on the semiarid interior steppes of coastal Morocco (in the plains of Haouz, the Sraghna, and the Tadla) forced the peasants to dig wells in order to irrigate some land. For several years they only cultivated fodder and fed animals; the production and sale of milk were later developments. Why? The usual answer is that there was no collecting center for the milk. In reality the notables were hesitant to sell milk because this was an innovation. No one wanted to be alone in doing so. In the last few years local-level acceptance of this practice has resulted in an intensification of agriculture and notables have come up against ancient customs: many disputes arose when irrigated parcels of land were invaded by the neighbors' flocks, but nobody dared erect fences. Everyone thought of wire fencing, but actual construction could have led to critical and sarcastic comments so nothing happened for a long time. Throughout rural Morocco, except in enclaves where capitalistic agricultural enterprises have developed, change has occurred slowly due to the notables' gradualism.[84] Such is the price they pay for their local sociopolitical involvement.

The notables respect technical traditions; but it is in the area of ritual practices that their devotion is most obvious. They maintain village mosques, see to the well-being of the imam and Koranic master, and do not hesitate to provide the village with a decent center of worship if none exists. They aspire to irreproachable observance of the commandments of Islam[85] with a dedication equaled only by their attachment to the great maraboutic rituals. Since the mid 1960s the revival of large-scale annual ceremonies held around shrines dedicated to the great saints of the country has created a stage (in the theatrical sense of the term) for the active participation of the notables, who receive public and symbolic support from the highest authorities in the government.

But only rarely do the notables function as a group and even less often as a class. Their collective action involves a local nucleus and does not extend beyond the limits of a network of dense interaction.

The government or the political center can, however, accustom them to a particular type of relationship with itself. For example, in the nineteenth century, before the French protectorate, there was a mixed attitude blending collaboration and distance: the notables sought favors from the monarch while protecting their local powers and privileges against the encroachment of the makhzen; through alliances with them, the royal house strove to maintain some local influence, even if it was unstable and ambiguous.[86] Nowadays the notables have consolidated their landholdings, thanks to the French protectorate, whose action prolonged itself after independence in this regard. But they still need the support of the administration to cope with the peasants' claims. This explains why the notables are sensitive to the pressures of political authority: it can endanger their economic base.

Beyond their typical relationships with the political center and with the peasants, the notables do not function as a class within the overall national political configuration. In this regard I cannot agree with the analysis of D. Seddon, who tries to describe political action in rural Morocco in terms of class.[87] The notables support the monarchy, but only inasmuch as it motivates them and, through its systems of favors, makes them behave in ways which are favorable to it. Notables can be found in the most diverse political parties; their political choices are guided by local factionalism and immediate interests. They act in a pragmatic rather than systematic fashion. Given their localized social integration, as well as their oral (Arab or Berber) Koranic or scholarly-scriptural culture, the notables are either outside or beyond other social and political ideologies. Moreover, those ideologies, which operate at the national or supranational level, lose their force when confronted with localism and Islam—the only formalized system favored by the peasantry. All of these factors account for the notables' desire to preserve the status quo. They may support the government machine which exists because of this status quo, or ignore it if it does not serve their interests; but they only organize collective actions if their way of life is challenged, whether by a brand of reformism they regard as too intrusive—as in the early days of independence—or by colonial aggression, as exemplified by their struggle against French penetration during the nineteenth and early twentieth centuries.[88]

Leveau did not fail to see the role of notables as a stabilizing force in the social and political system. He also correctly stated that the particular character of the political scene and political conduct in Morocco lies not so much in the force of pragmatism as in the revitalization of the tradition of the notable. Modernizing ideologies have been pushed aside by the renewed influence of the culture of the notable, which, as I have noted, has two foundations: Islam as locally practiced and a way of life governed by custom according to the notables' claims.

As a "stability group" the notables have a firm hold over the countryside. But this does not tell the whole story: the notable constitutes a cultural reincarnation which has penetrated almost all spheres of life, making his role crucial within the framework of our discussion. The figure of the notable informs success in public service, ministerial circles (in which a few notables guide others), political parties (majority and opposition), academic and intellectual circles, trade unions, and the business world.

The notables' political culture, however, appears pragmatic and devoid of ideology only if the concept of ideology is restricted to systems of social and political ideals engendered by the European humanist revolution. This restricted view becomes problematic as soon as one considers the Muslim faith and its impact on attitude formation: let it not be forgotten that Islam provides the faithful with a theory of the ideal society and its economic and political structure—a theory which ought to be illustrated by Muslim daily life, which, in a somewhat paradoxical manner, must prove the excellence of that very theory. The center of ideological life is thus not a coherent system of ideas and concepts, but rather the concrete set of comportments which the faithful display as rallying signs. It consists in the affirmation of the Creed, in fasting, in daily individual prayer and Friday communal prayer, in alms giving, the hajj, and sacrifice. It entails sexual abstinence, which in this context translates as distance vis-à-vis women; charity, which cannot clearly be separated from the social value of generosity; and respect for elders and tradition. Innovations endanger community consensus; if introduced they must be hidden, disguised, or even transformed to such an extent that they cannot be identified. If ever an innovation succeeds in imposing itself on everyone, it becomes a tradition.

The notables or apprentice notables must exhibit all these rallying signs, which for the most part refer to the famous five "pillars" of Islam. Many of them take advantage of their sharifian or maraboutic descent. Other signs of equal importance are grounded in the authority of the prophetic tradition and the social ethic broadly inspired by it: for example, an apprentice notable must submit to a master, a chief, a father, or an older person and put himself "at their service" if he hopes to reach a position in which it will be his turn to be served. This notion of service permeates daily life and mediates the transfer of these comportments from religious to political life. The respect due to older people and the deference one must constantly show to masters form the basis of the attitude vis-à-vis saints, and religious men in general, that a notable must support and venerate. The apprentice notables who will succeed are those who, on the one hand, epitomize these values in their conduct and, on the other hand, demonstrate their ability to capture the goods and services monopolized and distributed by an administration which, while apparently organized according to the principles of bureaucratic rationality, functions as a network of relations between notables.

At this point I can try to give a more precise picture of the authoritarian regime and proceed to an outline of its foundations. A notable is a natural leader, in the sense of a paradigm of authority naturalized by sustained practice. But what is of more interest for the purpose of this book is the congruence of the features described with those of the leaders who personify the nation. Note, however, that supreme leaders, unlike the ordinary notable, can avail themselves of decisive means, both coercive and symbolic. The supreme leader in particular is possessed of qualities of sanctity and charismatic descent which only a few other leaders share. Those who gravitate toward the royal household—advisors, government, political parties, unions, and the populace—are his "pupils." He is the "master," the "patron," the "lord." Becoming a notable means getting closer to this central figure and obtaining his consecration. The most important notables have direct access to the master himself, who is radiant like a shrine. Members of this inner circle of disciples take on the highly desirable task of interpreting his thoughts.[89] The directives implemented by the government and the decisions recorded by the parliament are in reality the result of consultations with this restricted circle of faithful. All of them are the sovereign's "servants" (khuddām). It should be noted that the dignified position of "servant" results from a long period of closeness and submission expressed in demonstrations of humility in the master's presence. This vital and dramatized representation of obedience is at the heart of the exercise of authoritarian power; in ritual and ceremony it takes the concrete form of prostration and hand kissing, which every notable must perform at regular intervals. Such images, enhanced by the court etiquette, enter every household through the media. The exercise of power, as a form of living energy, appears here in all the splendor of absolute and accepted submission.

Physical constraint alone cannot account for this form of command and submission, all the more so in that it is permeated with a degree of ambivalence which manifests itself not only in conversation but in coups and assassination attempts. For the master is also the one that others try to eliminate—in order to take his place—and who, as a consequence, must often chastise the disciples and keep them under surveillance. Hence the regular disappearance of servants who are too happy. This ambivalence or quasi-unconscious wavering between submission and rebellion seems to indicate that a powerful cultural schema is at work.

However, this set of attitudes could not impose itself if it did not have its source in the historical roots of the ethos of humility, submission, service, and gift exchange which were so characteristic of power dealings in the nineteenth century. The royal house is indeed an "exemplary center" in which one can observe these notions in the form of discourse practices which also exist—in a sacred form—in the mystical 'adab.

Dar-al-Mulk as Discourse and Practice of Power: The Cultural Schemata of Domination and Submission before the Colonial Conquest

The foundations of contemporary Moroccan authoritarianism can only be understood through a reconstruction of the historical cultural schemata it revives and perpetuates. The mechanisms of dominance and the principles underlying the exercise of power will then come to light. Some—those which, despite numerous upheavals since the nineteenth century, are still at work in the handling of peoples and resources—will be easily recognized. I will not, however, try to identify immutable mechanisms. On the contrary I will describe, in a subsequent chapter, their modes of operation in the novel context created by the colonial transformation. I have already documented, in chapter 1, how civil society was repressed and a new authoritarianism allowed to develop in postcolonial Morocco. In sum, if I discover some continuities, they will have to be justified only as a product of a historical process.

My reconstruction will be documented with examples drawn mainly from the nineteenth century; I will refer to previous periods only when necessary for an understanding of the background. I will not attempt to write a political history of the nineteenth century; this is still an uncharted area of research, which should be left to historians. But I will examine historical writings and other well-known sources in order to reach my own objective: a tentative theory which, without dwelling on the genesis of specific facts, seeks to shed light on their meanings. Such a theory will be based not only on action as reported in the annals, but also on the meanings the actors themselves seem to have attributed to it. An action and the meaning attributed to it may sometimes show apparent contradiction. It is precisely by following the meanders of consensus and contradiction that I hope to account for the political praxis of Moroccan society before the protectorate and to identify some of the most important elements which compose the cultural schema for power relationships, that is, the specific diagram at work since the fifteenth century.

The seat of power in Morocco is located in a capital city which the presence of a ruler transforms into an "exemplary center." The city as such does not incarnate the center of power; rather, the sultan does, and when he moves the center moves with him. This does not mean that cities incarnate nothing. On the contrary, we shall see that some of them play a crucial role in the investiture of every sovereign.

In theory the function is separate from the person; it has a label and a set of legal and conceptual attributes which give it an institutional character (sultanate, imamate, caliphate, emirate, etc.). Once an individual has been given a function, however, he seems to carry it out in a way that reflects his own personality and the country's customs. The reason is that, except for the general duties of the "elect" as codified in the shari'a, everything is left up to the circumstances surrounding a particular reign. For instance, the king can be seen acting as a personal host to visitors from the provinces, accepting their taxes as if they were gifts and expressing his thanks in terms of gift exchange, generosity, and relations of closeness and affection. The existence of a full-fledged royal etiquette is not incompatible with the prince's personalized and intimate attitudes and style in the presence of his visitors. The etiquette seems to allow this kind of behavior rather than restricting it.

All power is put in the hands of the sovereign once he has been brought to the throne. Historical sources do not mention any social institutions or instruments—apart from recourse to the ulema, which anyway is ambiguous—that can pass autonomous judgments or hold debates on royal directives. This does not mean that the prince ignores power relations between himself and the groups which constitute the society he governs, or that his directives are entirely and unanimously accepted and implemented. On the contrary, critics often mount successful resistance, either individually or collectively (rebellions, refusal to pay taxes, relocation in order to escape the prince's authority, support of counterpowers, etc.). But we are presently dealing with rapport de force, rather than institutionalized dialectics which are recognized and accepted by the partners.

The Conceptualization of Politics
in Terms of the Dar-al-Mulk

The term used in chronicles to refer to the prince and his entourage as the center is *dar-al-mulk*. Common language uses the terms *dar-al-makhzen* or *dar-al-sultan*. These terms deserve close attention: we are not dealing here only with an entity limited to a particular group, but with the power principle that operates everywhere, even in places in which the exemplary center is never present, in spite of its notorious mobility. In this chapter I will use *dar-al-mulk*, even though it is not the term most frequently used by the chroniclers, who were more inclined to speak of *sultān* (sultan) rather than *malik* (king). The crucial notions here are the ones connoted by the word *dār* (house) and by the root *mlk*, which revolve around dominion, property, and appropriation. The notion of *makhven*, hitherto favored by many writers, fails to conceptualize power and politics within the Moroccan system of governance.

The dar-al-mulk is the central element in the analysis of the conceptualization of politics. It is represented first of all by the domestic group around the prince (as the head of an ordinary domestic unit), which occupies the space most remote from the outside world. It also includes the group of servants in a broad sense which dominates the space bordering on the outside world. While the domestic group is open to the outside world according to modalities improvised by both, the obligations and rights of the servants are defined by law and tradition. This dichotomy, which is reflected in spatial arrangements, becomes obvious every time a man has gained so much influence that he must maintain some space to act in concert with others or to exercise influence over them; it is the classic opposition between *dār* and *duwiriya* in all "great households."[1]

Let us for now set aside the domestic group and focus on the other one. The group we have labeled "servants in a broad sense" is called either *dawla* or *'Iyāla*. *Dawla* has been translated as dynasty or government, which only serves to obscure the issue; it is rather, primarily, a *turn*, and by extension the group whose turn it is to take over community affairs. *'Iyāla* is a difficult term, in one of its meanings it refers more to an entourage and its whereabouts: all individuals who, in one capacity or another, move with those who have taken the fate of the people into their hands, but also the space and the people over which the dynasty claims sovereignty. The sultan, the army, and the bureaucracy constitute the heart of the dar-al-mulk. The high-ranking positions are filled by men with distinguished social ties and service records. Some of them took the title of vizier in the second half of the nineteenth century; but there is little specialization, except in the case of the grand vizier, the keeper of the treasury, an official in charge of military affairs, and a high-ranking dignitary in charge of grievances. External relations took on the form of a vizierate in the latter part of the nineteenth century, a period marked by dangers and tense negotiations.[2] Obviously there was concern for external affairs before that period. Under Mohammed ben Abderrahman the post was filled by a public servant, but there was no independent vizierate. The dar-al-mulk uses the services of a multitude of *kuttāb* (literally "scribes"), who are entrusted with various tasks, with preference given to ad hoc delegating of the tasks to be accomplished. The tasks are delegated according to experience, meaning, for example, that it would be almost impossible for scribes to serve in the army, which recruits from particular and "specialized" groups.

But dar-al-mulk is much more than a conglomerate of people performing tasks; it is also a society which includes occupational groups in charge of maintaining or organizing daily life, as well as individuals whose presence is indispensable for worship or simply for making the center complete. There are religious specialists, companions for games or literary pastimes, individuals possessed of baraka, and people to whom the prince has extended his hospitality or who have been asked by him to come.

The presence of an individual in the dar-al-mulk is often justified by what is perceived as a natural or quasi-natural bond, which, however, combines with some vague service. This applies to relatives, allies, and friends, any of whom may be called on for help at any time and entrusted with specific tasks. The presence of an individual in the dar-al-mulk may also be justified by a precise function combined with a vague natural bond (or a bond that one attempts to define in such terms). This applies, for instance, to military leaders who have been promoted to fulfill a particular function and whose bonds with the sultan are of a quasi-filial nature.

Hence, the privilege of being part of the royal house is defined either as a natural bond combined with vague service, or as a precise functional bond combined with a vague natural bond. In the first case it is a relationship codified in terms of nature, which has a prominent place in this society, namely kinship. All those who claim such a relationship serve the prince, but their functions are neither well defined nor permanent. The combination of these two principles is an explosive one, since rebellion is not exactly a crime, and since this kind of bond implies an obligation to share in the power.[3] The prince therefore faces certain inherent dangers. In the second case the prince must accept the necessity of placing great power in the hands of agents whose attachment is guaranteed through means other than kinship ties and values. Kin and nonkin must, however, coexist and cooperate in the service of the prince. But, while individuals belonging to the kin and affine networks are in principle bound by the loyalty resulting from these "natural" ties, all power agents owe their careers to royal patronage and live in a state of almost total dependency on the prince. So relatives and affines are bound by the morals of the domestic group under the authority of a patriarch (the prince or his substitutes), and the nonrelatives are bound by the privileges of membership in the dar-al-mulk. Both types of individuals stand apart from the rest of the population and perceive this cleavage as a privilege, a norm, and a necessity.

Closeness, Service, and Gift as Signs and Operators of Power Relations

The most important function at the center, just as in the provinces, is personal service to the prince. In the protagonists' eyes, such a notion does not contradict the other conditions of access to power, since attaining power requires making one's way into the khāṣṣa (the term refers to an elite and is often opposed to ʿāmma, ordinary people). But we must beware of the deceptive nature of this understanding; there is indeed a general distinction between ordinary people and those who are of a superior ilk due to their origins, knowledge, inherited charisma, wealth, and so on. Not all who are part of the superior order, however, are necessarily favored by the prince and the powerful. In the strict sense of the term, the khāṣṣa consists of those who have free access to the power center. Hence, one must distinguish an elite, which exhibits characteristics recognizable (if not always recognized) by everyone, from an elite engendered by political action. Ordinary language distinguishes this general khāṣṣa from the prince's khāṣṣa.[4]

In this system military leaders are recruited from the lineages of tribal notables or among former and current slaves; the other high-ranking government positions go to urban families which have distinguished themselves in the areas of learning, commerce, and public service, or which claim the same genealogical privileges as the ruling family (chorfa). It seems reasonable to assume that this mode of selection is based on the moral authority and influence derived from such social origins and/or practical life. And this real power, which must be acquired before co-optation by the dar-al-mulk, is clearly expressed in common language: those who succeed are "the people who bind and unbind" (*'ahlu al ḥallī wa al 'aqd*). However, the guiding principle remains personal service to the prince, and one's power increases in proportion to one's ties and proximity to him. Hence the relentless effort by people to be as close as possible. We can imagine this closeness (*qarāba*) as a sign of being chosen, for the favors sought, according to chroniclers, point to the preeminence of some servants over others: being allowed to sit with the prince (*mujālasa*), eat in his company (*mu'akala*), be in his antechambers.[5]

But closeness as a source of power is not unique to this system. It is also present in other regimes, whether they be democratic, republican, authoritarian, or totalitarian. What is specific to dar-al-mulk is, first, the elevation of this criterion to the dignity of a quasi ethic and, second, its weight in the handling of practical matters, given the rudimentary division of labor and the relative lack of distinction between areas of competency.

In other words, there is an ambiguous relationship between the exercise of one's competence and closeness. One indication of this ambiguity is found in the handling of what would today be called professional mistakes or failures. Closeness prevents such error's being punished or even being perceived as failures. The Moroccan army suffered what was probably its most important defeat in the nineteenth century at Isly (1844). Its significance derives, not from the magnitude of the disaster, which was to be surpassed by others, notably the one that ended the Moroccan–Spanish War of 1859–60, but from the fact that it was the first defeat to reveal the utter weakness of the sultan's armed forces on land. The campaign, headed by a prince of the blood, resulted in a total retreat. According to the chronicles, the ruling sultan consulted with dignitaries about strategies. One of them suggested removing the commander in chief. The sultan hesitated and consulted another dignitary, who suggested the opposite.

The prince was kept in his position, and the first adviser fell out of grace. Going even further, the monarch turned his anger on the other military leaders, whom he stripped of their functions, sent to jail, and humiliated (by having their beards shaved). They were, however, soon forgiven.

This is probably an extreme case, but it illustrates the fact that servants in the dar-al-mulk are first of all intimates. They may fall out of grace or be seriously chastised by their master. But it all occurs within the royal house, rather than being based on an assessment of their services by a third party. The prince cannot permit his choices and inclinations to be publicly contradicted without damage to his authority. Hence a vicious circle arises: the prince's personnel cannot be judged in terms of existing laws; at the same time the dar-al-mulk is responsible for ensuring compliance with Islamic law—which has developed notions of competence, integrity, duty, and so on, all of which are in conflict with the "ethics of closeness." The only way to resolve this problem is to recognize that the logic of the system runs counter to that of the law and must therefore circumvent it.

In the relationship between the prince and his bureaucracy there is a definite clash between the legal norm and the practical consequences of the notion of personal service. Islamic law and ethics make a distinction between gifts and wages—the latter being associated with work. Both wage and labor must be determined in advance, and every effort must be made to avert any hazards which could affect either of them and invalidate the transaction. But how can one conceive of wages for activities which are considered service rather than work? The bureaucracy is made up of servants pursuing closeness to the prince in order to obtain his favors, a competition which weakens everyone to the benefit of the sovereign and simultaneously destabilizes the whole structure by pitting government dignitaries against one another.

Given this notion of service, the reward cannot be wages. It is important to note that gifts coexist with wages, but clearly defined wages, when granted, are extremely modest; it is obvious that nobody is expected to live on his remuneration. In exchange for service the prince grants favors and benefits. And while the law makes a clear distinction between the prince's personal wealth and that of the community, it is not always easy to distinguish gifts coming from the public treasury—the *bayt-al-mal*—and those which originate in his personal wealth.[6] To the prince's gift corresponds his servant's return gift, since favors do not go just one way.

The coexistence of these two practices and the silence, in the chronicles, surrounding sources of remuneration for other personnel point to the central role of gift exchange. Wages introduce a contractual tie which is amenable to open negotiations, has theoretical time limitations, and clearly designates the contracted task. The case at hand is very different; and anyway cohesion is apparently not expected to originate in a contract. It is through gift exchange that a permanent and quasi-natural bond, beyond any contractual relationship, is reaffirmed. The term *sila,* which designates this practice, establishes it as part of the semantic field of kinship and its obligations. Such ties cannot be broken without the risk of severe social disapproval and divine wrath.

A gift reaffirms a mutual obligation of service and obedience, on the one hand, and protection through the perpetuation of royal favors, on the other. Loyalty is thus symbolized by the exchange of things visible. And in order for this central motive to be constantly obvious, it must be sustained by the circulation of objects. Although wages coexist with gifts, only the latter have the potential to create and sustain relationship. Hence the constant exchange of gifts between the dar-al-mulk and all those who come close to it. All encounters with the sovereign involve presents. And all religious ceremonies, royal parades, family festivities, and visits to the provinces involve presents to notables, chorfas, religious figures, armies, and public servants.

A distinction probably needs to be made between these two-way flows and taxation, the latter being controlled by laws and the operation of the government machine. But taxpayers may not see a real difference between contributing presents to the sovereign and taxation. At any rate the coexistence of wages and gifts has persisted into the twentieth century, and these strategies of generous exchange have operated continuously in government practices.

In this network only the populace does not receive any material gratification. When it behaves as a "good people" worthy of the prince, it receives his blessings—which in everyone's mind guarantees bliss and material abundance. But in exchange for these favors it must give part of its labor to a whole hierarchy of chiefs. The first source of funds for the community treasury is Koranic taxation, but there are also non-Koranic contributions: the *mouna* (exacting of supplies by campaigning armies), taxes levied on the *nāyba* (tribes which, unlike the so-called *guich* tribes, are not part of the regular armed forces of the sultan), and the vilified *mukous* (marketplace and commercial fees), the collection of which led to protests and sparked revolts throughout the nineteenth century.

Impoverishment may have been more widespread in the nineteenth century. But in spite of what postcolonial historiographers have said, the taxes levied in the countryside—as ordered by the political center and relayed by the local notables—seem always to have been imposed primarily on agricultural producers, that is, the peasantry. At any rate, it does not seem that this impoverishment was due only to the commercial opening to Europe or the end-of-war compensations imposed by the imperialist powers in 1860.[7]

The impoverishment of the prince's subjects seems to have been given the status of governing principle as early as the eighteenth century, during the reign of Sidi Mohammad ben Abdallah, at a time when the opening to Europe was apparently still under control.[8] The system in place enabled the sultan to levy resources, first, through canonic taxation and other contributions and, second, through confiscation. The latter method merits some discussion. During the same reign governors were often dismissed and returned to their functions several times or even imprisoned for a while after falling out of grace. How can we account for the sultan's conduct? The "servant" was probably not guilty of political conspiracy or military opposition, which would have been punished by a long period of imprisonment or death, since he was not only freed each time, but also returned to his previous position and status. Each time, however, his property was confiscated. It is tempting to think that this was a levy in the guise of punishment. The imprisonment of an agent of the prince for reasons of nonpayment of farm taxes cannot easily be distinguished from other causes for dismissal and confiscation; but it was common practice until the beginning of the twentieth century to imprison governors, caids, and other tax farmers for short periods of time to force them to pay. Temporary dismissal and confiscation of property (*attatrāk*) generated resources for the treasury. The treatment indirectly resulted in levies on people at lower echelons, since the individuals directly affected not only strove to recover what they had lost, but exacted more in order to offer more presents to the prince; such was the price if one wanted to recover one's position. Hence it does not come as a surprise that the late nineteenth century reforms resulted in more one-upmanship in gift exchange and an increase in the venality of public office.

Hassan I, a powerful prince interested in reform, wanted to bring some order to the system of territorial command. The positions of caid made available by the administrative changes he introduced were sold to the highest bidder. Such transactions followed the rules governing the exchange of favors. Moroccan chroniclers do not say anything about the sultan's personal fortune, although they sometimes mention the use of resources from the treasury for the conduct of business. In practice, however, no clear-cut distinction was ever made between the prince's wealth and governmental resources.[9] Later on, in the nineteenth century, government-appointed reformers were to work on differentiating competencies with financial management independent of the royal house. Such changes, which postulate a new fiscal system based on production and revenue rather than number of men and social status, culminated in the introduction of a new tax system (tertib), which was, however, later rejected.[10] The fact that these efforts ended in stalemate is symptomatic of the strength of a system actually based on gifts, services, and the privileges stemming from closeness to the prince.

Whatever the doctrinal assertions of Islamic ethics and law, and in spite of the efforts of some nationalist historiographers to minimize the above-mentioned features, Moroccan sources echo this mode of functioning specific to the dar-al-mulk. The monarch is definitely hated when he does not distribute favors. Whenever Islamic ethics and law pretend to manage the treasury, they in fact threaten the sultan's popularity; their rigorous application would make him appear a miser (bakhīl). Consequently, he is caught between rigor and generosity, but the power relation favors the latter. The dar-al-mulk discourse operates through the obligation of giving and the sacrifice of goods. When the sultan does not liberally use the treasury for gifts to his servants, they are unhappy. He loses their loyalty and takes the chance that his troops will choose to serve a more generous prince.

Terror and Administration: Between Gift and Contract

The Khaldounian model must be revised. The cyclical process by which tribal coalitions rose to political supremacy—under the leadership of a strong lineage blessed with esprit de corps (ʿaṣabiya)—was no longer at work in nineteenth-century Morocco and possibly not even in earlier periods. Since the end of the Merinids in the fifteenth century, power centers have emerged in a new way: the dynasties no longer come from a powerful lineage surrounding itself with ʿaṣabiya. The Saadian and Alawite chorfas have been primarily figures of holiness originating in religious brotherhood (zāwiyas) and the circles in which the example and memory of the Prophet are venerated. The descendants in the collateral branches certainly attempted to seize power in the nineteenth century. But they seem not to have been supported by other Alawite branches and, most important, they sought the support of the dissident tribes. The sultan subdued them with the help of a permanent army and the tribes he rallied; he also took advantage of collaboration within the groups assembled by the pretenders.

Attempts to seize power continued throughout the nineteenth century and into the early part of the twentieth century. The pretenders can be divided into two categories: either princes of the blood claiming the same Alawite primacy or tribesmen claiming charisma. Some individuals in the second category used their own groups as support and assembled partisans; however, pretenders could not move against the sovereign in power without the support of dissident tribes or rebellious cities. Others, who did not have their own forces and had to face an organized center as well as condemnation by the ulema, were relegated to the position of rogui or fattān. After being vanquished they were usually killed.

In dealing with groups that did not pose a military threat, the sultan associated his lineage with the exercise of power and consequent benefits. The destabilizing potential of the Alawite group, however, stemmed from the fact that its members could claim the same prophetic heritage as the sultan, thus undermining his claim of special privileges. Consequently the prince had to concurrently raise an army and win the loyalty of his own lineage through attentions and generosity. Prominent Alawite families were given large estates as well as privileges regarding the free use of peasants' labor, which limited the latter's freedom.

Sharifian descent functioned as a hub for all the mechanisms of the political center, which had no legitimacy without it. And the army was at the service of this Alawite lineage and its primacy. The classical

argument that the sovereigns acted as defenders of the Muslim community was made dangerously more real in the nineteenth century by
the humiliating progress of European forces. But we must pay close
attention to the more important question—that is, who was entitled
to undertake this duty? The chorfa were apparently successful in assuming the primary role and defending it with ideas, symbols, and
weapons.

The forces thus assembled in order to hold the seat of power were
considered primarily as an army of the sultan (*al jaych al sulṭānī*). In
ordinary circumstances its nucleus was built around the famous Black
Guard, the *ʿabīd al-Boukhari*. Next came the so-called guich tribes,
which had enlisted in the service of the dar-al-mulk in exchange for
land grants and various benefits or privileges, including the right
to contributions from the populations dominated by the politico-
military machine. A reform initiated by Moulay Abderrahman (1822–
1859) revived the Black Guard, which had been neglected since the
late eighteenth century, and introduced a system of regular pay for its
members as well as the rest of the army. Later on, the principle of a
professional army gained sufficient acceptance to result in a military
corps paid and trained according to the European model (*ʿaskar*).
However, until the early years of this century the organization remained at an embryonic stage; during its campaign the army still
counted on the rallying tribes and forced the groups in whose territories it traveled to feed the men and beasts of burden. Such was the
case in Hassan I's campaigns in the east, the Sous valley, and the Sahara regions and in the long fight waged by his successors against the
pretender Bou Hmara in the early twentieth century.

Whatever the intentions of their proponents, the nineteenth-
century reforms failed to introduce a contractual system capable of
substituting for other types of relationship between the prince and his
personnel. Everyone knew and used the contract as a legal form, but
its application beyond the areas of commercial exchange and personal
status had little impact on political relations.

On the other hand it could be argued that the proclaiming of
every sultan appeared primarily as a transaction whose principles
and forms had to be validated through explicit reference to those of
purchases and sales. The act of investiture performed by urban and
rural notables is called "sale" (*bayʿa*). However, the terms of the transaction are general and therefore inadequate as guidelines for the op-

eration of a bureaucracy, the daily management of conflicts, or the handling of taxation, to mention just a few examples. The modalities of this transaction remained unformalized, ad hoc in some way, and a candidate's success was in no small measure contingent on his social standing and armed force.

The acts of investiture originating from the major cities—particularly Fez and Marrakech—played a crucial role, along with other assets, in securing the adherence of the rest of the country. But for this allegiance to persist, its effects and symbols had to be constantly displayed and renewed. Dar-al-mulk required visible signs of closeness and obedience which took the form of exchange of rituals and material favors. Thus a practical relationship obtained, a rhetoric of gift annexing that of the contract and vice versa. Given such annexation, what is important here is the weight given to each as an argument in the competition for kingship.

Far from distancing himself from his own kin (as Khaldounian theory would predict), the Moroccan monarch—thanks to a strong army attached only to his person—actually cultivated his relationship with his lineage, lavishing honors and privileges on its members and attempting to extend the benefits of closeness to all who showed their willingness to serve him. Through gifts and multiple prebends, then, he attached the bureaucracy and the military to himself.

Marriage led to the establishment or renewal of kinship ties and alliances among the larger tribes. As for the Black Guard, it provided the *waṣṣīf* (a particular officers' corps) whose education took place in the prince's household and resulted in quasi-familial bonds between the partners—not to mention the ties formed with black concubines. The harem was not just a product of the lord's sensuality. Rather, through his wives and concubines the sultan extended to important constituencies throughout the kingdom the closeness which was so crucial to the conception of royal service. In the political balances of the dar-al-mulk "maternal uncles" of princes and potential kings would support their "nephews" and provide the necessary counterweight to the agnates' exigencies.

The periodic complaints and rebellions of the nineteenth century seem to indicate that taxation was heavy. As we have noted, in addition to canonic taxes there were the notorious marketplace and commercial fees as well as the exacting of supplies by campaigning armies. Supplies were also exacted by ambassadors and their numerous attendants when they traveled around the country. Within this system the setting up of an army capable of defending the autonomy and dominance of dar-al-mulk was not the only cause for heavy taxation. Even more responsible were the continual exchanges required for access to the center. One obtained the prince's favors through gift giving, which was by definition beyond the limits of regulations. And favors were granted in proportion to what was given—to the extent that protocol dictated the order of audiences with the ruler in terms of the applicants' social status and his generosity.

All this created an atmosphere of competition in which everyone tried to be as close as possible to the royal persona. The corollary was gift inflation. In the days preceding great feasts, dignitaries and public servants engaged in a race, with everyone hoping to reach the "sharifian gates" before rivals—since it was a privilege to be the first to see the "blissful face." The abundance and high quality of the presents were indicative of the submission and the allegiance which had always to be displayed. In this regard one of the most revealing facts is the dissident tribes' return to obedience. After imperial troops had pillaged, burned, and demolished villages, destroyed the trees, eaten the crops, and departed, with severed heads as trophies, or when a tribe could no longer endure a prolonged blockade, or, finally, when a modus vivendi could be found without any need for fighting, the gestures which marked the renewal of peaceful relations were always the same: sacrificing animals and offering presents—after which the sultan, if he was at the head of his troops, granted an audience to yesterday's enemies. This meant that he had forgiven. If some dissidents drew the prince's awesome wrath (*al sukht*) through their defiant actions or repeated humiliations inflicted on his troops, they could appease him—and themselves be saved and reintegrated within the community—only by means of some extraordinary sacrifice. They would throw themselves under the cannons and offer their bound wives and children in front on the sacred ground on which he was camping.

Nothing could be accomplished without gifts. Neither submission nor tax collection, peaceful worship, or the defense of the community could take place without the fundamental mechanism of gift exchange. This is precisely where the contradiction lies: defense and freedom of worship, crucial aspects of the Islamic contract for government, are apparently dominated by the gift exchange system, which is not governed by formalized laws. Gift exchange fed the treasury but also depleted it, and thus triggered the continuous levies. It maintained the "insatiable" nature of the makhzen, so often noted by observers, in agreement here with popular wisdom.

Some religious men and ulema refused to accept government positions or even to eat at the table of the prince or his personnel. By so doing they indicated their rejection of the practices of the dar-al-mulk and denounced the illicit nature of its transactions. However, they themselves could be said to be living off alms and gifts without always being concerned about the origin of the goods. And when they had influence they too were offered presents in exchange for their protection. Can we regard these offerings as voluntary sacrifice? If so, we must ask where personal will stops and constraint begins when protection turns out to be indispensable. There were always some people who took offense at these methods of government. But to obtain complete enforcement of their ethics of integrity and contractual exigency, Muslim rigorists would have had to erase some of the most crucial features of the exercise of power. Furthermore, some local values such as generosity and solidarity, which have been transformed into Islamic values and expanded to the level of the community ('umma), tended to reinforce the role of gift exchange in political relations. In any case, the inflationary cycle of the exchange of goods and favors was an iron law which was hardly influenced, politically speaking, by rigoristic Islamic ethics. And this is the law which is at the basis of numerous levies.

In such a system only the so-called secretaries (kuttāb) (and a few other types of personnel, such as the [limited] marine corps and the artillery corps) were specialized. The training of these scribes required many years in the madrasa, as well as an initiation to calligraphy and the manners of the Palace. Unlike military personnel, these civil servants were relatively rare and could easily be interchanged. The bonds they established with the royal house may have been more distant, but they were also more stable. The closer, more personal relationships the armed men maintained with the king could undergo radical changes; as relatives or clients, they did not hesitate to participate in factional struggles and to accumulate or seize new positions. Not so the scribes. Their fortunes were entirely in the hands of those who controlled the instruments of violence, most importantly the prince. Specialization prepared them for a change of master while insulating them from twists of fate.

Whatever reforms affected the bureaucracy in the nineteenth century—particularly due to more and more forced opening to Europe—their scope and consequences should not be exaggerated. The dominant feature still was the relatively undifferentiated nature of tasks, and the crucial steps toward more radical reforms were not taken until the beginning of this century, when the protectorate built a new administration and put the old institutions of the makhzen under custody. These institutions lacked formalized criteria for access and promotion, and the chronicles do not mention any particular curriculum or system of recruitment tests or exams. Further research may shed light on this aspect of the nineteenth-century Moroccan bureaucracy, which differentiates both it and the old Ottoman bureaucracy from the great Chinese and Japanese bureaucracies. Let us for now note only that appointments and promotions were based on a method of social selection congruent with gift cycles and the venality of the positions.

But can dominance be maintained merely through service, closeness, and gift exchange? There is no question that these central features operated not only in the dar-al-mulk but also in the country as a whole. The "exemplary center" was but one among many centers, albeit the most powerful one, in which the visible social arrangements could be articulated in terms of closeness, service, and the mutually shaping rhetorics of gift and contract. Establishing closeness and forming a community were at once a value and a necessity; but neither closeness nor service could be actualized without generosity (gift giving). The key was in serving God, serving the saints, and serving human beings. Therefore it is not surprising that, once he had achieved his position, the prince continued to operate according to this system, which contributed to the perpetuation of his power.

In Morocco (in the nineteenth century as well as today) a gift given to an equal constitutes a debt which the latter must repay. Whoever is not in a position to do so is deemed inferior. What about the prince? First of all, it is clear to everyone that *he* can transgress the rule of repayment without losing his preeminence. Moreover, offering a present to him is virtually obligatory and in some way conditions the encounter with him. The prince may, in practice, show himself to be generous and conform to the rule of repayment, but he is under no obligation to do so and, most important, he never repays an encounter with one of his subjects with a present—his status and power allow him to offer only his presence in exchange for worldly goods. In this case receiving does not create a debt to be repaid by the recipient; rather, it is as if the gift served to erase a debt which some obscure mechanism forces the donor to constantly renew within himself. It should be pointed out that this is the central motive of Abrahamic sacrifice, which will appear more than once as a cornerstone of this society.

Let us note for now that the present given to the prince makes up for inferiority in the sense that one party considers it its duty to offer this present to another party which offers only its presence in return. When the gift circulates in a society like this one (which is strongly stratified along status lines) it loses its reciprocating dimension and emphasizes dependence and inequality. Its stimulating power, which everyone considers indispensable for the construction of a community, can only maintain its force of attraction through charisma or the use of force. As soon as the latter changes hands, a new stage is reached in the gift cycle. Presents pay for other potential and long-lasting benefits, which the prince can only grant through organized coercion. The gift cycle then becomes a mode of ordering and administering human beings and things.[11]

It has already been mentioned that legality is on the side of the victor, whether he uses actual violence or other means to defeat or discourage his competitors. Once he has reached this stage, his sharifian status rises above everything else. Victory, which is presented by a strong party as divine election, transforms him into a powerful focus of baraka. From then on the combined effects of status and terror can operate.

Social status was based on criteria which individuals theoretically could not modify: birth, skin color, religion, origin, and to a certain extent occupation. It was impossible to abandon Islam for another religion, and converting to Islam from Judaism was rare. The law of *dhimma* maintained a clear separation between Jews and Muslims, sanctioning the Jews' subordination and limiting their legal and political capacity. But many important economic, political, and social ties crossed the line between Jews and Muslims.[12] Except for religion, recognized status categories were not clearly associated with particular functions, although they may have been associated with privileges. Color classification separated blacks from whites, but the normative boundaries were somewhat flexible; for example, the norm in many areas was that blacks were subordinate, inferior, and endogamous, but that did not stop white men from marrying black women nor did it discourage black men (although fewer in number) from marrying white women.

The chorfa were at the top of the status hierarchy and the poor, both black and white, were at the bottom. Between them we find tribal folk, townsfolk, and the descendants of saints (*mrabtin*). The last category was complex; in practice its members could be classified either on top of the ladder, right below the chorfa, or lower than the masses of ordinary men and women, depending on the authority of the charisma they inherited. The category of mrabtin differed from that of chorfa in that it was constantly open to new members, who could gain admission through individual effort.[13] But access to it was closely guarded by the voice of the people, which either granted holiness to an applicant or assured his failure; a failed candidate was subject to scorn, or mute pity at best, and in many instances was condemned by the ulema and the powers that be.

It is important to realize that status category and a person's worth were quite clearly demarcated. Status was difficult to change, but one could gain influence and rank through wealth, knowledge, or personal efforts to achieve charisma. One's worth depended on one's social connections, style of interaction, skills, and morality, as well as appropriateness and the willingness to perform useful tasks for the community. All of these could qualify a person for the highest standing within his community. In practice status emphasized difference while individual effort tended to bring about equality. Such was the rule in a society keen on "ontological inequality."

The presence of the sharif at the head of his armies, and his victories—which constituted signs of God's love for a lineage elected for revelation—preserved the preeminence of the chorfa and made them the mainstays of justice, which here consisted in maintaining the world order with its cleavages and hierarchies. Such divine election was a force of its own, bestowed upon the chosen ones, which went beyond material or intellectual status and success. It transcended the differences that it maintained, and people regarded it as the supreme form of accumulation, in the name of which they agreed to any gift giving or sacrifice.

However, the prince's position in and of itself, endowed as it was with charisma of a powerful nature (as evidenced by his victories), was clearly differentiated from his status. As a sharif he represented all individuals in this category. And his worldly triumphs, though epiphanies of spiritual power, simultaneously cast him in armed might. In either case he entered into competition with the great warriors and other charismatic figures of his era. Let us keep in mind that an old tradition attributed both miracles and military victories to invisible forces.

War and charisma, which were both associated with gift exchange, could elevate men to the highest positions of authority and create legitimacy that was not founded on closeness to the prince, creating power centers that might indeed enter into competition with him. However, to consider these phenomena as promoting participation is to forget that their movement did not dissolve in the center.[14] And if by chance they merged with the dynasty in power, which happened often enough, we would have to account for the fact in terms of the above-mentioned principles of domination.

Terror was a substitute for all the practices described so far when they failed. The recourse to violence was indeed a common method for curbing overt competition—which was also considered normal, as evidenced by the struggles that took place in the early years of every ruler's reign. Almost every sultan engaged in military action immediately upon his appointment. The *ḥarka* (movements of the army under the prince's command) was a major institution of governance; its forces produced a peripatetic center which constantly visited the tribes and the provinces as well as the major cities of the kingdom. Upon their return from large-scale battles, which were sometimes directed by the sultan himself, military columns (*sawga*) would attack minor pockets of insubordination.[15] (Without pressure, it was common for taxes to go uncollected.)

The army targeted both property and people, but fighting could often be avoided. Sometimes mediation led the rebels to repentance. At other times taking hostages or blocking the markets was enough to bring foes to compromise. Likewise prisoners, usually not held for long, were used as tokens for the purpose of negotiation.

More serious hostilities led to extreme actions by the army: the destruction of crops, trees, dwellings, and human beings. In the case of attacks which were definitely meant to challenge the prince, the army decapitated the dead and sent their heads to be displayed in the cities. Decapitation (*ḥazz*) and the display of heads was intended to fill people's hearts with terror. It occurred rather frequently in the nineteenth century, according to Moroccan and foreign sources. The following statement, for instance, can be found in a letter written in 1871 by Sidi Mohammed ben Abderrahman, at the end of his report of a glorious victory over the powerful Rehamna tribe in the Marrakech region: "And you will receive the heads of the dead for display at the gate of the city, to serve as an example to those who reflect on it and as a memory for those who can remember."[16]

Other procedures used by the makhzen to handle opponents and their bodies included putting them to death after a long public display. This torture was inflicted especially on pretenders not protected by sharifian status. By taking such actions the prince was asserting his rights on "the blood" of subjects who were no longer submissive. But he did not limit himself to this display of his death-dealing power: some sequences of the ritual seemed calculated to expel the pretender from the current category of the human. It had to be made very clear that one could not measure up to the prince. Hence this celebration of humiliation which went beyond death itself. Once the vanquished had been seized, they were brought to the prince, then made to face the court and the crowd.

There are recorded instances of this ritual throughout the nineteenth century. In the nineteenth and early twentieth centuries, there were three notorious cases, all of which fell into the category of fattān. In 1871, for instance, during the reign of Hassan I, Bou Azza al-Habri, a thaumaturgist and warrior, was seized and first brought face to face with the sultan, then taken around on a camel to be seen by everyone, the well-known practice of "promenading" (at taṭwāf).[17] Later, under Moulay Abdelaziz, the same practice was used after the Rehamna rebellion. It was described as follows in a letter by the grand vizier reporting the arrest of the guilty party:

> Our Lord—victorious by the grace of God—contemplated him and assembled around himself the blissful armies and troops as well as the notables of the city and the caids of the tribes. They examined him in this predicament. Then he was forced to mount a lame camel, paraded bare-headed in the

blissful *mahalla,* and slapped, as God's anger [*sukht*] struck him from all directions. He was then put in chains; after his feet, hands and neck were fettered, he was thrown into an iron cage like a wild boar or a ferocious dog.[18]

This well-regulated liturgy was orchestrated around the sultan and the vanquished in the presence of the court. The slaps and bare-headedness, in addition to the pain, deprived the victim of any attribute of manhood. Finally, being thrown into a cage reduced him to animality and at the same time enhanced the spectacle. Such celebrations of humiliation were definitely intended to be memorable, as clearly evidenced by the torture inflicted on Bou Hmara, a famous pretender of the early twentieth century. After the grim promenade the caged man was placed onto a platform especially erected for this purpose and kept on display in the center of the *mechwar,* or palace courtyard, throughout several days of "festivities and ceremonies . . . organized to celebrate his defeat and humiliation throughout the country."[19]

Michel Foucault unforgettably describes what he called a "ritual," "ceremonial," or liturgy of torture in eighteenth-century France. The cases I have cited of rebellion and challenge to the sultan in nineteenth-century Morocco differ from that of a famous regicide tortured and dismembered in a public square. But they also manifest a personalized confrontation between the sovereign and the condemned man, in which the victorious party takes public revenge on the vanquished.[20] Redress for the injury to the community was of course invoked. But reparation, if it was a factor, did not govern the form of punishment, as evidenced by the element of public display. The ritual which brought the vanquished rebel face to face with the sovereign is absent from the French execution. Nevertheless, in commensurability between sultan and rebel is vividly underscored even though the latter is constructed as a mirror image of the former.

When drawing such parallels, however, we must take into account the specificities of the particular societies. In the Moroccan cases the handling of the victim's body transforms his identity before he is put to death; he is first stripped of his identities as man and as human. But even though he is relegated to animality, the punished man cannot be dismembered and burned to ashes (as Damien was), because in this context human actions are bounded by the dictates of divine law. A man's powers, victory and defeat, and the application of torture remain contingent on God's will. Torture is a display, moreover, of a discursive asymmetry which may be only temporary; the agonistic processes of defining property and power place multiple allies in a ceaseless competition. At any rate the confrontation may not have been as uneven in nineteenth-century Morocco as in eighteenth-century France, especially since the armed forces in Morocco did not yet really give a clear advantage to the dar-al-mulk.

The use of terror was also limited by other factors. Prolonged warfare required logistical, organizational, and provisioning capacities which the belligerents lacked; it required completely specialized armies the cities and tribes did not have. Even the sultan's troops were only partially specialized. Social organization supported this relative balance of forces: it provided the people with means of violence the center could not suppress without depriving itself on the means necessary for government, that is, the tribal structure and the urban institutions. Hence the recourse to a postcaliphal theory of legitimacy reinforced by the promotion of sharafian status. This particular status also served to relate the Moroccan dynastic system to the primitive caliphate.

The solemn act of investiture (bayʿa) legally put the prince in the position of commander of the faithful. The conquest of power through force was only ratified if the bayʿa was implemented. A pretender who succeeded in carrying out this procedure thus became the leader (imam) of the community, setting himself up as the instrument of God and his "shadow on earth." Given this delegation of powers, which made the will of the community consubstantial with that of God, a sultan could rightfully suppress any dissidence since it jeopardized consensus; according to this logic, rebels "disobeyed God and his prophet."

The nineteenth-century Moroccan bayʿa implemented the realistic theory of power which emerged toward the end of the Abbassid caliphate, when the rulers originating from this lineage withdrew, to the benefit of the Buyid dawla. One of these dawla was in fact founded by the Alawites in the mid-seventeenth century. As already mentioned, *dawla* refers to a "turn" at power resulting from various circumstances, including the use of force. Moroccan jurists accepted this situation as long as the two main responsibilities of the imamate—defending the community and protecting Islamic worship—were fulfilled.

But was it an empty formula, as some have claimed? It does not appear to have been: the very ambiguity of the titles granted and the focus on sherifian descent seem to indicate an effort to relate the sultanate to the predynastic caliphate; moreover, as the nineteenth century brought radical changes with the European threat, the act of investiture included a list of concrete measures to be taken.

In the Rabat bay'a of Sultan Abderrahman ben Hicham, dated 3 January 1823, three titles are used: sultan, imam, and caliph. The text also mentions the "paramount caliphate" the signatories wanted the newly elected sultan to take on. Because of such precision the scope of competence offered to the sultan can be compared to the caliphate without overtly claiming it. Let us keep in mind that eastern Morocco bordered on the territory of the Ottoman caliph and that the Islamic world did not really have a supreme leader. So the dignity of the caliphate was extended to the sultanate. The uneasy juxtaposition of these titles is indicative of this process, as well as the jurists' capacity to differentiate the associated institutions.

And this document goes one step further: it identifies the community which "elected" an Alawite sultan in January 1823 with the community which made a famous oath of allegiance to the Prophet (bay'at al-riḍwān). And since the candidate obtained a written recommendation from his predecessor, the first "well-guided caliphs" were also invoked as antecedents. By appealing to the past, then, those involved bypassed the current unfortunate history of Islamic powers in order to avail themselves of the prophetic model. Sharifian ancestry thus constituted a definite step forward, although the coexistence of the sultanate with caliphal titles served as a reminder of the distance between the ideal and the real.

Another example is the act of allegiance presented to Moulay Hafid by the city of Fez on 5 January 1907.[21] Those were troubled times: the previous sultan had abdicated after being charged with unwarranted collaboration with the European powers and abuse of authority. French troops were already occupying part of the territory, and the reforms he had attempted were discredited on the grounds that they were fostering foreign penetration. This document, like the previous one, contains coexisting institutions—caliphate, imamate, 'imāra, 'uḍhma (paramount sovereignty)—but the title of sultan has disappeared. We can understand why the signatories made it their explicit objective to revive the primitive model of government (khilāfa), but its invocation alongside other models places some limitations on its scope. The sharifian argument, which is present, plays the same role as in the first bayʿa I analyzed. But there are some new specifications: abolishing non-Koranic taxes (introduced by the previous reformers), prohibiting collaboration with Christian Europe (dar-al-ḥarb), and allying with other Muslims, in this case the Ottomans.

Abdallah Laroui clearly shows that Moroccan jurists fully utilized the classical theory of the caliphate to characterize and justify the sultanate. This theory, he points out, limits itself to establishing criteria and defining the caliph as the one who is in charge of defending and propagating the revealed law, thanks to a community whose unity and integrity he must preserve; being timeless and devoid of meaning, this theory can justify any situation, to the extent that even an impious and immoral sultan cannot possibly be deposed.[22]

The position of Moroccan jurists thus lends itself to some confusion. First, we are likely dealing with a reformulation of the theory of the caliphate which sanctions a new state of affairs. The dawla legitimized by this theory—imposed by force and invoking God's will—is intended to regulate the politics of a divided 'umma. This fragmentation, which in fact had existed for a long time, was officially recognized at the time when the Abbassids were no longer able to force into allegiance the autonomous kingdoms founded by the Buyids.[23] From then on we have a theory which recognizes power seized by force but limits its exercise through conditions which are continuously reaffirmed in Morocco as well as in the rest of the Muslim world: maintaining cohesion and integrity within the 'umma by fighting domestic unrest and threats from abroad, while guaranteeing worship and the enforcement of Koranic law. By using this second theory, Moroccan jurists were attempting to dress their dawla in the trappings of the caliphate. This also accounts for the recourse to utopia; such an appeal can accommodate nonnegotiable conditions without attacking either the origin of this power or the modalities of its exercise.

We can thus better account for the point of view of the great jurist 'Abdelqader al Fasi, whose main objective seems to have escaped Laroui's attention. It was not due to some Shiite inspiration that this faqīh distinguished two different aspects of the Muslim sovereign's authority, which he called *caliphate* and *imamate,* positing the former as invisible and discontinuous and the latter as visible and continuous, within this particular Sunni tradition, a tradition which would have transferred, so to speak, the Shiite meaning of the imamate to the Sunni caliphate. Such a position leads one to consider as imamate what is actually a sultanian exercise of power. The prince is given the means to assume a quality which—without granting him a caliphal title—validates him as a guide accepted by the community. In other words, military victory and the consent of the community, which are two manifestations of God's will, establish him as an imam and in fact liken him to a caliph. So Moroccan jurists can be seen to have attempted reconciling, in a way, a theory and a practice which were historically divergent.

The Sharifian Motive of Intercession: The Mystical Body of the Prophet and Coercion Combined

In nineteenth-century Morocco the sharifian argument was forcefully invoked in the exercise of power and its legitimation. Prophetic ancestry is absent from Sunni theories of the caliphate, but in their Alawite form it conditions practice. In the act of investiture, in the homilies which accompanied (and still accompany) Friday prayers, and in the rituals which mark the Muslim year the presence of the chorfa provided an indispensable consecration. During the bayʿa they were the first witnesses to be named because of the grace stemming from their genealogy. Nothing could be done without their initiative.

This prominence was far from being strictly ceremonial. Crucial affairs of the state—dynastic squabbles, wars, and rural or urban unrest—required that their mediation be sought. Some sharifian lineages mediated between the sultan and his subjects (the chorfa of Ouezzane being one example). These transactions were carried out not only by branches of the royal family, but also by other groups who settled in the land before the Alawite conquest. The respect they enjoyed from the people gave strategic importance to the great sharifian shrines (Moulay Idriss in Fez, Moulay Idriss of the Zerhoun, Ouezzane, Moulay Abdeslam ben Mchich, Sidi Hmad ou Moussa, and so on). Every such group jealously guarded its genealogy and titles, as well as the material goods provided by the gifts and alms brought to the shrine. They also enjoyed special privileges: they were exempt from the taxes and contributions which ordinary people owed to the makhzen, and in practice they were beyond the control of the jurisdictions handling the affairs of the populace. Some of them were even granted the Koranic taxes obtained in their regions. These privileges, which existed before the nineteenth century, were renewed in similar forms until the early twentieth century. Important sharifian families acquired large landholdings, given to them by decree of sovereign. The most respected ones received the sila, a kind of regular allowance in the form of a gift, which was granted in the name of either kinship or some relationship modeled after it. The sultan himself would visit the great shrines and, like his subjects, pray by the tombs of illustrious saints; the belief was that one's intercession with God would ensure the success of his undertakings was widespread.

The chorfa participated alongside the prince in all great rituals. But it is in the annual celebration of the Prophet's birth (Mouloud in colloquial Arabic, *mawlid* in classical Arabic) that their ascendancy is at its most spectacular—a point which can be illustrated by the historiographer Ibn Zaydan's description of such ceremonies under Hassan I.[24] In parades and ceremonies, not only did the sultan's figure assume the attributes of the most powerful man in the kingdom, but it appeared as the manifestation of the Prophet's baraka: alive, beneficial, and dangerous, capable of single-handedly breathing life into the blissful kingdom represented by the crowds which participated in the ceremonies.

In the night preceding the day of the Mouloud itself, activity took place in the royal household. All high-ranking officials were gathered; so were all important men from the center and from the provinces; commoners, ulema, chorfa, and marabouts responded to the sovereign's invitation. The crowd entered the mosque of the *mechwar*, where poems praising the Prophet, some of which went back to the first centuries of Islam, were chanted throughout much of the night.

The chanting began usually after the *'icha* (last evening prayer), in the presence of the guests, who had positioned themselves around the sultan in relation to the focal point of the *miḥrāb;* this particular niche, from which the imam normally leads all canonic prayers, determined the arrangement. The sultan was seated to the left of the miḥrāb, and the chorfa positioned themselves in front of the miḥrāb, each man's physical proximity to the sultan reflecting his symbolic closeness to him. Across from them, on the right side, were the ulema and the *qāḍi.* The perfume burner was located at some distance in front of the prince. Further away and facing him were the singers, chosen from throughout the kingdom. Behind them came the rows of the secretaries, notables, and viziers; last were the governors, pashas, and military officers.

To put it briefly, the arrangement was as follows: first the charismatic community, then the bureaucratic machine. Those with functions in the royal bureaucracy were put in a secondary position, while priority was given to those who ensured the perpetuation of the family of the Prophet and to the ulema, the custodians of his teachings and tradition. However, at the miḥrāb, the focal point of worship were the descendants of the Prophet, not the ulema. The chorfa derived their primacy from the fact that their presence was a tangible manifestation of the Prophet's "mystical body."

The chanting continued late into the night. It stopped when the sultan left the mosque, followed by the guests, who proceeded to the reception halls of the palace and were served a sumptuous meal. There the sovereign was the first to be presented with a dish, which was then to be presented to the closest chorfa. This was a second sign by which the chorfa participated in the perpetuation of prophetic charisma. Commensality with the central figure of baraka put them above all hierarchies. After the meal the participants slept for a few hours. Those who lived far away lay down wherever they ate the meal. Then, an hour before dawn, everyone returned to the mosque and the chanting resumed. Poems glorifying the prince, panegyrics composed by poets attached to his service, soon succeeded praises to the Prophet. Then came dawn and daybreak prayers (*subḥ* and *fajr*), after which the master returned to his house. The guests left after the chamberlain's substitute had given them a one-rial coin sealed in wax.

The gift put an end to this night of apotheosis of the chorfa and, most important, of the sultan—as the head of a family whose power was grounded in the primacy of the Prophet's descendants through his daughter, Fatimah, and his cousin and son-in-law, Ali. The wax imprint of the coin probably marked an initium. The wealth and material prosperity which the sanctified sultan bestowed on his subjects was represented by this little coin.

According to Ibn Zaydan the same celebrations occurred during other Muslim feasts, and in particular during the Feast of the Sacrifice ('*īd al adḥa* in classical Arabic, *al-ʿid lakbīr* in colloquial). More details of these will shed light on important aspects of the royal house's symbolic power. All the factors already encountered (closeness, service, gift exchange, terror, the Islamic theory of the caliphate, and the promotion of sharifian status) when combined converge toward the synthetic figure of the sultan.

On the day of the great feast clothes are offered to the royal family, officers, governors, and notables. Important ceremonies take place in the *msalla*, a space reserved for the sermon and prayer preceding the immolation of victims. In the major cities of the kingdom it is adjacent to the royal palace, beyond the ramparts surrounding it.

In the morning the prince met with representatives from the tribes, who had come to offer congratulations and the customary presents, thus renewing their allegiance. In the meantime the official procession got ready in the mechwar. The prince came out of his house and crossed a first gate, where he was greeted and surrounded by the personnel attached to his household. These were the members of the "internal corporations," with the chamberlain at their head (*al hanati al dākhilīya*). Then he crossed a second gate on horseback. The royal music resounded, and the servants in the "external corporations"—those who are in charge of the activities of the court—came to congratulate him and wish him a long life; this done, they joined the procession, which moved in the order prescribed by custom and etiquette.

Six unmounted and harnessed horses headed the procession, followed by a small detachment of soldiers arranged in groups of four and the caid of the stables, who walked just before the sultan's horse. The prince paraded in the center of a rectangle, which apart from this small retinue remained open in front. The exclusive royal parasol was held high above him by a servant. The internal and external corporations marched around him, the former on his right and the latter on his left. Then came the ranks of the modernized army and behind them the other armed men (calvary and foot soldiers) from the tribes. The artillery followed at the end of the procession, with cannons pulled by draft animals.

The open front of the rectangle thus created provided a meeting space in which the prince was displayed. When the procession went through the rampart wall adjoining the msalla, the sultan came upon another crowd: on the left were the members of his government mounted on their mules; on the right were the tribal delegates. The central space of the msalla was free, with the calvary in the back. All assembled bowed in silence. The master greeted this multitude through the voice of the caid of the stables. Then the tribal delegates presented themselves to the sultan, who prayed for their well-being and blessed them. After the tribes came the royal litter, led by the great sharif of Ouezzane and the leader of the Nāṣiriya zāwiya, the flag bearers of the Black Guard ('abīd al-Boukhari), led by an uncle or a son of the sultan, with guns on their right shoulders. Finally, behind the Black Guard, came the government and the chorfa, followed by the army.

When prayers ended, the sultanian procession retraced its steps toward the palace according to the same arrangement, with the royal music playing. It stopped at the external gate, and the chorfa, positioned on the right, were allowed to throw themselves onto the sultan's stirrups and kiss them. Standing in rows on the left were the members of the government, who bowed and, after being greeted through the chief of stables, took their turns kissing the stirrups. Next the sultan approached the threshold of his dwelling, where he was presented with the traditional offering of dates and milk by the butchers' corporation. He ate some of the food, drank a little milk, and immediately passed them to the chorfa who led his armies and to officers and notables. Finally, after the sultan had entered his house, gifts were distributed to the singers and the chorfa. Then the caid of the mechwar greeted all the guests, signaling the end of this part of the ceremony.

However, the feast was still not over for the prince. After the 'aṣr (midafternoon) prayer, he would parade again in his finery at the center of the mechwar, which again filled up, this time with inhabitants of the city in which he was staying, who came to offer their congratulations and presents. The Great Feast of the Sacrifice was celebrated every year on the tenth day of Dhu'l-Hijja, a sacred month during which Muslims accomplish the pilgrimage to Mecca, where they sacrifice animal victims. On this occasion a sermon on the meaning of this sacrifice was followed by prayers in the msalla. After the prayers the prince performed the sacrifice on behalf of all his subjects, thus setting the example for all heads of household. The synthetic image of the commander of the faithful imposed by the processions just described was now augmented by two powerful and impelling motives: that of Abraham, whose sacrifice is at the foundation of the Muslim community, and that of the father who must imitate Abraham's sacrifice in order to maintain the community.

In all of these rituals the sultan takes on the features of a tutelary figure who embodies the miracle which gave back to people the real creed, the eternal Islam. Through a simple kind of symbolism the sacred prince acknowledges the participation of the chorfa in this privilege and allows the elite of the kingdom to benefit directly from his persona's holiness and from the emanations which flow at the time and place in which this liturgy takes place. The chorfa receive his gift of commensality and, along with the governing elite, are granted the privilege of kissing his stirrups.

However, participation and submission are one and the same. The ceremony brings together the entire kingdom to bow in front of its Alawite master, a focal point without whom the community would have no real existence. Through the founding figures of Abraham and the father, which in reality are fused into one, the royal house—the exemplary center—is constructed as the source of nurturing which saves the group through repeated sacrifices and allows it to maintain its existence.

The procession was a showcase for all the components of the campaigning army, articulated around a hard core, namely the Black Guard, a combat unit which provided protection for the royal house and guarded the sultan's tents when he was on the move. It is therefore not surprising that the Black Guard marched behind his litter. The presence of the chorfa and the heads of brotherhoods around the same litter was based on the fact that the movements of the army were preceded by mediators who would propose peaceful solutions to conflicts before any use of force.

Foreign observers have not failed to see the sacred character of the sultan's persona, thus concurring with the Moroccan chronicles, which underline the sultan's moral and spiritual influence beyond the limits of his territorial administration; his encampment was always treated as a veritable sanctuary, even in places in which the power of his bureaucracy was contested. Moroccan sources show that people approached the sultan for his blessing and treated him with respect even if he was defeated and taken prisoner. Postcolonial historiography, however, with its taste for the construction of a rationalized vision of the past, avoids any mention of the attitudes of anthropolatry which were definitely present in the royal procession.

The archives of J. Drummond Hay (a British minister in Tangier for many years in the mid-nineteenth century) contain a drawing representing the official reception granted to him by Mohammed ben Abderrahman. The sultan on his horse, surrounded by the usual pomp. Across from him are the ambassador and his retinue. Slightly to the left, close to the hooves of the prince's horse, some Moroccan figures are prostrated almost as they would be during canonic prayers.[25] Salafi and nationalist historians intent on offering a modernized picture of the country may claim that such practices are not related to the Islamic doctrine of power and that this prostration is not considered by anyone as real prayer. Nevertheless, it implies contiguity between God and the sultan, and (most importantly) those who prostrate themselves see no contradiction between their actions and the doctrine. Moreover, few guardians of Islamic law in Morocco can be found to condemn such displays of submission.

In parades and ceremonies the persona of the sultan is exposed to the public; but invisible barriers, in addition to the guards and courtiers, separate him from the rest of the world, just as taboos separate sacred beings and untouchables. He speaks little and most often through the caid of the mechwar or the chief of stables, who convey his greetings to people.

The other major taboo regards commensality; the sultan acts as if this was forbidden to him. He shares in the food only on some ritual occasions when the "interdiction" is partially canceled to the benefit of the chorfa and some notables who constitute the heart of the elite. His distance from others is made most explicit by the etiquette which cancels it; prostration and bowing accompanied by presents are the most common ways, along with sacrifices after a period of conflict. Then, once the taboo has been lifted, people act as if all constraints were lifted in order for devotional practices to occur freely: they throw themselves onto the sultan for beneficial contact, directing kisses to the hands and feet of the royal person. These ceremonies emphasize distance, inspiring fear of the monarch (*al mahāba*) and terror in people's hearts (*al ru'b*). The actions of this powerful figure add to the effect of his deployed armies to engender these two feelings which, alongside the love for the imam descended from the Prophet, are presented by traditional historiographers as the foundation of obedience.

Traditional historiographers agree with foreign observers as to the central nature of this figure. The pomp in parades and the deployment of armies combine into a picture of the sultan standing alone, on his horse, above the whole crowd, which is on foot. Many years before the drawing depicting the public appearance of Sidi Mohammed, the incredible presence of his father and predecessor, Sultan Moulay Abderrahman, was rendered by Delacroix in a large painting. Sketches left by the celebrated artist show him to have been progressively led to communicate the gradual fading away of the crowd into anonymity behind the formidable figure which dominates them.[26] Later, at the end of the nineteenth century, the mysterious, subjugating force emanating from the prince in a parade was conveyed by a writer present at the audience granted to an Italian embassy by Hassan I, a great-grandson of Moulay Abderrahman. In his words:

> The numerous suite that were gathered behind and about him appeared to be petrified. All eyes were fixed upon him; not a breath could be heard, and nothing was seen but immoveable faces and attitudes of profound veneration. Two Moors with trembling hands drove away the flies from his feet; another from time to time passed his hand over the skirt of his white mantle as if to purify it from contact with the air; a fourth, with an action of sacred respect, caressed the crupper of the horse; the one who held the parasol, stood with downcast eyes, motionless as a statue, almost as if he were confused and bewildered by the solemnity of this office. All things about him expressed his enormous power, the immense distance that separated him from everybody, a measureless submission, a fanatic devotion, a savage, passionate affection that seemed to offer its blood for proof. He seemed not a monarch, but a god.[27]

The ceremonies just described display some of the major means of government: violence, closeness, gift exchange, respect, and status advancement, as well as the renewed bay'a and the Islamic theory of legitimacy in which it is grounded. These rites and symbols are repeatedly displayed and endlessly constructed and reconstructed in ephemeral sets which function as power tactics.

The Paradigm of the Chief:
The Sultan as Saint and Warrior

The ceremonies I have just evoked glorify a central figure which is also synthetic: that of the chief. Whatever the (enormous) gap setting it apart from an "original" ideal of the leader that the community must obey, this historical and concrete incarnation is the one to which praise or dissent are directed. Before reaching supreme dignity the candidate to the sultanate must, like everyone else, ostensibly demonstrate submission: downcast head and eyes, service to the reigning prince, relinquishing of any display of authority or even virility in his presence. But once a man has reached the position of command, another personality emerges: solitary and aloof, he governs his subjects through the manipulation of violence, gift exchange, and closeness—in the name of Islamic law, which must accommodate these practices. We have already had some indications that this coexistence is perceived and accepted by some people, while others reject it. The repeated displays, however, reveal the existence of a lasting consensus about how a chief should look; we can see that a certain way of marking all matters of precedence—between fathers and sons, mentors and apprentices, masters and disciples—has come to acquire a lasting hegemony. This schema, which articulates the discourse of social arrangements within families, labor organizations, and institutions of learning and initiation, reaches its highest elaboration in cultural history—particularly in the lives and actions of the saints. I am referring to a specific elaboration which fills the gap between anthropolatric submission to the chief, on the one hand, and, on the other hand, Islamic law, which maintains a theory of the delegation of power, despite all evidence to the contrary.

Such a hypothesis sheds light on the sociological and cultural foundations of this style of domination, uncovering the sources of its instability as well as the basis of its astonishing revivals. It thus challenges both the theory of Oriental despotism, with its emphasis on religious beliefs, which has often been invoked to explain these practices, and the nationalist rationalizations which some have opposed to it. There are indeed two competing representations of the exercise of power in nineteenth- and early twentieth-century Morocco. The first sees only limitless absolutism, a cult of the prince, arbitrary decision making, and abject submission on the part of the subjects, who live miserable lives and bear the burden of heavy taxation. According to this representation the despot's power rests on an army and an administrative machine which repress any rebellion in a bloody manner; only groups that live in less accessible (mountainous) areas—the famous *blad siba,* which the colonial literature opposes to the *blad al makhzen* (submitted territories)—lie beyond the range of the sinister iron fist. Finally, the whole construction is seen to owe its perpetuation to "Islamic fanaticism" which is said to teach blind obedience to the prince.

Opposed to this familiar and distorted picture, we have the one proposed by postcolonial historians and ideologists.[28] According to them the sultan used more diplomacy than violence in his dealings with his subjects, and the revealed law (shari'a) limited the arbitrariness of political decisions. There is no question that some tribal groups refused taxation or rebelled against their governors, but they were not necessarily challenging the central power. At any rate, according to this view, they always recognized its religious legitimacy and often solicited its arbitration. Finally, in the late nineteenth century, foreign influence was strong enough to remove some subjects from the sultan's jurisdiction and stir up disturbances which limited the administration's control over his people.

Surprisingly, some empirical support can be found for each of these two, totally different viewpoints—which makes it difficult for either of them to fully account for the relationship between this society and its system of government. While the first one appears incapable of accounting for consent, the second cannot explain violence. Most importantly, neither of these interpretations draws any lesson from the crucial fact that the use of rebellion and forceful response were as widespread in the territories administered by the sultan's bureaucracy as in the dissident areas. A careful reading of the chronicles makes it clear that the armies of the central power were fighting a good deal in the plains (if not as much as in the mountains) and that the collection of taxes almost always required a display of force. Finally, the frequent uprisings in the cities are also seriously neglected.

In order to interpret such a level of violence, which seems coextensive with this type of administration, we must first consider the government machine itself and its working principle. Obviously the center can only impose itself if it is articulated in relation to social groups which have an autonomous life and organization; in itself, it

lacks a territorial infrastructure capable of defining individual identity in nontribal terms and thus making people submit to the will of the
state. A tribal group is a political entity with its own identity, headed
by a council or a chief. Each of these groups defends its territory, even
if that territory is prone to change and therefore not absolutely indispensable to its feeling of cohesion. More important, however, is
the fact that the center approaches them as constituted entities and
treats them as such when exacting taxes, imposing a collective penal
responsibility, or requesting troops. The tribes do possess an autonomous force, which they mobilize according to circumstances.

It should also be noted that such autonomous organization is not
specific to the countryside. The cities have their own militias. Neighborhoods are clearly individualized and can align troops in the case of
unrest. Different occupations are grouped into corporations (ḥanṭa)
which, in addition to their mundane common interests, have the patronage of a saint and an affiliation with a brotherhood; someof them
can be seen celebrating this spiritual bond or taking target practice.

So the makhzenian mode of administration is in fact articulated
through such local powers, which relay the forces of the center. But
since their growth and development has no clearly institutionalized
limits, antagonism inevitably arises. This accounts for the common
occurrence of violence and coercion. These local and regional centers
always originate in focal points of mobilization such as the kasbah
and the zāwiya.[29] Each of these two poles attracts partisans by offering either armed protection or charisma, thus channeling and accumulating wealth. Of course, they also compete for the control of men
and resources, and both have an ambiguous relationship with the central power (marked by cooperation and insidious conflict).

In each case the mobilization of resources and prestige is accomplished through family and tribe. To avail itself of a force sufficient
to impress others, the family submits itself to uncontested discipline,
laying the foundation for power through obedience and work under
the leadership of a patriarch who must be feared by everyone. The
need to accumulate accounts for the rigors of this very nonegalitarian
rule. Women and sons carry out the hardest tasks and are submitted
to a degree of parsimony in the apportioning of food. Women's por-
tions in particular are smaller than those of the patriarch and the other
men, while the patriarch must share generous amounts of food with
his peers. Accumulation is indeed paired with generosity and gift giv-

ing is a source of prestige. A head of family gains prestige by father-
ing numerous male children who are sent to take part in the sacrifice
of war. The women work for the elevation of men through their mod-
eration in food and their fecundity.

Such are the ways in which the "great houses"—or "great tents"
(in a nomadic context)—measure themselves and in which factions
are created in a tribal setting. As a second level of mobilization,
the tribe has three crucial characteristics: individualization, repetitive
structure, and perseverance in its own existence.[30] Whatever the force
of the sultanian bureaucracy, it can only temporarily limit the growth
of tribal powers, since ultimately it must articulate itself with them.
The individualization of these groupings, which constitute the social
texture, appears in their chosen names, which establish them as different from one another, and in the territory they use and defend, despite the fact that the solidarity of their lineages is more important for
their survival and that not all are necessarily settled.

Tribesmen share some ideas and feelings due to a common history and destiny, and they use their own institutions to guard their
possessions and maintain internal and external security. But although
they all have the same type of organization, none of the tribes will-
ingly accepts extinction by fusion with another. It could only result
from conquest, dispersal, or extreme weakening due to a natural catas-
trophe such as a famine or an epidemic. While tribes may have to
form leagues (*leff*), they keep their individuality. Their history is not
really known, but they have a theory of their own origins which is
modeled after that of procreation. All the tribes claim to be descended
from a chain of ancestors which ties them to some single ancient patriarch and sometimes to a matriarch; most likely they consist of ag-
gregates around powerful families. Finally, while tribes are not opposed to integration into larger groups (a Muslim community or the
administrative machine of a large state), they never merge completely
with any of these organizations.[31]

Tribal energies can be used in two different ways in specific undertakings: in the exercise of charismatic authority, which creates respect and centralizes resources or partisans, or in pure domination. In
the first case tribes' violence must be channeled to serve objectives
which are beyond their control; but their military commanders, who
are willing parties to their internal dissensions, are rarely credited
with such noble ambitions—hence the tribesmen's inclination to sup-

port prophets and thaumaturges. Only the military leaders, however, can head the intratribal or intertribal struggles for dominance or the conquest of commercial routes and fertile lands. Competition within the tribe itself aims at overt power and needs no other justification; generosity and military skill are sufficient. The struggle is seen by all as resulting from a break in the oligarchs' consensus due to cunning or force. Since tribes are such individualized groupings, this quest for power becomes a synthetic stake due to the limited space in which the confrontation occurs. Orders cannot be given to those who have equal status; only men who are stronger than others can force the latter into submission and a greater share of manual work.

But if ever the nuclei of political mobilization go beyond the first two circles (the family under the patriarch's orders and the tribe incited by the advantages of leadership), a new ideology of action becomes indispensable. The most commonly invoked motive is the defense of religion and of the Muslim community. At that stage one must either activate a charisma or attach oneself to a family which has inherited one: the scope of action then extends beyond local politics and puts this new center in competition with rival power centers.

This accounts for the instability of the system and a degree of violence (which, from the vantage point of the chronicles, is taken for granted) when the sultanian machine tries to suppress or utilize these competing powers. Whatever its hold on them, the equilibria remain fragile, since they themselves result from endless competitions in the nuclei of mobilization, which in turn coexist with the bureaucracy and the military organization of the makhzen.

The military machine strives to limit the effect of these local dynamics and stamp out the rebellion which arises time and again. Such violence is of limited efficacy for dominance, but its permanent use is nonetheless a necessity. It can be seen operating at the heart of the system, which it totally permeates; but at the same time it must combine with gift exchange and the game of closeness and attachment. Throughout this interaction the cultural schema of the relationship with the patriarch is activated in both the workings of the dar-al-mulk and the local nuclei of mobilization, which the dar-al-mulk must simultaneously watch, repress, and tolerate. But since power cannot expand or claim legitimacy without the help of charisma, the same schema—reformulated in the most idealistic terms in the master-disciple relationship—takes hold of the practices and tactics of power.

Master and Disciple: Identifying a Historical Diagram and the Sources of Its Sanctification

Tentative explanations of the persistence of Moroccan political authoritarianism have been based on a common postulate. In spite of their differences they have all attempted to account for the vitality of this political system by highlighting the crucial role of social and economic structure, giving no attention to the reasons which lead concrete individuals to accept or reject the principles and consequences of particular foundations. The action and ritual activated by the royal institution obviously express feelings, beliefs, and ideas which cannot be separated from political conduct. They appear as affects—regularly and publicly sanctioned by strong and vocal parties—in daily life and in the exceptional circumstances of feasts or the paroxysmal unleashing of violence. These affects are beyond open discussion; their practical rationality is such that one either conforms to them, in view of expected gains, or rejects them, aware of the dangers implicit in actions which the central authorities will consider infractions. The authority these affects sanction is frequently challenged. But the rebels either abandon all ordinary social arrangements (as is the case with wandering groups of dervishes) or tend to reestablish the same signs of domination and submission.

Individuals make choices and use means which, from their point of view, are rational in terms of both subjective and objective criteria, but they are not necessarily aware of all the logics implicated in their action. These choices and means form a structure of intervention which has a specific impact. Thus closeness, service, and gift exchange constitute the vehicles which motivate the interactions within and around the dar-al-mulk. Their concrete arrangements define positions of authority and submission; to reject them is automatically to adopt a defiant posture. Inversely one can spend a lifetime conforming and drawing benefits from them without having a clear theory of their operation in political relations. From this point of view one's behavior may be rational but not appear transparent beyond the mobilization of means and the identification of the objective. This explains why one never disputes service, gift exchange, or closeness as such, but rather the positions and duties of individuals confronting one another with their titles, their dignity, and the potential for violence which everyone tries to have at his disposal. Consequently the process in which and through which closeness, service, and gift exchange are activated—as well as the circumstances and contexts in which these three operators play their role in political co-optation or demotion—escapes the actor's attention. Success or failure would not, in any case, depend on their awareness. The most important factor is reasoned adaptation to situations in which one must display the signs of a request for closeness or a rejection of it. Then, and only then—in this highly risky endeavor—does it matter that things be submitted to analysis and evaluation.

The ascendancy of the political center is maintained through a constantly renewed competition between elites eager to obtain maximal closeness to the prince through service and gift exchange. Violence arises only when the regional nuclei of power, which are indispensable to the preservation of the existing order, create a challenge by rejecting the game of closeness. Even then, however, a selective practice of royal pardon gives those who rebel the possibility of a return to obedience which is no less spectacular than their challenge; such reversals constitute a source of prestige and stability for the dar-al-mulk. The cultural schemata of authority which are presently dominant in the society as a whole must (for reasons to be expounded later) be investigated at the level of those regional nuclei. I will therefore dwell for a moment on the issue of their structure and genesis.

Political Domination: Genesis and Structure

Scholars first took great interest in the *amghar* (tribal chief) and the great caid (the two figures of local and regional despotism), neglecting as a result the powerful "friends of God" and their great brotherhoods, the zāwiyas. Ignoring the saint, who coexists with the caid, Robert Montagne considers the latter as emerging from an assembly at the local, communal, or tribal level. The despot starts out as the "big man" of his lineage. If he shows himself skillful in local affairs and knows how to manipulate generosity and intrigue, he can count on the support of large-scale alliances (leffs), which according to Montagne are characteristic of North African societies, to help him subdue his rivals and gain supreme power over a set of tribes. As we can see, this kind of genesis links an obscure psychological sketch to a structural factor. Montagne has been rightly criticized for ignoring the zāwiya and overestimating the leff and chiefdom.[1] Ernest Gellner remarks on the extreme fragmentation of tribal formations and considers the local "theocracy" of the zāwiyas a particularly stable authority center grounded in the prohibition of military force rather than its use—a restriction which cannot be separated from the respect inspired by the manifestation and acknowledgment of baraka.[2] According to Gellner, the leff, local despotism, and the oscillation between the republic and the tyrannical chief are all well attested, but they do not account for the Moroccan social and political organization before the colonial transformation. On the other hand, the balance of violence and the action of the saint constitute a generalized structure which could perform in dissident lands the integrative role played by the government, with its monopoly on coercion, in state-run areas.

Both the scope and shortcomings of these two perspectives are blurred if one insists on opposing them to the presence of the sultanian state with its legitimacy, the cultural identity it claims, and the social groups supporting it. Indeed, reducing chiefdom and the zāwiya to simple "levels" of political and social organization within a society enjoying a significant degree of global political integration, as some postcolonial historiographers do, amounts to an anachronistic projection of the nation-state model onto a society which has relied primarily on religious unity.

The problem with Montagne's and Gellner's views is of a different nature. Neither was able or willing to give serious consideration to the cultural work which orients the actions undertaken by the local power nuclei, first to establish their dominance over a lineage and, second, to manifest and transmit the (divine) grace which is the other source of authority. This work is definitely at the basis of the mobilization of men. As we saw earlier, whether it is a lineage imposing its hegemony on a larger group or the zāwiya governing multiple tribal groups, these nuclei's ascendancy develops when they are successful at highlighting some difference.

At the outset the chief has the features of a patriarch, imposing on his extended family a discipline and hierarchy which govern the distribution of tasks and food supplies. Overt force and generosity assure him of predominance over his peers and set him on the path to local power. A zāwiya man submits to the will of a master, who rules his disciples' lives according to a system of ideas and practices related to those used by a patriarch within his family and lineage. Once they have achieved a position of influence, the chief and the zāwiya man acquire more and more resources and authority through the mobilization of other men. As soon as either of these two figures of masterhood manifests, through a demonstration of generosity and patronage which can no longer be rivaled, a difference which sets him apart from his contemporaries, he and the rest of the population enter the cycle of giftgiving and services.

It should be noted that no chief can achieve sovereignty without broadening the consensus which establishes him in the common perception as an entity defined by the Islamic creed; any pretension in this regard raises the problem of religious legitimacy. But in spite of theoretically being answerable to the shariʿa and its representatives, the ulema, this religious legitimacy must in fact, according to the diverse cultural forms manifested by Muslim ideals and practices, combine the legal sanction of the clerics and their tradition with the sanction of the holders of baraka, whose manifestation is precisely beyond the ulema's control. Whatever the historical background of this formula, in the late nineteenth century and to this day whoever obtains the legitimacy of the bayʿa also avails himself of some intrinsic holiness, or at least the holiness derived through frequent contact with and service to living and dead holy men.

Conversely, no zāwiya man or saint has ever become the community's commander without using physical violence. The advocates of the theory of segmentarity overlook the fact that when the local theocracies have tried to conquer the center, they have had to surround themselves with armed forces. The connection between spiritual and dynastic ventures is such that every governing body has to give special attention to the shrines of the elect of God. But an alliance with them is as dangerous as it is vital—not only because of the influence they exert over their adepts, networks of whom extend from the imperial cities to the most isolated villages, but also because the strong cultural integration provided by the doctrines and devotional practices of the zāwiyas and their masters make their collaboration indispensable. These practices have spread to everyone in the society—including the aristocracy of the ulema, who control canonic legitimacy. The virtuosi of the direct path to God play such an eminent role, in what must be regarded as cultural as well as social integration, that every governing body has to bestow on them visible and even ostentatious signs of respect. The festivals held around their tombs are honored by the makhzen, and the monarch's travels often include a pilgrimage to important shrines. Even more important, hagiography is there to remind everyone that the saints' miracles are more efficient than the sultans' armies.

If the royal institution and its legitimacy function in and through the hegemony of sainthood, as has been noted,[3] it seems logical to consider the master-disciple relationship in Sufi initiation as the decisive schema for the construction of power relations. Indeed, candidates for sainthood prepare themselves under the direction of a guide, whose imposed rule and hierarchical superiority they respect, to achieve in turn a position of authority. The rules thus sanctioned are primarily observed and enforced by men and women who scorn convention in their quest for the absolute. But they also operate in any interaction which involves precedence and apprenticeship. Therefore the use of cultural history—especially through an analysis of the hagiographic narrative—to account for these rules does not limit their scope; to the contrary, it demonstrates that they delineate everyone's horizon of discursive and nondiscussive practices.

Master and Disciple: Vocation and Separation

Relations between masters and their disciples seem to have achieved a high degree of homogeneity, at least regarding the most influential figures of sainthood. I will therefore deal with one case only: that of a well-known saint of the late nineteenth and early twentieth centuries. This biography will serve as a focal point for other information on the period and the doctrine, as well as other historical perspectives whenever the context requires them. The life and work of Sidi al Haj ʿAli, founder of the zāwiya of Ilgh, are pertinent not only to the Sous and the south, dominated by the prestigious city of Marrakech; on the contrary, the Sufi way they represent was widely diffused, in Morocco and elsewhere. We are dealing here with a man who devoted his life to the ideals and practices of the Darqawiya, a powerful brotherhood which led the politico-religious debate of the nineteenth century; in particular the followers of this zāwiya devoted their efforts to the defense of *dar-al-Islam* against the steady advance of French colonialism in the Maghreb.[4]

Moreover, Sidi al Haj 'Ali was not an obscure fakir. He traveled widely, paid visits to the successor of the supreme master of the order in the north among the Beni Zeroual, and had visions in Fez, where he stayed for a while in 1881 or 1882. He was born around 1850 in Ilgh, approximately 100 kilometers southeast of Tiznit; after spending the first part of his life in search of *'ilm* and initiation, he returned to his native village and founded his own zāwiya in 1884.[5] According to his biographer, his intense life and contagious enthusiasm made him extremely successful and earned him the respect of the powerful; at the same time they made him the object of a campaign led by a caid appointed by Hassan I, as well as some groups close to the famous Nāṣiriya brotherhood.[6]

'Ali, who is exemplary in terms of his choice of a brotherhood, his regional roots, and the stature he achieved, owes to his own son, Mukhtar al Soussi—a great *'alem,* sufi, and nationalist militant—an exceptional biography with numerous concrete details about interactions between the shaykh and his disciples, as well as the organization of material and ritual life in the zāwiya. Al Soussi can provide only a few first-hand accounts, since he was still a child when his father died.[7] But he had privileged access to family sources, as well as eyewitness accounts by fellows of his father and people living in Ilgh. These sources give the biography a degree of descriptive depth which is rare in hagiographic writings.[8] It enables us to follow the transformation of a young man into a disciple and of a mature and initiated man into a shaykh who exercised his masterhood during the reign of Hassan I (1873–1894), a period which epitomized some of the most salient features of the dar-al-mulk. 'Ali's career expanded under the succeeding sovereigns until 1910 and put him in contact with the political centers of the time—with the great caids of the south as well as with Ba Hmad, the famous grand vizier and regent of the kingdom.[9] The paradigm of authority emerging from my analysis will bring us back to the norms and practices operating in political power relations since, according to the biographer, state officials themselves compared their troops' submission to their orders with the disciples' submission to the rule imposed by this mystical master in the Sous.[10] Dar-al-mulk and zāwiya mirrored each other. In a way 'Ali gives us a chance to follow the lives of two masters and one disciple. Around 1870 we see a twenty-year-old boy give up everything to join Sa'id ben Ḥammou al Maʿdari, leaving behind him all desirable careers (and in particular the pursuit of the prestigious 'ilm) in order to save his soul.[11] He put himself in the position of disciple, and, in spite of the absence of great detail in the biography, we get a picture of his apprenticeship under the direction of a powerful (though illiterate) master of Idrissid descent who often experienced intense ecstasies. After the shaykh's death 'Ali succeeded in becoming the head of a new zāwiya to which he brought renown and prosperity.[12] His biography contains more detail about the relationship he then had with his *murīd* (disciples), his wanderings, and his management style during the twenty-five years which he devoted, in his own way, to the service of God.

Sa'id ben Ḥammou, who has remained obscure, must have been endowed with special gifts, judging by his divinations and his miracles. The way he attracted 'Ali certainly gives evidence of such supernatural capacities: the mere power of his gaze was sufficient to draw this young man away from his studies and make a murīd of him. The narrative provided by al Soussi in his scholarly *Maʿsūl* does not differ much from the one in his hagiographic writings, such as the *Tiryāq*, although the latter is more attuned than the former to concrete descriptions of an objectivized order. Nevertheless the *Maʿsūl* contains an additional piece of information: while contemplating his future disciple, unbeknownst to 'Ali, the shaykh is said to have uttered these words, which, while apparently expressing a wish, sound in fact like a decision: "There is no question that this body can only be meant to [receive] the light!"[13] The very same day 'Ali—by some extraordinary coincidence—came to put himself in the hands of this enthusiastic master in order to be initiated.

The novice was distraught by the influence of his master's gaze on his soul and body; he was overcome by a new energy of a self-alienating nature. He ran to the master and, so to speak, took refuge in the charismatic community. According to his biographer, "When he arrived, he had already been overcome and gone into a violent trance, to the point that his body almost dissolved. The *fuqarā* then submerged him [for a while] in a cistern filled with water; and he only calmed down after several weeks, during which he also abstained from eating."[14]

Let us dwell for a moment on this first step in order to understand its significance and scope; let us reconstruct the context and compare 'Ali's fate to that of people of the same age who have not made the same choice. Here is a young man who starts out by devoting himself to 'ilm. This decision in itself sets him apart from the majority of his contemporaries and launches him on a path which differs from the ordinary lives of cultivators, merchants, shepherds, and artisans. These others will stay in the village or, if they leave it, will be reluctant to leave behind their relatives and their customs. Their lives, unlike the one chosen by 'Ali, will be devoted to defending the group, its territory, and its norms. Not that 'Ali will leave everything behind; but he will have to distance himself from it all in order to go from one madrasa to another in his search for knowledge, guided by the reputation of places and teachers.

Nonetheless this departure from the ordinary is respected by society. It is an honor, a duty, and a privileged path to salvation to devote oneself to studying the sacred texts, disseminating the meaning of the ethics and the law (shari'a) derived from them. The community, as well as the powers which represent and defend it, recognize this function and guarantee its perpetuation.

But if a student, reaching the end of his apprenticeship and the beginning of adulthood—and expected to settle in an occupation and found a family—chooses to follow another path, to search for God through sufi exercise and illumination, the decision brings distress to the family and concern to the group.

There is no question that the saint is a familiar figure; but unlike the scholar in the Islamic sciences, he is engaged in an unpredictable quest. The development of his career is totally dependent on the grace of God, the work of his initiators, and endorsement by the people, all things over which the political authorities and the ulema have little control. The danger represented by the emergence of a saint is not even mitigated by the institutionalization of this figure, alongside the legitimate prince and the 'ālem, as part of the functional triad Berque sees at work from the seventeenth century on in the Maghreb.[15] To the contrary, when the initiate hears his calling, he bypasses all institutional guarantees and gains direct access to auctoritas. The community revivalism he advocates cannot easily accommodate the selection criteria which the state and its ideologists use against unpredictable surges of charisma.[16]

The distress of the initiate's family is therefore echoed by reticence on the part of the elite and powers that be. Not only can a new career crystallize a potential for rebellion; ordinary norms are also profoundly disturbed when someone declares his calling to sainthood. And when such a declaration comes from an ʿālem, as in the present case, it casts suspicion and discredit upon the ulema, since it constitutes an existential search which throws the guardians of law and tradition into the camp of routinized belief and practice.

Most important, the departure of a man for initiation takes the concrete form of a spectacular and immediate renunciation of the values which govern daily life. Instead of getting married he leaves his home and his village; instead of earning a living or accumulating resources he scorns money making, entrusting God with his needs; instead of settling down, giving allegiance to a territory, a community, a government, he wanders, engaged in a quest for a master and a charismatic group—traveling over spaces in which the only things that count are the traces of past revelation and the signs of future spiritual conquests.[17]

This is the path of all murīds; even the shortest hagiographic accounts show them all to have made this break.[18] The only difference is that ʿAli, due to his affiliation with the Darqawi order, was submitted to conditions so draconian that they appeared excessive to more than one contemporary.[19] He had to wander around the country, wear the tattered clothing (muraqqaʿa) characteristic of this brotherhood, to display a rosary with large beads, and to walk with a stick of a fakir. This was to implement the famous rule of "breaking of habits" (kharq al ʿāda).[20] This was ʿAli's third stage of renunciation: first he abandoned the ʿilm, then his family, and finally the ordinary clothing and gestures of daily life. ʿAli's father could not accept his choice, and his mother fell into despair when, after a temporary return, their son again ran away to respond to his religious call.

ʿAli was thus engaged—against his family's will—in a drama with irremediable consequences. The good student, who had clearly been destined for an elite career, was instead wandering around the country in repulsive clothing, giving no sign of recognition to anyone and paying no attention to those who approached and spoke to him. He went to marketplaces to beg—an act of extreme humiliation—and in his madness threw the alms he received into the holey bag he carried on his back.

The systematic new life 'Ali is entering, however, plunged his family into disarray. The situation reaches a tragic extreme when this madman comes to beg in his parents' village. This "challenge" unleashes such emotions that he is arrested, put in irons, and beaten— but to no avail, as 'Ali persists in begging for food in a loud voice, fasting rather than accept the food his mother offers him. For a time his family believes 'Ali is miraculously cured and happily celebrates; but then he leaves to rejoin his master. His mother goes after him but must soon turn back when she hears that her husband is dying. Could the loss of his son have hastened or caused this man's death?[21]

This period of 'Ali's life, which began with the master's gazing on his future disciple, continues with initiation around 1872 or 1873, followed by recuperation by his family, through 1879 or 1880, and his eventual return to his master.[22] 'Ali's hesitations probably led the shaykh to impose even harsher conditions on him after his second break. This is therefore most likely the point at which 'Ali stopped wandering around the country and returned to Sa'id ben Ḥammou al Ma'dari's zāwiya.

Let us examine more fully the implications of this stage in the biography. 'Ali goes away, refusing to take advantage of his knowledge. He leaves behind his village, as well as the dignity attached to the 'ilm. The list of teachers in his biography includes men of great prestige and political connections, but 'Ali does not intend to become part of the network. So we see that wandering in search of a master or under the guidance of one means not only turning one's back on worldly preoccupations and honors but also, and most importantly, leaving behind a whole set of spatial configurations—the family, the village, the tribe, and finally the state—which others accept or honor. They are left behind for other spaces, whose attraction results from feelings and norms not engendered by ordinary socialization. The new spaces have no borders; they are points of reference at which charisma flows through contact with a deceased or a living master. So the transcended spaces in fact are as many transcended relations. Family space coincides with the values and sentiments attached to the *ḥorm* and the risks attached to them. It is the locus of possible pollution, and preserving it consists in making it invisible and impregnable or, if necessary, defending it through bloodshed and violence. The village and tribe are the loci of exercise of one's exclusive identity and rights; safeguarding these frontiers, in other words, gives the measure of one's virility.

Sufi wandering obviously negates these areas of social and political identification. It forces the murīd to take a risk, leaving behind the shows of virility, and sometimes ardor for war and martyrdom, that enables other young people to settle in a permanent way as members of their community. Finally, wandering is not only negation of space but also negation of time, since the stages of ordinary men's lives no longer have any significance for the religious zealot. Mystical voyage creates a gap between him and other men by postponing the switch from dependent status to responsibility.

'Ali's attitude regarding this break took a more radical form than that of his predecessors, due in part to the rule of the Darqawa, but probably also in part to personal choice. According to his biographer, his wandering, begging, and accoutrement were shocking to people in the Sous, who were used to the balanced and serene demeanor of adepts of other brotherhoods, such as the Nāṣiriya and probably the Tijaniya.[23]

The violence of Darqawi dancing and ecstasy were alien to M'hammad ben Nasser and to his successors and adepts, who were contemporaries of 'Ali; there were also profound differences between Tijaniya and Darqawiya, which have recently been highlighted.[24] But whatever the force of the revival of ecstatic brotherhood, based on a break with the world, the secrecy of the divine name, and direct contemplation; whatever the apparent novelty of such transformations of the body, the breaking of its impulses, and the disdain for visible elegance expressed by the use of tattered clothing; whatever the distinctiveness of the fortress the Darqawi murid built, through his abnormal behavior, around a subjectivity exclusively oriented to God—we must remember that each of these features, far from being radical innovation, was in fact inspired by a *malāmatiya* tradition. Moulay Larbi al-Darqāwi, whose legacy fell into 'Ali's hands, explicitly vindicates al Majdub's teachings and example.[25]

The Absolute Gift: Transparency, Service, and the Renunciation of Virility

Let us now imagine this new man. Through spiritual exercises and ordeal he has reached the goal which the *tarīqa* is seeking: the destruction of his former ego (*al kharāb*)—the ego he is constantly striving to dominate (*qahr-al-nafs*) and repress (*qam'al-nafs*), whose sharp edges must be dulled through the "violation of habits" (*taksīr ḥiddat-al-nafs*).[26]

By the end of this crucial stage 'Ali has broken all his ties and surrendered to his master. He has become a "renouncer" (*munqati'*; a *mutajarrid*) about to spend many years in the company of the shaykh and his other disciples. He enters a life dominated by the education he receives from Sa'id ben Ḥammou and the constant service he owes this master as a young man aspiring to the direct contemplation of God. This service is called *khidma*; a disciple owes it to his educator and it must be accomplished according to the impeccable rules ('*adab*) which govern contact with the master. Such is the price for success and the hope for illumination; without service there is no salvation! The khidma dictates that a disciple must perform all the tasks ordered by his initiator, whether they be domestic activities or work on the land belonging to the zāwiya. The rigorous nature of this rule may sometimes be overwhelming, both for the murids and for their shaykh, who does not feel that he is in a position to modify it: khidma is God's will and no one could decide how long a disciple should work, or how strict the constraints should be. According to the biographer, 'Ali's initiator came one day to watch the painful harvesting work. In the heat of summer the fuqarā were cutting barley with no other instruments than their bare, bleeding hands. Being a good educator, he felt compassion for his young novices, which brought tears to his eyes; but he could not take the risk of freeing them from this service. To do so would mean departing from an imperative which is vital for admittance to the path.[27]

'Ali had to submit for five years to the conditions (*shurūṭ*) every candidate to the way of the Darqawa must observe on a daily basis.[28] His biography spells out these conditions in a brief (but highly significant) description of the brotherhood rule formulated in northern Morocco during the eighteenth century and practiced throughout the country (including the south) in the late nineteenth century.[29] When he became a member of Sa'id ben Ḥammou's zāwiya, 'Ali joined the company of the renouncers: he repudiated the ulema's garb, casting aside the *ḥāyk* (*ridā'*), burnoose, and turban for the Darqawi dress; accepted the conditions imposed on the fuqarā—silence, food deprivation (*al jou'*), individual litany (*dhikr*), and isolation; and with his brothers assumed responsibility for plowing, harvesting, wood collecting, building, and all other necessary tasks in his master's zāwiya. Serving a shaykh in this manner puts a disciple in a position to achieve success, something which mystics are known to have done since ancient times.[30] Later, once he has become a master himself, 'Ali reminds his own disciples of these conditions in an epistle written in 1887, only a few years after he left his master's congregation to found his own.[31] He asserts that dhikr requires isolation, which pulls one away from the vain company of men; isolation and silence drive away noise, which is the enemy of meditative effort—the more sound there is, the less meaning. As for communal dhikr, through body movements and modulations appropriate for uttering the sounds and syllables of the Word it aims at creating a void in one's conscience so that it can receive God. The rest of this work on the body and soul is accomplished through food deprivation, which contributes to repressing the ego. To cite the vivid metaphor used by 'Ali, who after his pilgrimage to Mecca became known as al Haj 'Ali, once the body has been prepared by food deprivation, dhikr instantaneously spreads the effect of the divine secret, just as everything burns when one starts a fire with dry wood. Eating parsimoniously averts the deadly dangers of satiation, which engender "tyranny, arrogance, jealousy, narcissism, hatred, lying and [love of] appearance."[32] Finally ascesis is radicalized and the soul provided with additional strength by the sleep deprivation which results from all these exercises, as well as the wandering, which demands physical effort, breaking with mundane matters, and learning about the diversity of the One.

However, all prayers would be in vain without the assistance of a living master (al shaykh al ḥay). Seeking his help in a totally submissive manner overrides all other conditions and constitutes the sine qua non for success.[33] So it seems that success, manifested by access to masterhood (which is the goal of every initiation), is first and foremost dependent on continuous closeness to the shaykh, as well as faultless allegiance to his commands and his person. This was the way young 'Ali saw it when he was a disciple and the way al Haj 'Ali would want it later as a master; he compares the shaykh to a father and regards the love owed to him as inferior only to the love owed to the Prophet. Even better, the intervention of a living educator can substitute for great individual effort since "gnostics [those who know God] are the true elixir and chemistry; whoever encounters them does not need to work very hard, whereas those who do not encounter them are like someone who strikes while the iron is cold and becomes exhausted without having achieved anything."[34]

Let us return to the biography in order to highlight some of the meanings such submission acquires. First of all, the same categories of service, obedience, and closeness which govern the master-disciple relationship also inform the attitudes of servants in the dar-al-mulk and (so it appears) the expectations of a chief regarding his men. From this point of view the religious elite and the political bureaucratic elite recognize identical norms. Finally, both murīds and government officials derive from their practice, and from the particular ethos they assimilate, a belief that individual effort is not enough; one must apply oneself within a framework of allegiance and obedience to a master.

These parallels take on even more significance if we pursue the comparison of lives dedicated to a search for God and lives spent in ordinary circumstances. 'Ali devoted five years of his life to the exclusive ideals of a brotherhood and the service his master. By 1884, when he began building his own zāwiya and thinking of marriage, he was thirty-four; if he had stayed in his village and accepted an ordinary destiny, he would have married and founded a household ten or even fifteen years earlier. But at the age when other young men married women probably in order to be served by them, he did the opposite and began serving a master. This decision constitutes an inversion of the "normal" course of life and can definitely be regarded as "transgression" if all the other deferments it implies are taken into account. A late marriage defers procreation; but in al Haj 'Ali's case, as in others, the interdiction of relations with women at the time of early sexual maturation contrasts with the multiple marriages made possible by his accumulated prestige and fortune once he had become a master.[35]

The biography of the founder of Ilgh contains little information on his life as a disciple beyond the stage of initial testing, except for a few notes on his service under Sa'id ben Ḥammou's guidance. But fortunately it contains rather detailed information on his twenty-five years of activities as a shaykh, enabling us to see how he governed his disciples and to reconstruct the attitudes he demanded from them, as well as the norms and rules he sought to instill in them. It also confirms the process of inversion initiated at the time when someone joins a charismatic community. At another level this information sheds more light on the parallels I established earlier between the ethos of the zāwiya and that of the dar-al-mulk.

Ilgh is home to approximately one hundred renouncers (*mutajarridūn*), including a few women who live apart from the men.[36] The first thing the shaykh demands from them is that they reveal to him all the facts and thoughts filling their existence. Nothing can be hidden in any case, since the holy man guesses everything. This implies confessing what one would rather keep secret; but the transparency rule is so rigorous that it overrides even the rule of absolute respect (*ḥayā'*) to be constantly shown in the master's presence. A sin must be expiated through the four famous conditions—isolation, food deprivation, silence, and the dhikr—which must be observed according to the modalities set up by the master; he decides on their application during periods of time not devoted to other tasks. Moreover, he alone decides on the probationary tests and "breaks" required of anyone who wishes to join him on the spiritual path.

Transparency therefore coexists with fundamental "stipulations." It brings the disciple's soul into unison with the master's, while the rigorous nature of the daily rule—preceded by the task of repressing the ego—discourages those with mistaken callings and functions as a filter. The only ones to go through it are those who will be elected because of their "noble ambition" (*himma*). Mukhtar al Soussi recalls a relevant scene from his childhood, which had probably been imprinted in his memory by the sight of those men submitting to the power of mystical discipline:

> When we were young, we used to observe the "renouncers" in the zāwiya; there were always about one hundred of them. No whispers or footsteps could be heard as they were scattered in all [four] corners of the meeting space called zāwiya and against the edges of its pillars and under its round walls. . . . We used to watch them at times when there were many of them together [*al jam'al ḥāfil*] and to see them lifeless as if there were no souls inside them any longer.[37]

The shaykh regularly orders a return (of variable duration) to these conditions, which the fuqarā' may also spontaneously impose on themselves. These commandments of the order are reenacted whenever it is deemed necessary, regardless of location: it can be in the zāwiya or in the place one happens to be when traveling. The stipulations may operate at any time except in a period of communal dhikr, during the season of agricultural work, or when the yearly festival (mousem) is an occasion for the *munqati'īn* to see visitors and pilgrims, as well as their brothers who are still leading ordinary lives (*mutasabbibīn*).

The assembly of disciples must perform a great number of seasonal tasks related to production or the maintenance of the zāwiya. According to 'Ali's biographer the pace of work is sometimes so exhausting as to put an end to some people's calling and create ambivalence toward the master. Some go as far as wishing him death or attempting to make it happen.[38] One faqīh who was not able to endure the pace of life testifies on the level of activity of the fuqarā under al Haj 'Ali's guidance, comparing them to "the jinn [who were at the service] of our Lord Suleiman, abnegating themselves, their entourage, and even their existence in order to submit to the shaykh who orders them according to his will and whom they follow with blind obedience."[39] One can imagine how busy they were with tasks which kept multiplying in proportion to the growing prosperity of the zāwiya, the master's prestige, and the number of clients and visitors.[40]

Some of these tasks, particularly in the area of production, are far from being specific to the religious order itself. In the large landholdings belonging to holy lineages or to other lineages on whom dar-al-mulk has bestowed favors, the work may be done by farmers and shepherds who are bound to their lord primarily through the *sohba*, rather than through contract.[41] It is difficult to give an idea of the vast extension of the semantic field of this word; depending on circumstances, it connotes friendship, lasting relationship, or loyalty and alliance. Its constraining force comes from the sanction with which it is endowed by common morals and faith. It also results from a careful count of the occasions when one partner or the other fails to meet higher obligations. Anyone guilty of overly frequent breaches of the sohba is excluded from economic transactions vital for his survival or loses his honor. A lord may be weakened through the loss of clients, and peasants may be left without protection in a society in which these networks are much more important than the bureaucratic apparatus, which has little influence on everyday life. In other words, sohba implies that the mighty give support to the powerless in exchange for their loyalty and attachment—that is, patronage.

Just as in its affinities with service in the dar-al-mulk, the master-disciple relationship seems to be related to the patronage system. If the relationship between a lord and his subjects takes on the features of the relationship between the shaykh and his fuqarā, we can expect all of these features to be accentuated in the paradigm of sainthood. After all, it represents the ideal of success: achieving direct contemplation of divinity through the patronage of a living saint.

If such is the case, it is understandable that the service demanded by an initiating shaykh, unlike that expected by an ordinary patron, can lead to the sheer negation of manhood and bring the male disciple to a radically altered state, namely femininity. The fuqarā living in Ilgh prepare the evening meal. Within a zāwiya this goes unnoticed; but for men of their cohort, apart from exceptional circumstances (such as travel or work away from home), the act of cooking would reflect badly on their masculine identity. This is not the only intrusion of femininity in the male disciples' lives. Those under al Haj 'Ali's guidance also collected wood and used a handmill to grind grain—a most typically feminine task. Other tasks make young initiates join the ranks of all other categories of servants, also bringing them closer to the opposite sex. When they are on the move, for example, they must make the master's bed, have water ready for his ablutions, and, sometimes, wash his clothes.[42]

The Colonial Elaboration
of Authoritarianism

The precolonial power relations and the master-disciple schema I have so far identified constitute a potent historical legacy. As I have tried to chart them through the study of historiography and hagiography, they give us access to the genealogy of Moroccan authoritarianism. However, neither the power practices nor the diagram which articulates them were simply carried over into the twentieth century. Such a view would obscure the specificity of the system as it was refashioned by colonial dynamics and the postcolonial struggle to define the newly independent nation. In this chapter I will discuss the colonial reconstruction of the diagram, which resulted in the elaboration of modern Moroccan authoritarianism. First, I will describe some of the social and discursive practices responsible for the emergence, in a new kind of objectivity, of the colonial structure with its grid of control and its disciplining techniques. Second, I will turn to the fissures which were produced by the uncontrollable proliferation of discourse itself. Such proliferation, I believe, accounts for surprising and unpredictable reappropriations and, thus, for the ultimate failure of the colonial as generalized panopticism.

Chieftainship and Technocracy[1]

One fine spring day toward the end of the 1920s, G. S. Colin, an orientalist of note, had some business with Caid Tiyouti. He reported to the latter's kasbah in southeast Taroudant, in the company of some officers of "native affairs" who, with the caid, were in charge of the regional colonial administration. By then a famous professor of Maghrebi colloquial Arabic who was also appreciated for his collaboration with the protectorate institutions, Colin was treated to a sumptuous reception. He and the caid struck up a lively conversation that lasted until well after the meal served in his honor. Colin impressed fellow guests and host alike with his talent as a linguist and his knowledge of Morocco—especially the caid, who very much admired French officers and orientalists who mastered both Arabic (the language of the Koran) and Berber (the language spoken in the area). At one point the conversation turned to the Koran. A marabout from Timguilsht, the scion of a lineage much venerated for its holiness and learning, asked Colin if he knew any verses from "the Book." Much to everyone's surprise, the young professor recited two or three. The caid's commentary went as follows: "That's a new one! Honey in dog's skin!" (*La'jab hada, la'sal f'jeld lkalb!*)[2]

If we believe witnesses' accounts, such meetings were common.[3] Everything points to a program of close cooperation between protectorate bureaucrats and indigenous authorities which imposed the latter's domination in both city and countryside. This model of complicity matured and underwent a series of changes between the two world wars. It proved to be effective during this period, despite the profound upheavals that were convulsing the country. And if the mass movement that brought independence to Morocco after World War II rendered this formula of complicity obsolete, the system itself—abhorred as a scandalous collusion between colonial and indigenous authorities—was resurrected once liberty had been restored. The new configuration, however, consisted of a renovated national bureaucracy which penetrated (and adjusted to) personalized networks of communication and embraced local schisms and regroupings. As it matured, the new system of control abandoned some colonial exactions which the new power holders and public consciousness could no longer tolerate. The upshot of such sizable changes was a bureaucratic and cultural "compromise," which between 1965 and 1975 reached a sort of classicism and provided the womb for the new Moroccan authoritarianism.

But before we get ahead of ourselves, let us return to the discussion between the French officers and "natural chiefs" in Tiyout. A new set of power relations is apparent. We can imagine a circle of notables, the *jmā'a* (i.e., the council) of the caid, seated before the officers. Caid and officers are the central figures and manifest a commanding presence. The indigenous chief is a man of arms and honor. Several years before, he had participated in brutal expeditions against the still unyielding tribes of the Auti Atlas Mountains, flanked by his brothers and his contingent. He now levies taxes and enjoys immense fortune.

Banquets like this one and the uninterrupted service of tea extend his generosity to passersby and sustain a network of negotiations and information gathering. Other chiefs like him held the Sous, with various outcomes, during the same period: Jallouli, Demnati, and, further south, Ayad Jirari and the descendants of Illigh, to name but a few. From 1917 to 1921, Si Tayeb al Goundafi—city pasha, representative of the makhzen, and one of the most powerful caids of the south, the "Lords of the Atlas"—had ruled over Tiznit. Accompanied by an officer and supported by a handful of regular troops, he was in command of his own troops recruited from the tribes. When the discussion between Colin and Tiyouti took place, the resistance, led first by Al Hiba and then by his brother, was all but defeated, its partisans having been pursued deep into the south. During this period, the French territorial administration held the chiefs and "their" tribes both in esteem and at bay.

In comparison to those who made their fortunes by what was once called the "politics of the great caids" (Glaoui, Goundafi, and Mtougui), Tiyouti appears to have cut a relatively modest figure. Several tribes came regularly to a weekly market situated at the foot of the master's residence. A palm grove irrigated under the watchful eye of the caid's assistants, a *mellah* that thrived with commerce and artisanal trade until independence, and an often-visited sanctuary were all signs of Tiyouti's less obtrusive, yet still effective rule. In addition to the resources derived from the palm grove were those from an argan forest and a common pasture. The taxes collected from the market, mellah, and trade associations contributed to the prosperity of a "great house." In short, Tiyouti's command was no less lucrative for its small size.

Some holy lineages supported the caid's power. Among them were the marabouts of Timguilsht, a powerful branch of the Nāṣirī brotherhood, whose main lodge is still active on the left bank of the Dra, south of Zagora. As early as the eighteenth century, this brotherhood extended a web of influence throughout the Maghreb and established means of gathering and disseminating information as far east as Egypt. Solidly attached to the reigning dynasty since the nineteenth century, the Nāṣirī lodges extended their influence even further, attracting elites and, in the Sous as elsewhere, fighting against the militant and anticolonial fervor of the Darqawa.[4] Caid and marabout occupy center stage in this drama, but other religious notables and the leaders of "fractions" are present as well.[5] The officers of the Department of Indigenous Affairs seated before the indigenous groups were still steeped in the dialogues and doctrine of indirect rule à la Lyautey; that is, they showed respect for Islam, for "the customs of the country," and they used the market skillfully, as both a place for contacts and friendly encounters and a seductive arena, made so through the display of commodities. Tea and sugar, both close to the heart of Moroccan tribesmen and women, were made equally available at low prices. "Applied" ethnology and orientalism played a central role in the elaboration of these practical truths about Morocco and its future.

Despite their differences, notables and officers knew each other well and collaborated in this work of "pacification" in the name of the sharifian monarchy under the strong guidance of the resident general. The caid-marabout couple had become inseverable; nothing could take place without the marabout. His baraka, influence, and firsthand knowledge of prevailing public opinion and religious sentiment were indispensable.[6] This specificity of the new French regime in Morocco consisted in placing indigenous chiefs under French tutelage and in concentrating power formerly wielded by village and tribal assemblies (jma'a) in the chiefs' hands. In fact, a change in this direction had begun well before the treaty of the protectorate (1912). In the second half of the nineteenth century, some families had already gained the advantage of modern arms and had carved fiefdoms for themselves, both on the plains and in the harder-to-reach mountainous areas. Others continued the process of accumulation thanks to their religious prestige. Moreover, the development of commerce with Europe stimulated activity in the coastal cities, while relay stations in the heartland sheltered intermediaries and merchants.

Chiefs and marabouts were the first to benefit from this shuttling back and forth of information and goods. Support from the center and, before long, from abroad added momentum to the pattern of consolidation and stabilization of material and political advantages. If in the past, family wealth accumulation had tended to run a course along which fortunes dwindled by the second or third generation after they had been amassed, there were now exceptions. Some families held tight to their power, influence, and fortune.[7] The famous pendulum swing between centralizing tyranny and local democracy, noted by the French anthropologist Jacques Berque, was brought to an end. From conquered plain to big city, French civil servants and native chiefs forced all who came within their reach to submit to their tight double tutelage. Cities were turned into municipalities, and pashas governed under the aegis of the new civil service machinery. In areas under military rule—that is, the Sous, the Atlas, and the Pre-Sahara (during the time we are concerned with and long after)—caids took their "command" from the regional Department of Indigenous Affairs. Of course, the village assemblies still existed, but their authority was limited to managing the soil, punishing minor offenses, and organizing religious feasts and official merrymaking. Nested at the bottom of the new bureaucracy, the caids now played the role of stool pigeon—gathering useful news about the community and giving advice to colonial authorities.

This consolidation and reorientation of power took place after World War I, when France turned toward its overseas possessions to revive its devastated economy. The French impulse to colonize was rekindled with new vigor, and with it the desire to conquer what was called the *dissidence*.[8] French administrators now controlled caids and notables with a more watchful eye than they had before. They viewed them as a useful tool, or else an administrative evil, needed to mobilize manpower for the massive public works projects undertaken by the "protectorate" in order to produce something worth protecting. Complicity between the new intermediaries and French administrators, moreover, put the burden of the *corvée* system of forced labor squarely on the shoulders of those who, unlike the caids and notables, lacked the influence or resources to bribe their way to exemption. So weighty was the burden, in fact, that on the eve of World War II, the new system of oppression was on the verge of bleeding the country dry.

I visited Tiyout for the first time in the summer of 1989. My wife and I made our way along a dusty trail that left the highway to the east, at the end of the Oulad Abdallah village twenty kilometers north to Taroudant. For a good half hour we wandered among the argan trees. Goats and camels kept each other company along the rocky paths, barely managing to get enough food from the strangely shaped argan boughs. As we crossed a ravine we saw an immense fortress overhanging two built-up areas: the old village with low houses, lost among the argans, cactus, and jujube trees, and the new homes that housed the village's bourgeoisie—*arrivistes* from the area who had made good in Casablanca or Europe. The fortress was in ruins.

By accident we met Hmida, an older former resident who had come for a visit. Hmida and I began to chat, and I received an unexpected response when we began to discuss the past:

"What comes from what is illicit [laḥrām] will always finish in destruction."

"When had it happened," I asked.

"At the end of the time of the French. . . . The Liberation Army [jaych at-taḥrīr] attacked. The master of the house disappeared and the rest of the family dispersed. So the people looted the kasbah. They took everything."

Later we went to buy some argan oil from one of Hmida's relatives. We were received in the main room. Here and there slabs of marble covered the ground. Hmida, again much to my surprise, made the following comments:

The marble came to this house from above! . . . The house was built with our sweat. I worked on it when I was young . . . the whole day long. At night the Moqaddem would call each of us by name to the kulfa [compulsory work duty]. Fathers sent their sons. . . . I carried soil, water, and mortar. We carried the beams, and our mules and camels carried the wood. We also needed mules and camels to work the road and bridges . . . and when we returned to the village, we also worked for the caid. . . . When our crops were ready, the first harvest had to go to the caid. Otherwise, you had to buy your freedom from the Moqaddem, the shaykh, or the caid himself. I lived through all of that. . . . Anybody who refused went to prison and was beaten. Have you seen the prison? It's there in the house. Later there was the French prison at Taroudant. . . . We preferred that one.

Hmida was just over seventy years old. He said that he had begun to work under his father with older brothers sometime between the age of ten and twelve, so we can assume that the events he recounted, involving his family, took place in the late 1920s and early 1930s. The conquest of the whole country had by then been achieved, and the evolution of a distinctive colonial political machine had laid bare the fictitious character of the protectorate treaty. The system that at one time had preserved religious values and the parts of the shari'a which governed personal status and individual rights had given way to the expropriation of land, the takeover of mines and commerce, and proletarianization. Until 1920, colonial administrators were supposed to rule indirectly, sometimes with rigor, sometimes without. Colonists' craving for land, French troops' efforts to gain control of resources during World War I, and the betrayals of indigenous chiefs obliged French administrators to make their way with care. At Azrou, in the Middle Atlas, for example, the *ḥakem* played the role of paternalistic Solomon, giving the region its first real infrastructure and fighting speculation. Such paternalism gained the respect of neighboring tribes, but it hardly hid the flagrant inequalities between Europeans and Moroccans.[9] In the Gharb, high interest rates posed problems that the ḥakem was unable to solve. Huge infrastructure projects and rampant colonization forced the peasantry, already beset with misfortune, into the labor market. It was the beginning of a proletariat that would become recognizable as such after the appearance of a further novelty—the *bidonville*.[10] Big public works projects drew workers from far and wide. Young migrants in search of work were drawn as if by a magnet toward Casablanca.[11] This movement grew stronger toward the end of the 1920s as the protectorate transformed itself into a system of direct domination, turning the country to big business. With the complicity of local chiefs, the new system short-circuited the former sharifian state. It tried to stem, if not stop, the exodus to the cities. Stories abound of families being chased or stopped en route. Extortion, trickery, violence, a patronage system, and the demand for labor reduced the flow. This is when Hmida left the region for Marrakech, and his brothers for Casablanca. It is fair to assume that colonization in the Sous and the development of Agadir into a major port kept only a portion of the Sousi youth who fled their villages or camps in the south.

To travel in space is to travel in memory. At least if, heeding the Derridean reminder, we refuse the dichotomy between the march and the memory, and if the very voyage that they constitute conflates them with writing. What happened, then, at the end of our morning with Hmida? We climbed the slope that led to the kasbah and entered through the main door onto a corridor filled with the sounds of squabbles. "That's the place for the guard [*l'assa*]." After crossing a second threshold, we found ourselves in the middle of a large, beautifully proportioned courtyard: "*ʾAd-dār!*" Guest rooms and halls were upstairs. "Many people used to come here . . . the feast days. . . . *Nsara* [Christian/French] *jninnarāt* [generals] and the whole world—right here! With their cars and everything!" The courtyard's columns were intact, and marble plaques attested to the luxe that the house once enjoyed. The stairway was made of polychrome stucco with painted woodwork. A hallway turned into a passage to a second and smaller courtyard: *"Ad-duwiriya."* I do not know how to translate this word— perhaps as the interior of the interior, quarters of "intimacy" that house women, kitchens, baths, and so on.[12] A hole in the wall allowed light to penetrate one of the rooms of the *ḥammām*: "The slaves heated water in the *fernatchi* on the other side of the wall and poured it through there into the ḥammām." Hmida provided further details. The caid's pride was his power, of course, and the cooking was like that found in the cities—tajines, Bastila. "He married women from Marrakech and Fez. Look at the *Ḥabashīya*'s quarters!" Ḥabashīya? "Only a few had a Ḥabashīya—a beautiful black woman. Hardly anyone could boast of having one!" With this commentary on the "Ethiopian woman," we left the courtyard to take a tour of the surrounding walls. The prison (*al-ḥabs*), next to the first court, contained several dark and humid halls and rooms: "The hotheads were tossed here and forgotten." Behind the duwiriya we visited another enclosed space: "This is where the troops [*al 'askar*] and munitions [*baroud*] were housed." We passed by large cisterns (*mṭafi*). The whole assemblage of courtyard structures, seen from the rooftops, was protected by a double surrounding wall with guard towers and throughways. Toward the southwest the view took in the souk, sanctuary, palm grove, and slightly above these, the old mellah; here what was once a Jewish village was now only ruins.

Local centers of power took flight from the *Siba* (revolt) at the end of the nineteenth and beginning of the twentieth centuries through a simple but flexible logic of expansion and contraction: When rivals or tribes laid siege, the lines of force were drawn in, and what was laid siege to was a single "house." Yet local centers also knew how to take the offensive by refashioning their internal reserves or waiting until they could join forces. Putting an end to this dialectic of contraction and expansion, the French protectorate promoted a new regime: the consolidation of such dominions became a deliberate political strategy. If, at the beginning of the 1930s, the new techno-bureaucracy brought them under more control and the colonists held them in disdain, still the destiny of the peasants was left to their whim.[13] The colonial state is this *sui generis* melange of new chieftainships, techno-bureaucratic structures, and disciplinary technologies. All are clearly colonial and not traditional or simply modern—there is no modern bureaucracy that we can oppose dichotomously to a "traditional" Moroccan form of organization. This experimental state structure, set up between the two wars, was at once technocratic, authoritarian, spectacular, and patriarchal. The planning staff of the chieftainship and its administrative techniques were at work both in the farthest reaches of the country and in its urban centers, at the General Residence and in neosharifian services—under the authority of two guardians, the resident and the sultan. This twofold guardianship made it easy for the French to collude at the local level with businessmen and with the owners of large, newly mechanized farms. Such collusion, needless to say, further reproduced the system and the particular tensions, violence, and irredentism it had to face.

There were no colonial farms in the immediate vicinity of Tiyout. Not far away, however, between Taroudant and Agadir, colonization swept aside the peasantry and colonists appropriated peasant farmland. On the eve of war, the Sous plain had come to be called New California. Like many of the old timers, Hmida remembered the beginnings of this beautiful estate, which is now held by a Moroccan owner:

> There were jujube and argan trees. They worked the fields their ancestors left them. One day the shaykh told them that the makhzen wanted the land. They came en masse to tell the colonists' friends [ṣḥab al-muʿammir], whom they had never seen, that they wouldn't give up their land. The *mokhaznis* came and cleared them away. They were taken to prison at Taroudant. The ground clearing began. . . . Unpaid tribesmen and workers built the buildings and cleared the land. Their wives brought them food. Their animals were put to use transporting materials. . . . Many left the area.

Stories like Hmida's are told throughout Morocco. And where we do not find memories of forced labor, we still hear tell of plundering and forced land sales. Berque, for one, observed the Gharb at close hand and described with compassion how law and custom were refined and manipulated for the colonial settlers' benefit. He also detailed the dealings of chiefs and brokers, as well as the peasant's resistance, acts of violence, and forfeitures. More recently, we heard similar stories from the Haouz: the monopolization of farmland by

colonists and the consolidation of large estates in the hands of chieftainships and marabout lineages.[14] Until the time of the decisive
struggles against colonization (1952–1955), colonial planters, caids,
marabouts, and notables (or "religion magnates," as a British author
calls them)[15] amassed social and economic advantages in the shadow
of the new colonial state.

The goal of the preceding narrative is not to outline the genesis of
a specific mode of production. Such a mode—what some would call a
formation sociale—has been the subject of endless discussion that I will
not rehearse here. Instead of hashing out an analysis in terms of feu-
dalism, caidalism, or theories of unequal and dependent development, I am interested in locating the specificity of the colonial, first as
a political practice—a practice of bringing together men and women
who otherwise considered themselves different (and opposed) by life-
style, religion, race, or political stance.[16] Oppression and confrontation developed as a body of knowledge about race, society, work, and
ethics in the form of an ethnoscience or (on the Muslim side) in the
form of transcendental knowledge about human worth and destiny
and positive knowledge about history, community, and nation. Both
forms of knowledge seemed to imbue difference with an irreducible
quality. Yet we should not think that such difference presented an in-
surmountable barrier. To believe, for example, that the *savoir* generated by the ethnoscience and the positive historiography of the nationalist narrative created two views foreign to each other would be to
forget the meanderings of authorized discourses, the parade of concepts and words as they gloss over the very social surfaces that give
ambiguity its impact. Such concepts are reformulated in unexpected
fashions, transfigured in other cultural creations. Sometimes they
seem to disappear, but they soon come back into view fully upright,
spilling out as if by miracle. Has the ever-increasing power of the media in the twentieth century become a decisive determinant in this
highly volatile dissemination? I cannot express an opinion on this
point. Indeed, a separate ethnography would be required to treat the
subject adequately.

In colonial Morocco, as in the rest of North Africa, the same colonial situation glorified racial difference; yet it also broke down such
difference through "mixed" marriages,[17] the discourse of assimilation,
the mutual aping and adjustments of colonizer and colonized, and the

profound dialectic of internalization of each other as stereotype and as agent to be dealt with in daily life. The point of contact between colonist and native exhausted the clerks' pigeonholes: common practices—forced labor, new agricultural contracts, corruption, work in difficult conditions, armed service—gave all categories a characteristic instability. The plundered *fellāḥ* became transformed into an "idler" (a *fainéant*). But what about the fellāḥ driven to forced labor? He, as the colonist well knew, worked hard and threatened his oppressor.

Surprising inversions also destabilized the colonial discourse. For example, Muslims spoke the language of contract, law, and right while the colonists, who championed the same notions in their legal discourse, more often spoke the language of custom, practice, tactical maneuvers, and brute force. Wherever status, rights, or resources had to be acquired or defended, the colonist nativized and the colonized Europeanized. Relations of power rather than racial platitudes produced and exemplified these oscillations and inversions. Some French officers tried to limit the exactions and monopolies to which some caids had become accustomed, in the name of what they called justice; but nobody cared to know if it was Christian, Muslim, or some other form of justice that was invoked. They were unable to suppress the kulfa, the *twizas,* and the *sokhra* (which plagued the peasant until the end of the protectorate) or the expropriation of resources by native notables, French colonists, and French companies.[18] A majority of caids and notables, particularly in the countryside, were devoted to French rule and the new "modern order." But hardly any of them lived in villas or apartments in the *ville nouvelle* where the Europeans lived. And very few Moroccans of any condition wore the habits and hats of their French partners.[19] This despite the fact that in other Muslim countries, nationalist and modernizing revolutions imposed European dress and headgear in the hope of achieving westernization and the ideals of the modern nation-state.[20] Moroccan notables acted as if the colonial model were undeserving of imitation.

Similarly, in the sphere of the agricultural enterprise, few adopted the French modern farm. Was this an economic calculus? Was it because of the benefit of free, forced labor? Maybe. Yet in production as well as in reproduction, consumption, costume, and dwelling, the Moroccans clung to their differences. These differences, however, represented not such objective and permanent divides as would separate two cultural species but, in fact, points of confrontation

particular to the time. In terms of tactics of power they constituted in-
dicia of belonging and betrayal. They also shaped leadership irrespec-
tive of the colonial segregations. But one can go beyond tactics of
power to stress that differences such as these are a play *in* difference
as well as a play *of* difference. In this process, inscription is inseparable from argument and justification, and the work of both introduces
a radical instability in the dichotomous production of a new country
and a new civil society on parole. Dichotomous categories produced
Morocco anew. This production went hand in hand with the elaboration of colonialism in other colonies and "mother" countries in the
nineteenth century. This accumulation of colonial *savoir* entailed the
figuring of "cities and tribes" as well as a particular kind of colonial
countryside, social relations, cuisine, government, and so on.[21] It entailed the invention of the very term *North Africa* to designate countries until then called Marrakech, al-Jaza'ir, Tunis (themselves the
products of particular admixtures of *savoir-pouvoir* before the Ottomans, under the Ottomans, and, for Morocco, alongside and in reck-
oning with the Ottomans). Everything existed before colonial domination; what colonialism invented were new connections between
things and words and unprecedented controls over bodies and souls.
A new center of power with both a native sultanate and a French residence was produced. An etiquette, a tradition, a regulated formula
for succession came into focus, and within this "order," the unceasing
work of division into knowable parts. It was not until the new-style
guards' music and orchestra were themselves produced from scratch
that the parade could begin.

The indigenous chief and the district officer were created as a
specific pair at work and working on such institutions as the bureau
(*al-ibirou*), the market and market court (*maḥkma, guelsa*), the palace,
the kasbah, the shrine, the religious festival, the ceremony and the
banquet (mousem and *fijṭa*). Everything had to be made anew or reconstructed; colonial power counted heads (of humans, livestock,
etc.). It made maps and located and fixed life in them; it fixed, at least
in theory, masses of humans in territorial quarters.[22] It immobilized
"scenes" and "types" in the period's paintings and postcards. The
protectorate was itself produced: *ḥimāya*. A new name generated by a
semantic bead game that turned unsought (and so-called) protection
into an unnameable novelty: a Christian guardianship in dar-al-Islam.

The central institution of the protectorate was the "Residence," a unique social construction among other unique social constructions, whose purpose it was to reconcile the interest of colonists and "indigenous populations." The first and most prestigious resident general was Hubert Lyautey; a supporter of "indirect rule," he was responsible for much of its initial success.[23] Lyautey's successors, on the other hand, either could not or did not wish to moderate the direct and brutal control over resources and population. The new institution of the "general census" constructed the population as a source or as a force to reckon with. The resident general assumed basic command of military and bureaucratic forces; his title came to be written with a capital R even in midsentence. He was also the Resident Commissioner, a title from which the "Commissioner" was often dropped—making him simply the Resident. What a fine invention this title was! Residing at the top of a famous hill, he dominated, on one side, the Bou Regreg and its valley and, on the other side, the *ville nouvelle* then under construction and, further off, the *medīna*, or "Arab city." He was also in close proximity to the sultan, whose palace within the Almohade rampart could be seen from the loggias of his magnificent residence. He was simply residing presultan. The title Resident did not refer to any activity; he (there was never a she) was simply the Resident. Not—God forbid—a general governor or a proconsul. No, simply a Resident General. In Arabic, the term is translated as *al Muqīm al ʿamm*—the "resident, or sojourning, general." In any case, we are speaking of a new type of resident, a unique exemplar, as well as a generalized residence. This resident plays with the ubiquity of a saint, who, it is well known, is likely to have pit stops and rest stations (*maqām*) far and wide. The Resident General sets up his offices everywhere; like a saint, he is all knowing and can even predict the future. In Moroccan Arabic, his strange title may be rendered as *Saken* (inhabitant). The land inhabited by him is therefore *maskūna* (in Moroccan parlance)—possessed, alienated—by occult and dangerous forces. As for the Moroccans, they find themselves in the predicament of the *maskūnin*: inhabited by the Other, seized by trance, transformed and alienated—possessed.

Colonial *savoir* "inhabited" them as well. A vast accumulation of knowledge—often unwitting mastery over the native, with its own institutions and reference points—had been gaining ground since the nineteenth century. Its privileged sights and sites, which were first evident in Algeria, could be found not only in the French university, both in France and in Algeria; they could be seen in the famous Institut des Hautes Etudes Marocaines, in the Azrou Franco-Berber school, in such central administrative departments as the Department of Indigenous Affairs, in the tourism office, and so on. "On the ground," this knowledge operated within the ḥakem bureau, in the local technical and administrative offices, and in the military compounds. It also operated within the specific articulation between chieftainship and technocracy. The colonial knowledge and discourse circulated through government circles, both French and native, and through the very democratic institutions of the "protecting" power. It was a currency that could be spent in judgments that the politician, businessman, or the officer could apply in simple dispensations.[24] The economy of this discourse consisted of key oppositions like the now familiar Arab/Berber dichotomy and its many transformations: Arab despotism/Berber republican liberty, Arab respect for Islam/Berber attachment to pre-Islamic custom, Arab ties to the East/Berber ties to the West. The paths along which such oppositions traveled were well worn by metaphors that rendered the Berbers as a people who had little in the way of a past and, without the intervention of the Other, would have nothing in the way of a future. One heard talk, for example, of the "regeneration of a people still squatting on their haunches." This example condenses many of the presuppositions that buttress the symbolic economy, privileging the observer's point of view. Such an approach is a confrontation, reducing to coordinates plotted on a simple grid all that comes into view, thus giving the viewer the powers of creation and regeneration and depriving the object (i.e., the native) of the gaze—of almost everything except the possibility of being transformed by another. Morocco and the Moroccans became a virtuality to be shaped by French power and know-how.

This particular science posits diversity only insofar as it can be used to build separate and homogenous entities. The Arab or the Berber appeared as categories and representations in the coming into being of a specific politic. How could it be that such simple reductionism could avail and sustain its claims? Edward Said responds that "the scientists, the scholar, the missionary, the trader, the soldier was in, or thought about the Orient because *he could be there* or could think about it, with very little resistance on the Orient's part." Here we have a logic that unifies what would be multivocality into the voice of a unitary Oriental Other, a logic that shows us what the Other can or must be. S/he is not to be argued with. S/he does not come to dispute the self-image of the Other, but on the contrary, to speak *of* him with exclusive authority—that of *savoir-pouvoir.* One writes *on* or *about* Orientals, and, when they happen to be called to speak, they seem to do so in a single voice.[25]

I have already noted that ethnology and orientalism came, over a relatively long span of time, to constitute a dense authoritative corpus, and that in the Maghreb the bulk of the key texts were produced at the end of the nineteenth and in the first half of the twentieth centuries. In reading them closely, however, one has to keep in mind that the homogenous and homogenizing colonial discourse does not always keep its word. Instead of a single discourse, we find several discourses, which contradict each other. The writings of Massignon, Berque, and Rodinson, for example,[26] answered those of Renan and Montagne. What we read under all of their signatures appears as commentaries on Arab and Berber voices, presented in glosses and translations. One can see in them a colonialist project or a power discourse, or else the proliferation of writing subverting both project and discourse. But unless we want to reduce them all to a oneness we dub "logic of the Enlightenment" we should remember that Massignon, Berque, and Rodinson shook and threatened the colonial discourse by accepting that their actions were part of all the power fights and tactics of the time. Theirs are writings which evince an empathetic respect for others' (not the Other's) words. Did Massignon, Berque, and Rodinson provide a *contre-pouvoir* that was already at work in French society at large? Without a doubt. The dilemma that remains is that whatever the approach, the words of others always bear the signatures of the ones who write them. Despite everything, however, there remain "resistances" and discrepancies in the discursive logic itself. Some of these discrepancies stem from the difficulty of the subject/ object relationship, which breaks down in the very movement of its establishment and reassertion. This involves responsibility, effort, suffering, hatred, and so on—that is, questioning, emotions, and justifications which cannot be written off. The constant reversal of positions in the unstable and confrontational subject/object relationship seems to be what really matters in writing. It may help us to break with the disturbing isomorphism between the absence of agency in discourse and writing theory and the denial of that same agency by the colonial power.[27] It may also help map the discrepancies in the colonial discourse itself, an example of which I want to examine now.

In 1951 L. Justinard, a relatively well known but minor figure in French orientalism, published a biography of a famous caid. The author, then in retirement, had played an important role as officer, liaison, administrator, and orientalist and had been both pro-Arab and pro-Berber. He had translated works written in Arabic by Berbers: a story of travel (indeed, of flight) and a treatise on mysticism, to cite but a few examples.[28] The book I am concerned with is a biography, the title of which reveals a programmatic strategy: *Un grand Chef Berber, le Caid Goundafi.* Chief, *Berber, Caid*—each a localizing word. And all under the signature of Justinard. The voice of the colonel (Justinard's rank when he retired) authorizes all the categories. The events and the protagonist met their ostensible end in 1928 when Goundafi died. Yet they lived on in Justinard's papers; these were lost, but one of them was found again in the middle of the war (1941) and printed as a book ten years later. Why the delay? It is not an easy question. Maybe Justinard needed to wait for his retirement in Sale to write the biography.

Whatever the whims involved, the preface by General Juin, new Resident General of Morocco, gave order to caprice. In the twenty years following Goundafi's death, a new nationalism—manifested in the *latif* against the Berber Dahir (1930),[29] the action of the Committee for Reforms (1934), the creation of the Istiqlal party, the demands of 1936, and the protests of 1944—had succeeded old-style upheavals, such as the war of the liberation in the Rif (1922–1926), and scored decisive points against the colonizer. Moreover, this movement called for an end to the protectorate and total independence under the leadership of a monarch capable of rallying the people and repudiating the abhorred treaty of 1912. When the people thronged to see him in his public appearances, so feared by the French between 1927 and 1950, it was not the colonially constructed specter of the sultan and the sultanate which they saw, but the king and the kingdom. "Long live the king!" shouted the crowd (*Yahya al Malik!*), and such words amplified by the nationalist press became rallying cries.[30] Indeed, we can still trace the battle lines that then separated the nationalist party, on the one hand, and the urban labor unions and secret organizations, on the other. And at the heart of the large party that Allal al Fasi led, both ideas and generations came into sharp conflict. Still, a united front ensured the restoration of the monarchy and provided a clear target for the French, who were aided by notables and tribal chiefs leading a corps of "Berber horsemen."

The colonial coalition directed the horsemen to camp at the city gates of the capital as the time drew near for the king's deportation. We may never know what Si Tayeb al Goundafi's attitude would have been had he been there to see his descendants placed in the bosom of the protectorate. However, the publication of Goundafi's biography at that very moment could only have been part of a strategy. There he is: chief, great caid, Berber horseman, ready to duel (albeit posthumously). He stands with his peers behind the man who—at least according to colonial hagiography—represented them all, al-Haj Thami Glaoui, Pasha of Marrakech, the real king of the south, whose shadow fell over the king on the international scene. In popular writings and ethnographies of the day, "the Goundafi" was positioned behind "the Glaoui."[31]

The images and metaphors which we saw at work on the colonial corpus structure the narrative. The Berber caid rebels in his fortress. Although he does not challenge the makhzen too openly, he is autonomous. The image of the fortress—an eagle's nest where circumspection is the rule—tells the whole story. The hero is cast in this discursive landscape: master of ruse and intrigue, ruthless with his enemies. The account mentions his Koranic education, but just enough so that the rough edges of the young horseman (who is figured with all the qualities of a knight) remain salient. However colonial this metaphor may be, there are also metaphors recycled from local sources, first written in Arabic by Moroccans. These are the authorities "cited" to authorize what Justinard has to say; authored anew by the colonial writer, the tropes are all too familiar.[32]

Justinard's approach thus constructs a Berber, a Berber country, a Berber chief, and a Berber religion.[33] The map is complete; everything is arranged within its four corners so that those who have the powers of decision can maneuver without a hitch. Justinard conflates his own action with that of the first Resident, Lyautey. He is there—they are there—to pacify, to unify, to transform.[34] The Berber, like the Arab, is rendered an object of wills other than his own. He will be quartered in the space of the map that traces tribal borders. His space will be judged by the amount of resources it contains; it will be neutralized, dominated by the highway, the wireless telephone, and other means of communication.

Justinard's writing, in fact, interpolates an objectified description with first-person narrative. Poems and particular quotes sometimes intercede on behalf of their tellers. The writing charms with its variety and endears by evincing a subjectivity that is not afraid of unburdening itself. The other is objectified, but the writer approaches him as closely as he can, shares his life (again, there is no "she" in this confrontation); the native moves on the scene, alive and speaking. Despite all of this, the author places himself outside of the description, which is given within the linear structure of the narrative. The book opens with a photo of Si Tayeb and closes with a map: two objectifying spaces par excellence, spaces of pure representation—at least in the eyes of those who offer them. These spaces have a specific impact, providing the categories and the metaphors with an additional "effect of the real."

But in spite of the author's concerted efforts, his words appear to follow their own desires. The Berber, Justinard knew, was also named by the category *Amazigh*.[35] But are not both categories historical constructions, constructions in permanent flux, redefinition, and negotiation? Today's use of Amazigh resonates with the vibration of a radical freedom, but this redefinition may well have precedents in an old dialectic in which Berber/Amazigh stands vis-à-vis Phoenician, Latin, and Arab. At any rate, it is difficult to escape the impression that Berber and Amazigh are two slogans in the historical Arab/Berber dialectic, and that Amazigh, as conqueror, vindicates an assertion of freedom vis-à-vis not only Arabic speakers but also peoples (Phoenicians, Romans) who predate the Arab conquest. The word *Berber* (*barbar* in Arabic) is also the construction of the Arab, the Muslim, the conqueror, the mapmaker—the describer and narrator of his day. It is a sprouting word which is found in many places, including literature written by Berber/Tamazight–speaking writers.

Justinard wanted to render a portrait in living color of the Berbers and their chiefs, a portrait in which everything stays the same, in which social history can forget itself in a tableau of natural history. Those who live with the officer and make up his retinue are from another age. The hero, Si Tayeb, for example, is an "homme du moyen age." The imperial history of the Berbers is evoked through the consecrated historiography of Ibn Khaldoun, but the evocation does nothing to alter the received wisdom of the Berber cum biblical archaism. It is a regressive description that, like many others of its day, implicitly recovers the vestiges of the Roman presence in Morocco, or explicitly recognizes a parallel between Roman and French colonization. Scipio and Lyautey, same program.

In his youth the future caid is raised with a firm hand. He receives Koranic instruction and is imbued with a respect for fatherly authority; but he is also something of an adventurer, given to horsemanship, war, and gunpowder play. He acquires wisdom in *aḥwāch*, where music, dance, and poetry come together. Habitat forms character; he acquires rigor in response to the rigors of the cold and the mountains where he lives. He becomes a cultivated knight, but remains a warrior who enjoys galloping between kasbahs. Although he knows the Koran, he is hardly a pale-faced *ṭāleb* (Koranic teacher). Even when he later joins a confraternity, he stays a warrior, a chief like the founder of his lineage. He is constantly aware of the dangers of tribal revolt and of the risks inherent in the delicate and difficult relationship that must be maintained with the makhzen. Like him, all Berbers, according to Justinard, are "in love with their independence," "have little confidence in the word of kings," and are "resigned to God's will and patient in the face of misfortune."[36] Other traits, however, are also salient: violence, a lust for lucre, dishonesty, and a taste for the pleasures of the senses. Justinard notes these, but remarks that the caid was advised not to continue those loathed exactions which fall under the rubric of *frīda*. These and other dissonances create textual tensions to which I will return.

Such are the Berber, the Berbers, and the Berber chief: pinned to a new linguistic and literary map. The Berber's energy must be captured and used within the limits of a plan that pervades and encloses him, a plan enhanced by a new management of ethics and bodies to which the war (1939–1945) gave an imperious character: the armies devoured the men who composed them, and famine and epidemic devastated the entire population. The map's grids were made more systematic with food rationing, and other controls over resources, population, and movement.[37]

The disciplines that prepare and accompany the submission of the colonized have been described in other social settings, in colonial contexts and Europe alike. They first appeared in North Africa (in

Egypt and in Algeria) in the nineteenth century and in Morocco at the end of the nineteenth and the beginning of the twentieth centuries. Timothy Mitchell, writing about Egypt, groups them under the suggestive heading of "enframing," the building of a specific framework of *savoirs* that renders the dominated highly visible.[38] I would add that, in Morocco's case, the frame making and the frames also constituted interpretive vehicles and traps. Doesn't the word *frame* itself work as a framing device that entails such traps? As a framework-trap, discourse ensnares and encloses its objects; but as a juxtaposition of words, discourse can not prevent their proliferation, nor preclude the uncertain directions they go. The colonial construction of "Berber" encloses the dominated in the categories and grids. For example, Justinard cites a poet on the subject of airplanes and T.S.F. (wireless telephone):

> These *roumis* [Christian/French] carriers of calamity make rumors rise on the ground and in the heavens from a trunk where they keep their wings and saunter with sunbeams. Bringer of doom, the king of the Christians has a big stick in a silver sheath hanging at his side. He takes walks with his big stick under a sun that he has beaten down low beneath the plain, a sun that he has forced to yield the secrets of night and day. I no longer know where to turn.[39]

In Justinard's book, the voice of the vanquished intermingles with that of the author, as well as with those of the officer, caid, and tribesmen. And although history is denied, the Arabic historiography that is cited—Ibn Khaldoun and al Nāṣiri—imposes its own authorial voices on the French author. Certainly the fabric of the plot is woven with a warp and a weft of motif and motive taken from elsewhere and given a new texture. But despite this *quadrillage*, this framing and pinning down, the words and texts that shape this collage escape domestication. Because of such unravelings, the bulk of colonial anthropological knowledge and know-how—which gives the account its architectonics and its truth claims—is unable to fit in preestablished templates. To do so would require one to accomplish an impossible task: to metamorphize into objecthood the unravelings and the voids resulting from the collision of words and wills.

Since the end of the eighteenth century the proliferation of texts has fashioned an "imaginary museum" where letters (in both senses of the term)—Arabic, Berber/Tamazight, French, Spanish, English—intermingle and cut across each other. On this confusion some order is reluctantly forced. But no sooner is this done, than the letter extricates itself and moves on. Jacques Berque has shown how between the two wars a (deceptive) archaicism beat the colonist and the modernizing discourse at their own game.[40] Was this archaicism an example of regression, of resistance, or of escape? It is impossible to tell with any certainty, even with the salafi and nationalist counterdiscourses that surfaced at the same time, in 1930, in the revolt against the famous Berber Dahir.

All that was objectified resisted long and hard in the Sous that Hmida of Tiyout knew, although, as the poet indicates, no one knew where to turn. On the steep, ragged slopes of the Kerdous, facing the "pacifying" troops, the text of a "passive front" that bears Justinard's initials is contradicted by the military column (harka) which bears his signature. Knowing that they would soon be facing the great Caid Goundafi, pasha of Tiznit, invested with the power of the sharifian state in the Sous and supported by the French military and bureaucratic machine, the partisans drilled under Al Hiba, a *mahdī*, or "master of the hour," who had been instructed in the shari'a and was their supreme guide for jihad. Opposite them, the "great Berber chief," supported by the regulars of the reformed sharifian army and flanked by the captain who would become his biographer, rallied his tribal brethren into a complex network of concentric circles, organized them, and took them into battle. The mahdī challenged the legitimacy of a monarch protected by a Christian power. His adversaries called the mahdī a pretender. In 1912, at the gates of Marrakech, many of his *mujāhidīn* went up against the superiority of French arms. They continued their effort during World War I and afterwards, in the Anti-Atlas and the Sahara. Caids who had rallied behind the French served as intermediaries between the mahdi and protectorate authorities.[41] But the "mother country" again struck up its politic of conquest with the help of the caid. Si Tayeb al-Goundafi occupied the flank of the De Lamothe column in 1917, which was supported from behind by contingents from Mtougui and from Glaoui. The mujāhidīn resisted the intense bombings at Ouijjane and, later, the shots from the rear. In this war of the south—whose theater, until 1934, was the Saghro, the Dra, the Anti-Atlas and the Pre-Sahara—death was considered preferable to surrender. Whatever the reason for this preference—it is hard to distinguish here between religion, magic, and political ambition—it cannot be denied that those who opted for death over other choices realized one of the "limit experiences" that can "liberate" one's death, to use the words of Foucault.[42]

In any case, there is the text of the colonel-biographer, which is riddled with unexpected gaps. Resident General Juin, in his preface, dubs the Berber voices which cross the text *folklore*. Justinard does not use the word, although he cannot conceive that the Berbers were his contemporaries. How can we explain the presence of voices whose speakers are recognized in the rest of the book, albeit not by name, but denied in the preface? The colonizing nation-state turns the Other, an other impossible to deal with because it lies both inside and outside the nation, into a beautiful spectacle to contemplate, the "beauty of the dead."[43] On the inside is a particular people with its inventions and popular culture; on the outside, ethnics, primitives, Orientals, and so on. To this answer we should add that even this dichotomy cannot survive the nation-state colonizing *en marche* with native troops and native personnel, and it cannot survive the native building of a new nation-state shaped within the colonial discourse. Yet identity as will resuscitates the "dead." As a mummy which would stand up to take control of the mummifiers, the resuscitated seizes upon the very ethnosciences which purport to immobilize it. Silences, refusals, returns, popular, anticolonial demands, mass passivity and lack of responsiveness, and riots—all take power-knowledge by surprise. Did not Berbers leave the Berber to assume the fighting energy of Amazigh? Did not the Arabs break off the Arab by being endlessly on the move, wandering between noble, idler, creator of civilization, Muslim fanatic, mystic, bedouin: Writing nomadism challenges fixed categories and blurs them in unexpected poetic configurations.

In the case of Morocco, identity gaps and glissandos during the protectorate's early days extended beyond biography and ethnography and pervaded colonial discourse. The fixation of the natives within categories (tribes, *ḥaḍarīya*, trades and trade organizations, etc.) by powerful research programs and the deliberate politics of "conservation" resulted in a reworking of ideas such that these ideas could be put to new administrative uses.[44] Attempts to update and upgrade what was "preserved," however, destabilized the very colonial project which made such attempts possible. Colonial society and power propelled themselves to center stage by reforming and reworking indigenous cultures as a frame and a background, but doing so made them appear small and weak, conspicuously exposed in comparison with the larger Arabo-Berber society. Hence the latter came to the foreground, pushing the colonists to the background. Native society and culture appeared threatening as it stood both in the heart and in the periphery, threatening and confusing colonial science and power. Anticolonial voices inspired dissenting young orientalists in the 1930s, at the peak of French colonial domination. It is as if the uncontained and uncontainable proliferation and reception of texts were energized by a dynamic comparable to the one which keeps perception oscillating between foreground and background.[45]

Colonialism, Authoritarianism, and Civil Society

In the 1920s, while Goundafi waged war in the Sous, the French state completed the organization of the colonial institutions and resumed the systematic war effort aimed at reducing dissidence. The period after World War I was favorable for the task, and allowed the French military, which controlled the new territorial administration, to exert a more punctilious control than ever over indigenous chiefs. Si Tayeb saw his command reduced and was later to experience a humiliating fall from grace. Such reductions would eventually diminish the control and territorial scope of even the greatest of caids, with the exception of the Glaoui. And while Taroundant-Agadir was receiving its first quota of colonists, other regions like the Haouz, the Sais and the Gharb, colonized earlier, were subject to an ever more rampant confiscation of farmland by the French.[46]

Si Tayeb Goundafi died in 1928 in a state of disgrace and piety. The Sous that he had known—the Sous of Caid Tiyouti and of young Hmida, the two protagonists with which I began this account—was quickly transformed, like the rest of Morocco. The 1930s was a period of crafting, of honing, and finally of perfecting the arts of colonial domination. Perfection was achieved by the "reduction" of the last pockets of resistance, with direct administrative rule propped up, above all, by the "natural chiefs" and local councils (jma'a). This technocratic structure managed colonists, natives, schools, hospitals, and other resources, and an army was quartered at strategic locations throughout the newly pacified "territory." This political and social engineering effectuated a particular sort of revolution, one founded on a specific *rationalizirung* that managed both center and periphery with a calculated combination of ritual and planning, expenditure and exaction. Each combination was to reflect a very specific purpose of the powerful metropolitan state.

The Algerian experience was decisive in determining the shape of the Moroccan political landscape. In 1843 Jules Cambon, then Algeria's governor general, lamented before the Senate that the French administration no longer had "intermediaries appointed by the indigenous population." According to Cambon, it was necessary to re-create a structure for the natives. Lyautey seemed to have meditated on this lament. Forgetting neither the lesson learned from the troubles on the "Algerian-Moroccan border" nor the one learned from J. Gallieni, Lyautey conceived a plan intended to rework the structure of Moroccan society and to win the allegiance of Moroccan notables. He was aware of the philosophical and ethical contradictions of a project of co-opting native elites, as well as its advantages:

> How can a regime which in its purity represents a form of administration and politics barely acceptable to a liberal mind (or even to a mind that is somewhat imbued with simple justice) evolve through intelligent change and, thanks to an adjustment to a central power (a power that would tolerate it only grudgingly) preserve a capital of prestige that would be useless, indeed dangerous, to sacrifice.[47]

Indeed, for Lyautey, losing this capital, or substituting another form of authority, the regime might well become a laughing stock. So the famous resident general embarked on his program of "intelligent change." This program was somewhat reshaped during the 1920s. But it did not change much in the subsequent decade, during which it was forced upon and generalized throughout the country, albeit in varied forms. The formula was economical and thanks to its capacity to force the French and the notables to adjust to each other, it survived well until the independence of Morocco (1956) and beyond. Its rationality and economy stemmed from the fact that it allowed the seizure of individuals as individuals (for labor or other duties) while, thanks to the notables, it governed them cheaply as groups. Administrators could thus establish group boundaries thanks to a forced *quadrillage*, the establishment of which was the work of the same powers who shaped and were shaped by the ethnoscience.[48] Finally, such groups served as administrative and cognitive frames through which the technocratic structure managed the Nomad, the Arab, the Amazigh, and their fictive kin.

As an order, the new state, a precise, authoritarian social manager, gained the admiration of the nationalists, who simultaneously fought it as a foreign power. One such nationalist, who had carried out an immense cultural and literary quest in the Sous, said explicitly that his southernly venture had been motivated both by nationalism and a desire to preserve for posterity a patrimony threatened by this "new and extraordinary order."[49] This thought was doubtless shared by other nationalist leaders. In this case, it came from a Berber 'ālem (the son and biographer of the famous Sidi al Haj 'Ali, whom we have already met) with a fierce loyalty to classical Arabic and Islam, who collaborated in the work of setting them straight against other languages and religions and the colonial politics of division and denigration.[50]

In these new circumstances, a reelaboration of tradition can be seen. The chief protagonist is still the notable, but he is different from the precolonial notable. He is now a sociopolitical mediator who is less dependent on mobilizing his lineage. The support of a solidly entrenched central bureaucracy, the acquisition of durable goods, and his participation in the new economy assure him a new form of preeminence. In brief, his patronage has acquired a stable base. This new patronage is not a simple continuation and extension of the old version, superimposed on the bureaucratic rationality. On the contrary, it would be wrong in this instance to oppose bureaucratic rationality and patronage. From its inception, the new bureaucracy is pervaded by the notable and its mediational style.

This new tradition, the technical, authoritarian, ritualistic state buttressed by the notable, survived the struggle for independence. The events of the long struggle are well known, if often rendered in overly linear accounts that fail to follow the twists and turns of the battle lines within the nationalist and colonialist camps. The breaking down of this narrative of the nation has begun, however, if unevenly.[51]

It is not my aim here to tell a new story. By laying out a map of some of the landmarks of the old story, I intend, rather, to evoke the contradictory textures of clashing discourses, wills, and desires. Until what we might call the "hinge years"—the Rifian revolution (1920– 1926 and the 1930s)—battles against French and Spanish invaders were led by tribes under the direction of charismatic leaders. It was not that the cities gave up without a fight; the uprisings in Fez alone contradict such a claim. Instead, the tribes defended the cities; but the cities, on the whole, did not come to the rescue of the tribes. Beginning in 1930, a new form of militancy appeared with increasing frequency—new because urban, oriented toward older forms of ritual practice, directed by salafi ulema, and finding its expression for the most part in the mosque (first, as we have seen, in the memorable laṭīf against the Berber Dahir).

In Sale, and then in Fez and elsewhere, protests against the Dahir reunited those who shared neither geographic origin nor language. This short-lived piece of legislation disavowed by the leader whom the colonizers called the Sultan Sidi Mohammed Ben Youssef, intending to govern Berber tribes by custom, as codified by the colonist, and to supplant the shariʿa, the use of which it reserved for cities and Arab tribes. The dynamics of the Dahir's imposition and the protest which it triggered revealed the power-knowledge of the customary and "natural" chiefs, who effectively came together despite the failure of the great caids' policy in the Middle Atlas and the new limits placed on the Caid's power.[52]

The attempted imposition of the Dahir was a new phenomenon, and one that was met by urban resistance. The rejection was total; the Dahir was withdrawn. Their goals achieved, the nationalists regrouped around the throne, calling first for reforms (1934) and then for complete independence (1944). The so-called traditional urban mosques housed the protests, which crept into religious ritual. Casablanca—new industrial city, chief colonial port, economic capital— offered unprecedented freedom of movement and communication, which fostered the development of unions, a new style of commercial and artisanal organizations (the ḥnati), and a new, dynamic group of professionals.[53] Coming together with the cultured bourgeoisie of the "old cities" was not always easy and did not always work smoothly, for the birth of this civil society took place, paradoxically, under police surveillance. As in neighboring Algeria, the nascent Moroccan civil society was initially raised within and by the colonial civil soci-

ety, but it soon strayed from the earlier institutions and major decisions. In the dynamics of the struggle, colonial civil society appeared
for what it was for the colonized—a construction and an illusion.

The inception of these spaces of liberty for the oppressed could
also be seen in the modernized countryside. In large-scale agriculture,
men and women from tribes and village communities learned to work
as laborers, that is, for fixed salaries on fixed schedules. The hiring
practices of the cities were almost unknown here; hiring took place
within small cells of permanent workers-supervisors (*cabranat*). The
work was hard, exploitative; more often than not discipline was enforced through physical violence. But salaries were regular and there
were breaks. Along with the forced labor of the *corvée* system, the regularity of salary work began to undercut the authority of the caid, the
shaykh, and the moqaddem. After World War II, insubordination and
the phenomenon of "fleeing for the city" (*lahroub lamdīna*) multiplied:

> It was during the harvest. We had had a good year. The
> *jarrāy* pressured my Father. At night here was always the call
> to the kulfa. We had already lost our camel. The authorities
> took it to carry wood. That afternoon my brother and I har-
> vested the *glass*.[54] The night before the jarrāy had called him
> to harvest the shaykh's fields. I hesitated a bit the next morn-
> ing. Then I told myself, "He is not going to go and that's all
> there is to it." The sun was already high. My brother and I
> were out there bending over our threshing and the harvest
> was going well. I saw the shaykh come on his mule. I contin-
> ued working like nothing happened. He gave his mule a kick
> and approached. "Your brother must go!" "Sir, we're in the
> middle of bringing in the crops. Let us finish this field and
> then he'll go." "No! He is coming now!" "He won't go!" I
> responded. "He won't. He won't." Then, "You'll see what
> you've got coming!" After that, the shaykh left in the direc-
> tion of El Kelaa. I ran along another road to see the shaykh of
> the Jews. The caid's *khalīfa* never refused him a thing.[55]

These memories of a Sraghna peasant echo Hmida's account of the
events that took place on the other side of the Atlas, at Tiyout. In the
case from El Kelaa, however, the story takes place after World War II.
The Americans had landed in Casablanca, the manifesto of 1944 had
run its course, and Jews everywhere in Morocco had acquired new de
facto rights. Such changes were felt throughout the country. A new

generation of rural peasants and urban bourgeois were in the process of laying bare and challenging the limits of prewar technologies of control. Something like an internal civil society produced these refusals, whose energies were spent in militant, armed revolt or in hope of a new life under "a king of our own" after the colonists' departure. The increase in fighting in both villages and cities kept the notables' rule over the "natives" in check. In 1953, the king's deportation revealed the extent of his popular support and the political defeat of notables who had fallen from grace. It was a defeat that took place in much the same way as it had in Morocco's easterly neighbor, Algeria.[56]

This defeat did not invalidate colonial *savoir* as such. A positivist science inseparable from the power relations that produced it, the colonial politic had produced static and essentialist concepts and metaphors, bringing to a standstill what had been a changing social landscape. Some of the voices that did not pretend to separate the "science of man" from politics and ethics, and who repeatedly extolled the virtues of liberation, failed to make themselves heard. In the preface to Justinard's book, the resident general who masterminded the coup against the very popular king still spoke fondly of the early days of the protectorate, when a French captain could become a "*Chleuh* [Berber] Captain" and one could hear the sounds of "certaines chansons de geste" sung by the officers to whom the book was dedicated.[57] The biography and its preface thus were meant to perpetuate the "memory of great men" who oversaw the colonial beginnings. It is *le temps retrouvé*, or time regained—synchrony in diachrony. How distant this belle epoque seemed in 1950, and consequently, how endearing! One cannot help but think of a heroic and innocent era, one of births and beginnings; the accursed history which had followed lent this moment, lapsed forever, all the force of an origin myth, whose return naturalizes the day-to-day business of oppression.

The account of Colonel Justinard, hagiographic in many respects, portrays a man who has his highs and lows, his good words, his wisdom, and his edifying end. But in the photo, taken enigmatically at the threshold of his *riad*, the old and fallen caid is dressed all in white and framed within the ogival arch of the door. He bears the modest posture of a body swathed in dress robes, the collars of which can be seen under a medal choker that sports a cross. Other medals are fastened to his djellaba: one on the right side of his chest, two on his left shoulder. A cord that runs around his neck and wraps across his body nestles a dagger (*kūmmiya*) in a sheath on his left side. We cannot see his left hand, but his right fingers clasp a string of prayer beads. The djellaba almost reaches the ground on his right side. Its folds are hiked up a bit on the left and reveal a pair of *balgha* on his feet. A thick beard covers his face. Si Tayeb's head is tilted slightly toward the right and covered by the hood of the djellaba. His whole demeanor breathes something like embarrassment and awkwardness.

The aged and pious Si Tayeb obviously had a hard time giving himself over as a spectacle. The photo gives the distinct impression of a man whose door is rarely opened. When it is opened, it is only after the ringing of the doorbell; at that time the doorbell on this princely house in the heart of the medina would have been an innovation and sign of distinction. Behind his silhouette, frozen like an icon, nothing can be seen except deep darkness. The colonial photographer no doubt has been kept at arm's length, outside the riad. We do not know if the old man immobilized by the picture found, like his biographer, the protectorate's debut "endearing." He has left us with no statement on the subject, neither in his mother tongue (Tamazight) nor in colloquial spoken Arabic nor in written Arabic (he knew both). His way of life (never westernized), his piety, and his tax excesses escaped colonial control. But he played scrupulously the role of the loyal caid of the protectorate. Here too Si Tayeb wears, in a highly visible way, his colonial symbolic capital. But at the same time, he seems to disavow it. Djellaba, robes, dagger, prayer beads, balgha, medals—Si Tayeb appears like a collage in which the cross and the prayer beads play at cross purposes. The medals disfigure the djellaba; their juxtaposition produces shifts in being and meaning. It also imparts a comic effect, and we might laugh if this strange panoply were not a signature of colonial drama with its actors and horrors. One major actor is at the center of this picture. But the spectacle is pushed, rejected, outside the house, and the character is shown against the entrance of the house, inside which nothing can be seen but the deep darkness of the corridor. This interior darkness is not a substance, but perhaps a refusal and a will. The framing of the whole picture produces shifts which confound the traps of both colonial and anticolonial interpretation.

Si Tayeb, as a collage, seems to indicate something of the risk and mystery in which all historical existence is entangled. Risk and will subsume the gap in being without annihilating the difference that un-

settles it. They redefine each moment of life past and, without exhausting the past, give a person the exorbitant sense that the world
belongs to him or her. Who then is this Goundafi? The great caid cum
collaborationist, once part of the network of notables who invented a
double tyranny, less Oriental than colonial, that toward the end of the
1930s extended its grasp into the heart of the city and countryside?
A greedy and a bloodthirsty despot? Without a doubt. Even colonial
hagiography cannot relieve such men of their earthly sins. Fridas,
extortions, spoliations, unceasing demands from a lord hungry for
power, competitions, intrigues: all ruin any hope for idealized reconstructions. But what should we make of the prayer beads that never
left this man's side? And what should we make of his prayers with the
troops and his mystical devotions? Sense shows its elusiveness and
we are left adrift with words.

First of all the name itself: Si Tayeb. The *Si* connotes "sire" in
Moroccan Arabic. Then *Tayeb*: "the good." This "Sire Good" says it all.
Here is a Berber, like most Arabs and Berbers, bettered by the language of the Koran, and thus identified with a sacred genealogy. Justinard says (and knows) as much. Thus, for him, this "Sire Good" is
also "Amazigh." Berber/Amazigh put together sound like a program:
the Barbarian–Conqueror–Free. This program features something of
a musical medley, a percussive duet of two wills. Two historical constructions (barbarian/free) bound by a dialectic of power. An Ariad-
nean thread runs from the historiography of Ibn Khaldoun through
colonial historiographies, weaving the Berber into history in a particular fashion: a builder of empire, a staunch Muslim, the one who
evolved a "high civilization" in the Maghreb, this West of the Arabs.
His actions are defined by words and metaphors that, even today,
connote barbarian–civilizer–historic agent. But must we still oppose
him to Amazigh? To do so would only multiply shifts and confusion.
Berber as barbarian–civilizer–historic agent can be subsumed by
Amazigh. But the latter will never cast off a slightly defensive connotation. Justinard, the connoisseur of things Berber, cannot eliminate
this difference that defies the construction of stable identities. In 1922
everyone thought, according to Justinard, that Si Tayeb would make a
substantial contribution to the fund being raised to build the mosque
of Paris, a typically Lyauteyian project. Yet Si Tayeb refused, and
without saying a word had the mosques of Marrakech refurbished at
his own expense. Thus whatever meaning(s) one may give to his ac-

tion in the Franco-Moroccan colonial context, the Berber–barbarian–pious Muslim–Amazigh takes swift leave of the realm of the thinkable. The colonial product finds itself *en porte à faux*. It was unthinkable that Si Tayeb would not contribute to the Paris mosque, but this is exactly what he did. Instead, he made another gift, a gift by which perhaps he called for the return of another Morocco.

At this point it might be useful to explore some of the implications of Foucault's analysis of the relationship between power and *savoir*, rarefaction of the enunciated, and production of knowledge. Such a production is inseparable from objectification and control over body and soul. But in another direction, Foucault encourages us to listen to speech that springs from the likes of Pierre Riviere. From his cell, Pierre assumed an authority and spoke against the discourse which at that very moment was constructing his madness and criminality. I do not know what befell Riviere's memoir right after he wrote it, but it is striking that what he wrote is still proliferating in the writings of others, including those of Foucault.[58] The interstices and invisible lines of such encounters of writings are the spaces within which speech happens. These spaces seem to offer sites for the work of power as well as to impose limits to that work.

At the height of colonial conquest, words bump up against one another and meanings butt heads even when they pretend to ignore one another: The words of those who were pitched against each other delineated two camps and invited the often blurred divides. Was one colonial discourse opposed to one nationalist discourse? It seems not. One strong colonial line was backed by a powerful bureaucracy an a modern army. What we might call protectorate colonialism opposed nationalisms, liberal colonialisms, and the humanisms that issued from certain French quarters. It did not, however, sin by positing a simple false vision that we can symmetrically and easily oppose to a true vision. Instead we are faced with a historical construction that refused to recognize itself as such, one that alienated those who spoke in the name of the oppressed majority but could still move those who apparently subsumed the whole under the new Franco-Moroccan order. As for the historical validity of the nationalist discourses, such value can only be measured in terms of its effects— the motivations it produced among the masses who were ready to sacrifice themselves to shake off oppression. This absolute engagement, despite the semantic bead game of shifting meanings, moved into action masses of Moroccans—the Arab–Amazigh–Berber–barbarian–Muslim–imperial peoples who created the civilization which in the Maghreb inhabits the *longue durée.*

The nationalist critics of colonial despotism were born and raised in the shadow of a new civil society, relatively free but under surveillance, and flanked by an enslaved peasantry, itself pegged in radically new ways on the colonial map. This probably is the specific invention of colonialism, as the creation of *sui generis* order, in Morocco and perhaps elsewhere. The collaborationists, or traitors, as they were called at the time, stood guard over the new civil society, watchdogs in the guise of native notables. On this point, the cleavage which sets collaborationists and nationalists apart cannot be bridged. Was there, in fact, any common ground these enemies could share? The question may appear sacrilegious at first, but it gains currency once one remembers the reconciliations which took place after independence. Some basis must be found for these reunions. During the glorious return of King Mohammed V and the royal family, the crowds were electrified by the king's charisma, and the notables (who, along with the protectorate administration, had engineered his exile) were forced to retreat to the margins. But much to everybody's surprise, the protectorate network came to prostrate itself at the feet of the king. The famous Glaoui came thus, the same man who inherited a near principality against which the lineage of Si Tayeb had warred for generations. The greatest caid—the most Parisian of all of them, it was said—had reigned over the south and been pasha of Marrakech for decades until the early days of independence and freedom for the majority. He finished his days in sickness and humiliation, his property sequestered. Some of his companions were killed in the main square of Marrakech; the crowd burned some of these fetishes who had for so long hung in uneasy balance between it and the colonial machine.[59]

At the same time, Allal al Fassi, the great nationalist leader, received massive popular ovations all over the country. Along with other leaders, he knew how to anchor the popular struggle around the monarchy and maintain a unified front. If one went in search of the two most radically antithetical personages, one could not find a better pair than Allal al Fassi and Thami al Glaoui. Everything Ihaj Thami stood for was transcended by Allal al Fassi or was foreign to his experience. Allal al Fassi exemplified a new Islamic universalism; Ihaj

Thami exemplified localism. The former was a man of culture who fought with the pen, the latter a political animal who imposed his will by sword, ruse, and cash. One exuded urbanity, the other the austere condition of a mountaineer upbringing. Whereas al Fassi was reserved and studious, Ihaj Thami was known for his taste for the good life and the pleasures of the flesh. One man reflected on Islam and European values in order to draw a specific lesson for the future; the other believed in Western might with blind faith. In the one we see a readiness to sacrifice, in the other a passion for opulence and the power pushed to sacrifice. I could go on with these antinomies, but they do not tell the whole story. These two men, opposed as they were in so many ways, shared a respect for the canonical rites of Sunni Islam, as well as a distinctly Moroccan way of life. In the drama of the struggle for independence, civil society—through it, language and other cultural practices—transcended for a while the forms of factionalism and submission to chiefs. Such behavior still persisted, but it seemed on the wane. Civil society transferred and changed, in a manner that seemed radical and decisive, the rapport of patronage. Patrons and patronage were thought to be things of the past, of the colonial past in particular. They were exemplified by the colonial notables, rejected and buried forever. In fact, however, even within the nationalist movement, the system and its values were only occulted— simply archived, so to speak. As the postindependence political protagonists felt their way, by trial and error, along paths full of traps, what was archived returned as a tacit reference. In this context, the patronage system slowly regained its credibility and reassumed a primacy sanctioned by traditions.

When Allal al Fassi went to visit the largely rural town of El Kelaa in the first few months after independence, the jubilation, affection, and deference that greeted him showed the love the masses felt for a man who had done his country an invaluable service. As a bystander, I saw the shapes that this respect took among the militants— the shapes of bodies and their skill at improvising the aesthetic and social forms their submission to al Fassi required. Such forms differed little from those sketched above in my discussion of the meeting with the caid. The *za'īm* did not demand abject forms of submission. He in fact discouraged the kissing of his hand and did not demand other such displays of ritualized affection. No coercive means were used in the encounter with him; his action and courage alone had invested him with auctoritas. Thus, although the za'īm never resorted to the coercion that was Ihaj Thami's stock in trade, he was met with the same forms of submission as the "lord of the Atlas."

During the summer of 1954, less than two years before independence, one of the Sraghna's greatest caids—a friend of the pasha, a famed hunter of man and game, a polygamist, and a distinguished horseman—prepared himself to do justice in his court (*maḥkma*), which dominated the weekly souk. In front of the caid, shimmering in the afternoon sun, a copper teakettle simmered. The caid's retinue crouched about him on rugs. Musicians had just struck up an 'ayṭa when rumor of a bomb suddenly struck the crowd of plaintiffs with a panic that dispersed them in utter disorder. In the souk, the multitude moved back and forth like sea waves. Then the panic came to a halt. News that the bomb had been found buried under the *galsa*, the space in which the caid was seated, and had been unearthed and dismantled spread just as quickly as the first rumor had. A bit of smoke from the wick had seeped up from the ground and betrayed the bomb's location. The caid proved to be unflappable. Moments later, two men with hands tied behind their backs were poked, pushed, and prodded before him. Everyone understood these were *waṭan* (nationalists), suspected of having planted the bomb. As the huge crowd watched, the caid ordered the men to be "plucked." His militia forced them to their knees and pulled out their beards tuft by tuft; blood ran down their cheeks. Then they were thrown in a car and sent to Marrakech under heavy guard. The incident was the subject of much discussion in the subsequent months.

What strikes me in retrospect is that the loss of honor signified by the public plucking assumed the same importance in day-to-day discussions as what might seem to be more pressing topics—the political climate, nationalism, torture. These themes were by no means absent from conversations, and the caid's actions unleashed a great deal of resentment. But repeated commentaries on the event held that even if the men had been found innocent, they could never return to the village after suffering the humiliation of a public "shaving." The new generation made light of the old men who "put their honor in their beards." The habitus at stake in such localized and localizing altercations collided with national debates on change, revolution, and the end of colonialism's *techne* of despotism. Skepticism, changes of opinion, practices classed as revolt and deviance, critical assessments of society and its mores—all shook the habits and habitus of the past.[60] Such criticism and reevaluation, never absent, continued and was amplified in new terms. They had taken a dramatic turn during the nineteenth century, but had tended down to a more clearly defined path after half a century of colonial rule and reflexive returns on and to the Self. The za'īm himself accomplished such a reflexive effort, engaging in a conscious and accepted dialectic with the West as it was understood by his salafi generation, a fact that has been neglected.[61]

But these examinations of conscience were denied entry in certain quarters. Only a few solitary voices denounced the excesses of fatherly authority.[62] Yet such authority was not reconceived, and although disobedience and autonomy became part of a burgeoning consciousness, precedent retained its influence over present practice. Science and experience alike were subjugated to a rationalist critique that never passed from theory to reflective practice. By means of an intellectualism buttressed by emotion, the return to the Self after the (physical) departure of the French provided both the energy for the struggle and a limit to questioning and criticism. Freed from direct colonial surveillance, Moroccan civil society preserved the tracks of its first meanders. Patterned after hidden and semiclandestine battles, it proved little given to public debate. Nothing could have prevented its striving to go public after independence; sheer will and the errors of experimentation could have enlarged the ambit of permissible debate, and might, consequently, have provided a radicalized reflexivity and eradicated some of the elementary forms of obedience and submission that had come to be taken for granted. But it was not to be.

Despite the grave risks taken before independence, when the dust of the battle settled, Ihaj Thami refused exile. Like our caid from the Sraghna, he opted for a life of discretion. Such notables, compromised for a while, began a process of reconciliation with the new social setting and the powers who took over from the French during the first years after independence. Secret organizations killed some and caused some to vanish; such, for example, was the fate of Caid Tiyouti, whose once grand home we visited. But the better part of the network survived the storm.

There was no historic fatality that could *automatically* restore, across political camps, the forms of submission and preeminence expressed by both the cultivated bodies of the militants and the crowd.

The choice of men and the volatile early years of independence forced those who were given to protest to choose between two varieties of authoritarianism, one with a socialist bent and the other guided by economic liberalism in the service of the new state. The inherited protectorate apparatus, quickly restructured, regained control over the basic resources necessary to found a properly political economy. Given such conditions, the gains and entitlements of civil society eroded at the same time that the system of patronage—after having been submitted to the egalitarian ethic of battle and projected as the exclusive stigma of the procolonial camp—reasserted its credibility. Indeed, patronage proved to be such a reassuring and familiar face, that no one—not even those with the most militant of pasts—seemed capable of escaping its temptations.

As Laraoui has pointed out, what happened after independence cannot be accounted for as the "resurgence of a precolonial system." The relations of power and its peculiar rites that we have seen at work, both in the nineteenth century and before direct colonial penetration, were reinterpreted and "reread" in and by the science of the protectorate.[63] And if the regime that succeeded it was its continuation, it would be an error to stop the analysis at its dualistic facade. To do so would be to miss the specific, authoritarian montage whose forms took shape between the two world wars; that authoritarianism evolved and draped itself into a new legitimacy after independence.

The Cultural Schema, Its Saliency, and the Structural Tension It Mediates

Although al Haj ʿAliʾs biography straddles the nineteenth and twentieth centuries, the power relations it brings to light should not be regarded as memories of a bygone era. Enshrined in everyday discourse and practices, the master-disciple example not only continues to inform political interaction in present-day Morocco but still appears hegemonic in comparison with other modes. Far from being driven away by a new legal rationality, the master's authority pervades bureaucracy. For in spite of its spectacular development in the last hundred years, the bureaucratic apparatus sees its rules constantly subverted by concrete codes of interaction geared toward building closeness through gift exchange—that is, through the same procedures we found at work in the master-disciple relationship. These procedures can be observed in lobbies and offices as well as in relations with the supreme leader.

Let us recall some characteristics of the regime before returning to the social and political salience of the master-disciple relationship. First, it retains a monopoly on strategic decision making and arbitration between factions, made possible by an ever-present threat of violence (the police and the army) and the manipulation of economic benefits; such manipulation reflects a political economy which literally neutralizes the market's potential to liberate participants from these practices. Second, at the center of the system is a leader surrounded by an entourage of disciples who cannot achieve success without some kind of authorization which only he can give. Third, there is the promotion of a particular culture, namely that of the notables. A notable becomes master of his estate only when he has obtained the agreement of higher masters after visiting them regularly, exchanging favors, and giving evidence of good and loyal services; this inevitably forces him to go through displays of ritualized submission. The norm of service, which has a strong affective dimension, extols these ways of doing things and imbues them with ethical as well as aesthetic value. Such are the salient features of this form of modern authoritarianism, which in addition claims religious legitimation, as summarized in the Islamic formula "the community of the faithful." The latter concept, as a formalized ideology, does not clash in the least with the empirical (and not always explicitly formulated) notions which govern power relations between notables and apprentice notables.

The expansion of this system (to the detriment of reformist efforts during the first years of independence) was in no small measure due to the work of the royal house, as well as domestic and foreign networks which assisted it in rallying the people.[1] Another factor in the consolidation of this system was the paralysis created by factionalism and divisions in the parties and organizations stemming from the political movement of national emancipation.[2] At the center is the bipolar figure of the monarch, who shifts, as required by circumstances, between two incarnations—as figure of holiness and as source of violence—without any transition or apparent contradiction.[3] Added to the charisma inherited from his ancestors (baraka) there is his personal grace, evidenced by miraculous escapes from potentially fatal situations, such as wars or coup attempts.[4]

As baraka became a quasi-official creed, holiness as energy grounded in a specific location (a shrine) and as object of veneration, which for a while had been contested, made a strong comeback. This trend has continued since the late 1960s, thanks to the moral and material support provided by the postcolonial dar-al-mulk. Yearly festivals around the great marabouts' shrines have become official events to which the government delegates ministers and high civil servants. Many saints are officially venerated: among others, Moulay Idriss in Fez, Moulay Idriss of the Zerhoun, Moulay Abdeslam ben Mchich, Moulay Bouchta Lkhammar, Moulay Abdellah of Tit, Sidi Ben Abbes in Marrakech, Sidi Rahal in the Haouz, Sidi M'hammed ben Nasser, Sidi Salah in the Dra, and Moulay Ali Chrif in the Tafilalt. Royal gifts are bestowed on their shrines, and their offspring and servants gain entry to the inner circle of the political and administrative system. Some of them are granted frequent and generous visits by influential members of the royal family or even the sovereign himself.[5] It should be noted that the shrines adopted or reactivated by this new religious policy are scattered throughout the territory, in cities as well as the countryside. In the capital the mausoleum of Mohammed V is a center of pilgrimage and devotion, as is that of the great sultan Moulay Ismail in Meknes.[6]

But the brotherhoods and the kinds of interaction they shape and use as a foundation for their perpetuation are not vindicated by the royal house and the Moroccan officialdom alone. Keep in mind that the young nationalists who headed modernization efforts and the independence movement in the 1930s belonged to "the old families abundantly represented in the hagiological armorial of Morocco."[7] One of them, Mukhtar al Soussi, the son and biographer of al Haj 'Ali, also became a nationalist, a modernist, and an advocate of salafi reform. At the same time he wrote in defense of the Sufi way, and sought to establish the legitimacy of its methods. So this advocate of enlightened Islamic reformism was concurrently justifying, in a forceful manner, the principle of absolute and blind submission to a master in mystical initiation.[8] A disciple must submit not only to rational injunctions but also to injunctions which seem to violate the exercise of reason. For al Soussi, this is the "normal" mystery of a master's guidance, which should be accepted; it should be taken as a psychiatrist's prescription is taken, because the master is a "physician of the soul," whose reasons may not be clear to the patient.

It does not matter whether or not this argument is valid. The author had a ministerial post and was adviser to the Crown at the time of his death in 1962. Is this an atypical destiny? There is no question that the life of this highly educated man from the Sous has been somewhat different from the lives of bourgeois in Fez. Beyond the dissimilarities, however, the attachment to mysticism in personal life and to its practical *adab* was widespread among the leaders of the nationalist movement.

Some observers have been struck by the structural similarities between political parties and brotherhoods.[9] Parties and unions thrive on oppositions and negotiations between warring factions, but both are tied to supreme leaders who remain the masters of their organizations for life, despite changes in context, ideology, or policy, and despite any vicissitudes or failures.[10] The formal structures of mass organizations are in fact superposed on network and clientele practices governed by criteria of allegiance and faithfulness akin to those operating in the brotherhoods. It is as if the desire for change, which is obvious in the major political parties and unions, operates on two levels:

on the one hand, it reduces the influence of religious brotherhoods, and on the other hand, it extends to political life, on a larger scale than ever (that of the nation-state), the comportments typical of mystical initiation and master-disciple relations. Parallel to the modernization of structures is an unprecedented diffusion of specific ways in which and by which the leaders and their followers must recognize themselves.

It should also be noted that the influences of mystical orders can be felt in commerce and handicraft as they are still practiced in all the great imperial cities and in rural marketplaces.[11] In both cases these activities elude control by the unions. Finally, tanners, blacksmiths, weavers, bricklayers, and shoemakers still maintain strong bonds with religious orders and patron saints, not only in places like Fez, Marrakech, and Meknes, but also in other cities.

Master and Disciple: The Diagram in Cultural History

The present salience of this schema of leadership is better assessed if one realizes that the advocates of radical Islamic reform join either a brotherhood or a new-style charismatic community headed by a venerated master. The phenomenal success of the brotherhood formula is perfectly illustrated by the Boutchishiya: in addition to its main lodge in the Oujda area, which is the residence of the paramount shaykh, it has branches scattered all over the country, particularly in Casablanca, Fez, and Rabat. While the groups advocating government by God and scrupulous enforcement of the shari'a are not necessarily constituted within the institutional structure chosen by the master of the Boutchishiya, their organizations invariably reenact the potent paradigm of the prophet, with his guidance of devoted adepts. At any rate the master-disciple relationship articulates all power relations and tactics. The schemata of submission, ambivalence, rebellion, and access to masterhood are enacted on a daily basis, in the present and historically all at once. Hence the special position of this living archaism, which operates at the heart of Moroccan authoritarianism.

The specific power relation I have described owes its strength to a constant and repetitive reassertion of the master-disciple relationship, which is itself enshrined in mystical initiation. It has imposed itself as a pervasive motif in the biographies of saints since the fifteenth and sixteenth centuries. The biography of al Haj 'Ali is only a recent manifestation of a genre, already flourishing in the eighteenth and nineteenth centuries, which actually defines the stages and conditions of access to masterhood (and therefore to power). One of these conditions is that the apprentice saint must find a living master. He may not invoke a dead master or claim to have received his education in dreams. The requirement of initiation by a living master, which for a long time was an object of controversy, was forcefully endorsed in the fifteenth century by the influential Ibn Khaldoun, whose opinion seems to have rallied a majority of writers up to the present time.[12]

A calling often emerges at some transitional stage: at the end of puberty, after brilliant studies in esoteric sciences, just before entering a trade, sometimes just before getting married. In other words, in most cases, at the threshold of full manhood. Some have to abandon their trade and offspring to start on this venture, while others embrace it after falling out of grace or suffering some misfortune. I have already described the contrast between a candidate for sainthood and an ordinary man. Here I will pursue the discussion of the most dramatic change the initiate undergoes, that is, the abdication of virility.[13]

If we combine the requirement for a display of modesty in the master's presence with the clearly feminine activities carried out by the disciple, we can only conclude that we are dealing with a process of feminization. Other observers have remarked on this process at different times in the history of Morocco, but we still lack precise information on its scope and the way to interpret it. A disciple's feminization amounts to a shocking departure from ordinary norms, the culmination of a set of atypical behaviors.[14] It is loaded with significance: a man defines his identity through sharp opposition to feminine identity. The deviation is made even more explicit by other requirements and taboo violations often associated with it. For example, only the master can authorize a disciple to marry, and the transmission of baraka sometimes involves bodily contacts which go against public morals.

The transmission of baraka is done through channels such as these: teachings, silent or chanted incantations, dancing and trance states, food sharing, contact with the master's hands, garments, or other possessions, fainting, screaming, and even neighing.[15] But in addition to these techniques—some of which, while not violating accepted norms and practices, are still surprising in terms of my own sensibility—the master may spit into the disciple's mouth or place his tongue in it and order the disciple to suck, or the disciple may ingest the master by swallowing defilements from the master's body. In a celebrated case, a disciple who was washing clothes dipped into the water a shirt which had absorbed pus from the master's body during a long illness, then rinsed it out and drank the water. The drink brought him the supreme consecration.[16]

Finally Westermarck gives evidence that contact with the master's body may go as far as sexual relations:

> Sexual intercourse with a saintly person is considered beneficial. . . . Supernatural benefits are expected even from homosexual intercourse with a person possessed of *baraka*. I know of an instance in which a young man, who was regarded as a saint on account of the miracles he performed, traced his holiness to the fact that he had been the favourite of a shereef. . . . So also an apprentice is supposed to learn this trade by having intercourse with his master.[17]

The disciple is so to speak impregnated through a teaching process which resembles procreation. The master transforms into a saint the young man who rushes to him in a sense-awakening encounter; he basically feminizes his disciple in order to produce charisma: it is a metaphor of insemination, gestation, and birth.

This last feature clearly sets the candidate for sainthood apart from ordinary men, but at the same time it links him with other apprentices and especially craftsmen. The fact that all teaching situations include some aspect of the master-disciple relationship I just evoked brings the disciple's experience closer to ordinary life. This is the perspective in which to reconsider the similarities between the bond a saint establishes with his young recruits and the father-son relationship.

The disciple becomes a woman for a while. But his submission does not exclude either feelings of ambivalence or awareness of the transitional nature of this role. Quarrels arise between the shaykh and the murīd, as noted in the hagiographic literature and seen in the current life of the brotherhoods. Nor does it preclude dissent and violence. The biography of al Haj 'Ali discloses a case of attempted murder, just as the biography of a mahdi reveals the master's distrust of some overly ambitious disciples.[18] It must be pointed out that, from this point of view, the way a disciple relates to his master is not radically different from the way a son relates to his father. It entails the same kind of submission interspersed with outbreaks of disobedience, which may lead to heartrending separations. (Near-lethal fistfights between son and father are common events, especially in the countryside.) Moreover, both groups impose a double standard and expect two different types of behavior: agreeable and modest in the father's (or master's) presence; virile and domineering in relation to others, in particular women and boys of the same generation.

So mystical and familial ethics appear as replicas of one another, each reinforcing the other one; both require above all the qualities which define will and noble ambition. But as I have stressed, these qualities are for a long time to be put at the service of a father or a master, and the same person who must display this zeal must also conform to the norms of modesty. This contradiction forces every individual to endorse within himself two selves in permanent tension. It is thus not surprising that the second self, which is at once kept under pressure and sublimated, will arise forcefully as soon as separation from the master or the father is accomplished. The parallel between these two situations is significantly emphasized in the hagiographic literature, in which a disciple must consider his master as his father and put the obedience he owes to the former above that which he owes to the latter.

When the initiation has been completed, master and disciple can no longer cohabit. The initiate's own will bursts out openly and he devotes his energy to establishing a new foundation and producing abundant offspring. The first total inversion is reinverted, as submission is replaced by authority and passivity by overflowing virility—which according to some is a sign of divine force. This again clearly resembles the reversal required of a son when he separates from his father or when the father dies.

Crapanzano, who duly remarks on the double requirement imposed on the son in his relationship with his father, establishes a link between this situation and the feminization postulated by the transmission of baraka.[19] Here, I wish to mark with more clarity the boundaries of this temporary transformation. In fact, while the master dominates with all of his authority and appears ruthless, he also often displays tenderness and motherly attention toward a disciple who is being tested. This shows the master to be ambiguous indeed—a father who impregnates his son but also cares for him as a mother would. Of course the disciple is as ambiguous, or more so: he is given feminine tasks while being inculcated with habits of bodily control (thirst, hunger, endurance, abstinence) and kept away from relations with women.

In the final analysis the master and the disciple, inasmuch as they are figures of ambiguity, appear to be in contact with the invisible (this is the meaning of the *walaya*) and to combine within themselves the two principles (feminine and masculine) of reproduction. It is precisely their continuous presence, in the form of uninterrupted emergence of charisma, which maintains Moroccan society. The ideal community, modeled after the one engendered by prophecy, thus continues to drink from the sources of life through the miracle of androgynous figures.

The affinities between a group consisting of a master and his disciples and that comprising the royal house and its head may now appear more clearly. All the more so since a mystical master attributes to himself the title of *shaykh*—which designates anyone who claims some preeminence, whether he be a master in exoteric and esoteric sciences,[20] master artisan, tribal chief, neighborhood chief, father-in-law (for a married woman), older person, or elder. This suggestive polysemy is an additional element in the long list of categories which establish a link between the life of the brotherhood and ordinary social and political life. Furthermore, the exclusive paternity claimed by the shaykh vis-à-vis his disciples is comparable to that exercised by the sovereign vis-à-vis his subjects. If this seems to be a valid claim, we still need to ponder the role ambivalence plays in social and political action, and to ascertain that a fundamental bipolarity indeed characterizes the structure of behavior.

Ambiguity and Authority: The Rite of Passage as a Test

The schema of authority seen in the master-disciple dialectic is therefore the same as the one which shapes all precedence relations, including the superior-subordinate relationship that forms the backbone of modern bureaucratic and political order. Its work is visible at the global level of hagiographic history and generally speaking in cultural history; does it appear also in other spheres of life?

Apparently so, for the same figures of basic ambiguity, the same fundamental bipolarity conditioning the access to manhood—that is, to a power position—can be seen in situations which, while localized and microsociological in nature, recur in time and space.

Transitional periods in individual or collective life are marked by rituals, two such instances being weddings and end-of-the-year celebrations. At the beginning of the festivities marking the alliance of two families, presents are brought to the bride's house. Interestingly, a transvestite (or at least a symbolic representation of transvestism) can often be seen at the center of the procession. A man dressed as a woman, wearing makeup for the occasion and covered with jewelry, performs suggestive dances prefiguring the union of the sexes. Thus we have inversion at the beginning of ceremonies which sanction marriage as a crucial rite of passage. This cannot be attributed to mere chance, since the inverted dancer occupies a position which could have been filled by a female dancer.

This dramatization of ambiguity can also be seen in canonic rituals. The Feast of the Sacrifice is universally celebrated in the Muslim world. Together with the 'achoura, it brings the lunar year to a close and opens the new one. Thus it is the collective "rite of passage" par excellence. In Morocco (and not long ago in the whole Maghreb), a masquerade takes place either the day after the sacrifice of the victim or at the 'achoura; it varies in length (particularly in Morocco) from two to eight days. This ritual of the "man with the skins" is still observed in many places in the countryside as well as in urban working-class and popular neighborhoods; the ceremonies have been described by various authors, but their reconstructions and interpretations have been marred by preconceived ideas. I will now summarize the essential aspects of the ritual as I have witnessed it.[21]

The village is totally in the hands of the youth, since the older people are required to leave in the morning. In the houses there are only women and young girls; the tasks they usually perform—taking care of the cows, collecting hay or wood—are on this occasion accomplished by older men, an instance of role inversion that provokes laughter. In the late morning, after long preparations—interspersed with jokes, simulated sexual chases among young men, nonsense, and obscene jibes addressed to the mothers—a biped creature covered with skins and wearing a goat's head rushes into the streets.

The space used to dress and make up this character is a soot-darkened room adjoining the prayer room of the mosque, a room ordinarily used for the ablutions required at worship time and for the ritual washing of the dead. From here Bilmawn, the man with the skins, is thrown out in a cloud of ash. Four young men costumed as Jews (udayan), one of them a rabbi, follow him, and he is preceded by another young man costumed as a slave (ismagh); all of these figures carry sticks. Dancing and music constantly accompany the masked figures, and custom dictates that all young men and women, without exception, form a procession behind them. Those who are wearing masks chase the other young men, who make a show of resistance, and hit them repeatedly with their sticks; the man with the skins deals sharp blows to them with the goat's feet hanging from his sleeves. As the music and uproar continue, the group makes its way into every house, turns it topsy-turvy, and pursues the women in a playful and obscene way. The slave chases away those who come too close, and the children flee like a swarm of sparrows when he pursues them.

Before leaving each house the Jews and their rabbi demand and obtain presents. Sometimes they negotiate, in a partly joking, partly rude and pressing manner. The most common offering consists of flour and eggs, but it is not unusual for the beggars to snatch a chicken or a rabbit. The man with the skins runs after the young people to deal them blows, while the slave and Jews constantly protect him. He in turn is insulted and jostled, and people do not hesitate to hit and harass him if he lets down his guard. The Jews, who wear repulsive rags and shake their long beards, constantly proffer obscenities.

In midafternoon an improvised theater in the center of the village presents various scenes from daily life, such as plowing, harvesting, and getting married; but everything is acted out in reverse and at such a pace that the picture of ordinary life assumes a strongly burlesque character. Muslim invocations, as well as the Koranic verses marking activities and worship, are parodied and their meaning subverted in this recitation. The original words are erased and replaced by terms referring to sexuality or to bodily emissions and secretions.

Bilmawn for his part constantly changes identity: he is alternately the bellows of a blacksmith, fanning the fire which dilates the plowshare to be repaired for the plowing season; the cow that pulls the plow and gets mistreated, insulted, and poked in the anus with a long stick; and the wife of the landowner (who in fact is the rabbi). This last incarnation fixes couscous while putting on makeup, and the fieldhands (actually the Jews) take turns copulating with her—each punishes his predecessor for the sacrilege he has committed, throws him out, and immediately sleeps with the lascivious woman. When she takes the food to the fields where the harvesters are working, she trips, spills everything, and thus wastes all the goods that the men accumulate through hard work. Then she and the rabbi indulge in frolicking under the watchful eye of the slave and the other Jews, who do not refrain from addressing comments to the public, particularly to the women standing on the terraces to watch the scene.

The fieldhands sow ash and compare furrow cutting to sexual penetration, the sowing is immediately followed by the harvest (!), canonic prayers are said with faces turned to the west, and the Holy Book is recited in reverse order in a ridiculous and incomprehensible jargon. These scenes, which everyone sees as indispensable in the man with the skins' play, are sometimes followed by a kind of revue. It may be a staging of local scandals, a satire of locally contested innovations, or scenes of grotesque misery. Then the house visitations resume and dancing continues until late in the night.

A brief description of Bilmawn is in order here, since he (or she or it) is the central character in this masquerade. As I said earlier, he is covered with skins. It must be emphasized that these are the skins of victims which have been sacrificed and therefore consecrated in a feast which, for the people, is an orthodox Muslim ritual. Bilmawn is fitted with male genitals in back, hanging over his buttocks, and on his chest is a single enormous breast which everyone regards as an enviable female organ. He has marigolds on his head, as a young woman would, and these flowers have a local connotation of music and love. Neither the slave nor Bilmawn says a word. The latter only cries out once in a while, in a specific way which cannot be confused with any other sound or identified with any known zoological species. Finally, the procession always takes place in the same order, with the slave opening the way in front of Bilmawn and the Jews around him. Actually it is a parade of a playful kind, with loud music and noise, in which those who by mistake find themselves in the way of the masks risk punishment. The Jews utter insults and comments, rant at the crowd, sing obscene poems, and sometimes stage a highly visible display of homosexual love on the terrace of a house. As Bilmawn touches children and women during his expedition, he brings blessings and cures disease, since he is possessed of active baraka. And the parade itself makes the new year bountiful and propitious.

Let us stop the description here. What can this ritual teach us about ambivalence and rebellion and about the conditions for access to masterhood? Two structural tensions, mediated by an ambiguous creature, sustain the "plot" of the masquerade. But let us be clear that they are not reflected in the theatrical play; rather, they are transfigured and stylized in the ceremony so as to rise, as a work of imagination, above the confused manifestations of everyday life. This gives them an aura of reality which obsesses our minds, transforming them into a set of pictures which arouse emotions that cannot really be activated by daily reality.

The first tension lies in the opposition of young people and older men. The elders must here leave the village in the hands of the women and young men who ordinarily carry out the most laborious tasks under their firm guidance. In addition the cohort of marriageable young women is mostly "appropriated" by the older generation, which thereby threatens the sexual and social accomplishment of young people, or at least delays it. This practice is made possible by the great differences in marriage age of young women and men, the women always marrying much earlier and often to much older men.

The second tension is of course the one opposing men and women. The men in the masquerade appear as creatures with unbridled desire who are often, however, impotent and ridiculous; as for the women, they correspond to preconceived ideas of insatiability and unfaithfulness. But the antagonism is even deeper, for we are dealing with a society which traces descent patrilineally. Manhood is defined by, among other criteria, the authority exercised over a woman, the maintenance of her inferior status, and the procreation of sons. But women, who are so discredited in the masquerade, are at the very center of the procreative process. What alternative is there to using women as conduits to procreate children, even though the children must belong totally to their fathers? But the fragile nature of this arrangement is obvious to everyone in daily life, where the wife's lineage always threatens the father's prerogatives, especially concerning the children. Generally speaking, how can woman, this indispensable intermediary, be accepted in a process which is so vital for the reproduction of men?

On the one hand, a man must fight (with other generations) to obtain a wife; on the other hand, he must do without her. The elimination of women, through glorification of the bond which unites men, is carried out under the authority of a monstrous and ambiguous creature who—I might say for that very reason—is possessed of religious powers (baraka). Thus Bilmawn's behavior vindicates everyday life in its accepted form and with its aporias, which remain open-ended but at the same time are bounded by a clear framework manifested in the occurrence of ritual displacement.

The initiation of the youth is carried out every year under the direction of this deviant creature, which is, however, possessed of charisma, a feature it shares with all initiands and initiation masters. Bilmawn's procession—with its etiquette, its small guard of slaves and followers versed in profane creation (poetry) and religious lore—evokes all chiefly processions; all the more so in that two of their usual features are the parade and the exercise of violence. Finally, let us note that gift giving also takes on its "normal" dimension of tax exaction within the specific power relations acted out here.

The powerful schema of the chief is also present here, offered to the gaze of everyone, as the young men conquer power (albeit temporarily) by driving away the elders. As mentioned earlier, the canonic sacrifice takes place the day before the masquerade; the fathers' generation carries out the immolation of a victim, which establishes and binds the household and the (local and universal) community of the faithful under male authority. Tradition requires that the sovereign cut the throat of the first victim, with the rest of the nation then following him. This gesture commemorates that of Abraham, the exemplary patriarch who accepted the order to offer his son's life to God (symbolically, it turned out, since he was stayed by an angel, who substituted a ram). The masquerade inverts every aspect of the sacrifice and also—logically—of the power center in relation to which the rite of sacrifice is performed.

So mystical initiation, a process which can be reconstructed through cultural history, converges with sacrifice and masquerade (which can still be observed today) in some crucial respects: both entail ambivalence, the disciple's seeking access to the saint's masterhood through a period of inversion, the son's conquest of the father's position after a lifetime of submission. There lies the cultural diagram of access to authority which informs all precedence relations and particularly the relation to the chief.

However, neither inversion rituals nor the process of mystical initiation (at least in some aspects) are specific to Moroccan society. Nor is male domination. Furthermore, men and women have engaged in ceremonies analogous to those I just described in a great variety of societies which are distant from one another in time, space, culture, and historical development. Finally, while both the master-disciple relationship (with its temporary inversion in the disciple) and the reversal of behavior and norms in play and rituals are in many places associated with male dominance, it cannot be said that this configuration always co-occurs with authoritarianism. If that is the case, should I not abandon the interpretation I have so far advocated.

It is often said that Moroccan society is not the only one in which males dominate females. This argument is commonly invoked against those who dwell on the "inferior status" of women. It is certainly true that in many Western and non-Western societies men still retain privileges linked to gender. This is denounced by feminist movements all over the world. It remains the case, nonetheless, that gender inequalities are stronger and have more severe consequences in Morocco, where they are inscribed in the letter of a revealed law. This is a crucial difference from other societies, especially those run according to man-made laws. In this respect Moroccan society belongs, albeit with some important nuances, to a bloc of Muslim societies where the inequality between men and women is comparatively both stronger and more difficult to challenge.

If one agrees with this assessment, inversion and feminization take on a much more dramatic meaning than elsewhere, and the specificity of the system I have described lies first of all in the extreme aporia created by their coexistence with patriarchal norms and practices. The female principle is negated and hidden, but it is always there, threatening the male order and simultaneously conditioning its reproduction.

Other societies in which this male/female relationship obtains occupy the Indian subcontinent to the east. A brief comparison sheds some light on the meaning of this structural tension—which I argue lies at the heart of authoritarianism—because India presents an extreme case of the phenomenon of inversion in the disciple. A comparative study by Max Weber contains the following remarks on the subject:

> The bond between the teacher of religious or philosophical wisdom and his disciple is uncommonly strong and is regulated in an authoritarian fashion, particularly in the sacred

laws of Asia. Everywhere the disciple-master relationship is classified among those involving reverence.

Weber gives a number of examples along these lines: the ethos and attitudes in German fraternities, the *famulus* and his *magister,* as well as the love relations known to exist in these or similar institutions. He concludes as follows:

> All the Greek poetry of pederasty derives from such a relationship of respect, and similar phenomena are to be found among Buddhists and Confucianists, indeed in all monastic education. The most complete expression of this disciple-master relationship is to be found in the position of the *guru* in Hindu sacred law. Every young man belonging to polite society was unconditionally required to devote himself for many years to the instruction and direction of life provided by such a Brahmanic teacher. The obligation of obedience to the *guru,* who had absolute power over his charges, a relationship comparable to that of the occidental *famulus* to his *magister,* took precedence over loyalty to family.[22]

We can now address the issue of specificity in a more precise way. What is indeed specific to Morocco, as well as those societies I regard in this respect as part of the same cultural configuration, is the obligatory passage through feminization simultaneous with an apparent radical negation of it. In this sense there is a contrast between Morocco and India, namely, the affirmation of the feminine presence as a divine principle of continuity in Indian religions and cosmologies. Morocco and India also differ in the nature of their political regimes. In India the introduction of democracy has so far succeeded, while in the societies I have compared it with national liberation movements have resulted in modern authoritarian systems and democratic experiments have so far been incomplete or short-lived.

We can now better understand the transition through womanhood on the path of authority. The initiating shaykh, or saint, definitely constitutes a metaphor of human energy and strong will, two supreme values of Moroccan discourse. But maybe the shaykh is even more a source of life, in the sense given to this term by Hoccart. His success is measured by that of his foundation, the new community he creates, which can be seen fostering cities and creating prosperity. His baraka then takes a form which is visible to all. As a source of life the saint helps reconcile the principles of procreation. This explains why the disciple becomes a woman for a while under the guidance of a master who once did the same.

This is a good point at which to recall that, through a set of historical circumstances which so far have not really been analyzed, the Moroccan monarch has come to embody (possibly since the eighteenth century) concurrently baraka and force, holiness and coercion. Isn't he treated as a source of life by political actors?

The integration of the two principles of procreation (man/ woman) involves here the exclusion of one of them; the disciple's inversion in the presence of the shaykh functions as a sign of devotion to a masculine/feminine figure, and impregnation and procreation are the two key metaphors in the making of a saint. Consequently the unquestionable and highest authority (that of a saint) is embodied in a chain of men whose procreation does not involve women. The deviation engendered by this situation—which can be seen in the initiation process—would then be the price this society has to pay in order to bypass female power.

Such circumvention is understandable if one reformulates a previously indicated structural tension. On the one hand one must procreate in order to maintain the agnatic line and ensure the continuity of the patriarchal system. On the other hand one must accept the fact that procreation involves women. This is a normative scandal. A master and his disciples strive to take away from women and give to men the credit for this continuity—which justifies the paradox of access to authority through the process of feminization.

On the Comparative Potential
of the Paradigm

My final remarks will concern only Arab societies, which constitute an ensemble consolidated by powerful historical and cultural bonds. These bonds are evidenced by the profound repercussions which every change in one of these countries automatically produces in the other countries. In each of these societies the crucial fact until the last few years has been the perpetuation and reinforcement of the authoritarian state. A timid orientation to change has been emerging lately; but it is still uncertain.

The rulers have chosen different bases for the social and economic development of their societies: liberalism, socialism, or a third way based either on a version of Islam or on a theory of cultural specificity. The types of legitimacy they have invoked are admittedly different—some traditionalist, some revolutionary—but each has been trying to accommodate or speed up social change. Arab countries admittedly have faced protracted tensions and/or wars with each other and with non-Arab neighbors; they have also had to deal with internal conflicts. Finally, prior to *perestroika* and the fall of the Berlin Wall they were classified as either "progressives" or "moderates" and defined themselves as such.

All these differences, however, cannot hide a fundamental similarity regarding the mode of exercise of power: everywhere monarchic regimes or single-party systems invoke direct representation of something called "the masses," and ignore or repress any political alternative. The authoritarian structure is characterized by a central figure's claim to single-handed decision making regarding the aspirations and future of the society governed. It persists as an underlying mechanism, as a stage on which regimes and elites come to act and then disappear.

Monarchies fall, one reason being that people clamor for democracy. But they are succeeded by single-party rule and autocratic presidents. The latter can modify the economic and social orientations of the political formations they lead or even make them adopt economic and social measures contrary to their initial program. There are many instances of such reversals. Particularly spectacular was the 1972 return to liberalism, dubbed *infitāḥ* (literally, opening), and decided by Sadat, who had been a self-effacing disciple of Nasser during the whole reign of the great *ra'īs*. The striking phenomenon is that the authoritarian structure remains unchanged, seemingly immutable, in spite of the most radical revisions of previous policies and doctrines.

The authoritarian structure can take diverse forms and be based on different or even contradictory ideologies: absolute or quasi-absolute monarchies, military dictatorships, single-party regimes. Saudi Arabia, the Emirates, and Oman are absolute monarchies, Morocco and Jordan quasi-absolute; Libya, Mauritania, and Algeria can be classified as military dictatorships; Tunisia, Syria, and Iraq are single-party states supported by military machines. Obviously there is also significant variation among these nation-states. For example, Tunisians and Moroccans enjoy a measure of freedom of expression, whereas Libyans do not. The former have (until recently) pursued economic liberalism with planning and state direction, the latter an Islamic variant of socialism. Important differences could be found between all nation-states falling into the three above-mentioned categories. Authoritarianism and the preeminence of the army in maintaining the political order remain common features.

Ideologies can be diverse and even contradictory, as a comparison of Libya and Tunisia perfectly illustrates. Upon further examination one also finds differences within one and the same ideological bloc: the use of constraint to maintain values and behaviors regarded as "authentic" (Saudi Arabia); recourse to an enlightened Islamic "tradition" to justify a combination of patronage capitalism and slow social reform (Morocco). In the so-called socialist bloc, Khadafi's revolutionary Islam contrasts with laicism in Syria and Iraq. At other ideological levels the only differences lie in the degree of militancy—as is the case for unionism in its North African, Near Eastern, and pan-Arab forms. Some states avail themselves of a pan-Arabism that invokes a great hegemonic past (as in the case of Italy). Libya is presently the main instigator of this type of pan-Arabism. But there were comparable strands earlier in Nasser's Egypt, not to speak of the Ba'thist parties' nationalism.

So we seem to be dealing with a structure which is definitely operating everywhere. Let us identify its components by examining five dimensions of the exercise of power and leadership:

a. Decision making is restricted to a small group of men, only one of whom really emerges on the public stage.

b. Society is dominated by an extensive and ramified system of repression and cannot avail itself of institutional means of control over the government machine.

c. Government requires total conformity with what it defines as the "people's customs." This goes hand in hand with the requirement of absolute loyalty to an ideology defined largely on an ethnic or a religious basis, or both.

d. Government is reluctant to recognize linguistic, confessional, or regional diversity, or any other forms of pluralism, promoting instead a leveled and homogenous society in which all individuals are moved by "duty to the nation." However, when confronted with pluralism, the authoritarian government adopts a dual line of conduct: it either denies or officially ignores diversities, and simultaneously tries to manipulate them and to present itself as the only authorized mediator between them.

e. Obedience and the performance of duty take the shape of ostentatious submission to a chief. Behavior in all bureaucratic relations is modeled after this relationship: passivity in a subordinate corresponds, at every level, to activity and authoritarianism in the man above him. This dualism is omnipresent: everyone is alternatively a chief and a subordinate. Everywhere this type of interaction erases the legal and institutional mediation of the relation of domination.

Some of the implications of these five points will help us outline the structure. The two fundamental problems raised by the relation to one's chief—see (*a*) and (*e*) above—amount to those of ambivalence and violent succession. For the chief is defined by the privilege of being surrounded by collaborators who are entirely devoted to his personal service. As a "truly free man" he does not have to contribute any particular work. This attitude is found everywhere despite the socioeconomic upheavals brought about by the twentieth century.

The chief must control the machine, which he does through a

small group of devotees and the co-opting among them of a few disciples who are closer to him. These are who the media call the "strongmen" of the regime, the ones who direct domestic and economic policies. The chief monopolizes foreign policy and rarely intervenes publicly on concrete matters. He is there to correct his disciples' mistakes in a spectacular manner.

Master and disciple are in an ambivalent relationship; and in transitional periods, given the absence of formalized succession rules and the lack of stable institutions that would allow a civil society to act as a counterweight, one may go from total obedience to one's chief to murdering him. The tension between two poles is thus resolved until the next cycle. Such a duality, as we saw earlier, characterizes the attitudes of social actors in everyday authority relations. This form of exercise of power does not mean in any way that the authoritarian state should be regarded as something which has its own life outside society. On the contrary it must be emphasized that the ambivalence of the chief-subordinate, master-disciple, and father-son relationships operates at the very heart of social life.

However, despite its closed-circle tendencies, the political center must seek elites for the direction of its affairs. The present development of the government is in sharp contrast with the small number of institutions that characterized archaic power centers, as well as the relative simplicity of the organization put in place during the period of direct imperialist domination. These new developments involve (or at least involved until the 1970s, for some countries, and until the 1980s, for others) a great deal of social mobility. The two main avenues for change in status or social class are education and the army. Elites are rapidly co-opted and achieve success rather promptly because insidious conflicts between potential leaders and personal attachment take precedence over the (necessarily slow) acquisition of technical skills. So the intelligentsia is absorbed en masse by the government machine and undergoes reclassification, declassification, or even physical elimination. In such a context local insertion of the state power is achieved through the co-opting of elites on account of their social origins, as well as their regional, religious, ethnic, and kinship ties. But this insertion, even though fragile, is achieved, thanks to the consolidation (or creation) of a network of notables.

There are three other integration mechanisms: accelerated economic development, ideology, and armed repression. But economic development is limited by the prebendary nature of the groups in power—a feature related to the mode of co-optation and the rule of loyalty described above. It is also slowed down by unequal exchange and dependence on other countries. Consequently there are regular social outbursts, which are repressed by force.

So the army is at the center of national life, and the chief must necessarily come from its ranks or give proof of martial titles. The military institution thus becomes the royal road to social mobility; but in the absence of a civilian basis the chief cannot really use it as a foundation for his authority. So the ruling group is caught in a contradictory game: on the one hand, it must use the army to contain public opinion, and on the other hand, it must count on civilian political alliances to escape a deadly reinforcement of the military.

This process also involves playing regional, religious, and ethnic groups against one another. The supreme leader incarnates the nation's unity, and according to his ideologists chaos is an ever-present danger should anyone imagine changing him. So the authoritarian government is caught between a desire for total homogenization of national life and the indispensability of diversity if the chief is to fulfill his definitional function as mediator of differences.

There are two possible ways to blunt, if not to resolve, this contradiction. The army's task can be either to defend the nation or to consolidate it; the latter undertaking necessitates the support of what is usually called the popular masses. This is where ideology enters the picture. Conflicts, either with non-Arab states or with Arab states accused of betraying the pan-Arab ideal, can be used to justify internal authoritarianism. The construction of an Arab supernation is an ideologically powerful notion which is often reinforced by the shibboleth of an Islamic alliance in which the leadership role is implicitly granted to Arabs. In this conjunction of identities the ethnic factor intersects with the theological one in the worldview constantly rehearsed by the media.

It is important to note that the government presents itself as the exclusive source of ideology and that it requires external signs of loyalty: two simple examples are national costumes and a proclaimed mystique of cultural heritage in a broad sense. Its fundamental premise in this regard seems to be that this ideology must be said to be *ours,* coming from us and not from some foreign source. Thus the government will stigmatize other systems of ideas—alternately liberalism or socialism, and sometimes both—as "foreign." When a system of ideas is accepted, it must necessarily be "ethnicized." Such was the case, for instance, with Arab socialism.

When taken to the extreme such conceptualizations can take on a sacred character, in the sense that ideological purity translates as avoidance of any foreign contamination. This takes us back to the dialectical relationship between *pure* and *impure* which is at the basis of extreme religious cleavages, and in particular the attitude of one sect toward another. Controlling individuals, reducing contacts with the foreign, and, generally speaking, closing off the territory controlled by an authoritarian government were, until very recently, all important aspects of this worldview. In practice, however, one must compromise with societies to which the ideologies of authoritarian Arab governments are alien—a contradiction which is becoming more and more serious, given their level of technological and scientific dependency.[1]

Thus the essential characteristics of Moroccan authoritarianism show it to be, despite significant differences, no more than a variant of the modern Arab authoritarianism. Moreover, some remarks on two other Arab societies, the Algerian and the Egyptian, will help us realize that the master-disciple relationship may still be very much at work there too. Of all Arab countries Algeria and Egypt are perhaps the most radically affected by change since the nineteenth century, yet the paradigms of domination and submission do not differ there from the ones I have described in Moroccan society. Modernization itself can now be seen as a reelaboration of the master-disciple relationship diagram and the practice of government through the notables are not specific to Morocco; the colonial elaboration of authoritarianism took place along similar lines in most Arab societies.[2] This production of an authoritarian political structure in colonial and postcolonial circumstances has been obscured rather than highlighted by some current interpretations, such as the one which accounts for it in terms of a marriage between patriarchy and modernity dubbed "neopatriarchy"; these notions perpetuate dualistic analytical categories (tradition/modernity, rationality/irrationality, and so on) and miss the specificity of the phenomenon together with the formidable tensions at work within it.[3]

In Algeria as well as in Egypt, the religious brotherhoods and the veneration of saints remain part of life. In Algeria, the network of brotherhoods and marabouts in spite of everything maintained some influence and underwent a revival in the mid-1970s. Furthermore, the master-disciple relationship has remained omnipresent in Islamic reformist circles, and it is to these that Algeria owes the formulation of the nationalism that prevailed during its liberation struggle and in the postcolonial process of reconstruction of an Algerian "personality" and state.

In Egypt, the institutionalization of the brotherhoods and their subordination to a new, strong and centralized state took a decisive turn in the nineteenth century with the reforms instituted by Mohammed Ali and his successors. The new organization of mystical orders would follow such a powerful development that at the beginning of the century these would be managed by a true official bureaucracy integrating the central lodges (zāwiyas) and their subsidiary branches in the small towns and a multitude of Egyptian villages. Measures taken under the Nasser and Sadat regimes finally, partially succeeded in increasing the integration of these pious institutions to the structures of the state and modern economy. The impact of these reforms and the transformation is such that today, after experiencing a decline in the 1960s, the Egyptian brotherhoods seem to have reestablished a firm influence in the popular classes, where they compete with the currents of new radical Islam. The growing audience of the brotherhoods has been occulted by the concentration of recent research on the so-called Islamist movements, most of it grounded either in some view of modernization or in the notion of an Islamic threat.[4] According to a recent estimate (1982) Sufi organizations in Egypt command the loyalty of some six million followers.[5] Although the notion of followers can cover various degrees and modalities of adhesion, we can nonetheless note that neither the single-party state (Nasser) nor the political formations that have issued from the infitāḥ were able to win over so many people to their fold. Finally, the grand annual celebrations (the renowned *mawālid*) that gather the brotherhoods around the sanctuaries draw immense crowds of rural and urban participants. In Cairo in 1989, the *mawlid* of Hussayn, second in importance only to that of the Prophet, brought together a crowd estimated to number half a million. The feast of Tanta, held in honor of Sidi Ahmed al Badawi, brings together upwards of a million pilgrims, and in Dassuq, the sanctuary of Ibrahim al Dassuqi has also been the site of a great assembly. These grand ceremonies are presided over by officially recognized authorities from the brotherhoods, and the Egyptian state is represented by ministers or other high-ranking officials.

As a cultural reference, the master-disciple relationship, as manifested in the initiation and discourses of sainthood, is by no means the sole space where a relationship of domination is played out. We have already remarked on the importance of the father-son relationship and the configuration of power in the family and in the work sphere. The discourses of sainthood provide the symbolic anchor for all these relationships. That is not to say, however, that absolute coherence is required. Both in the circles of ulema and in those of the Sufi the authority and the necessity of a master in initiation have been (and continue to be) the subject of serious debate. The biography of al Haj 'Ali, on the other hand, clearly illustrates the popular reticence and resistance with which charismatic voices are met. Lastly, there are all the crazed saints and all the "enraptured" (*mejdoub*) who do not follow the classical path of initiation.

All these contradictions and conflicts notwithstanding, the discourse of sainthood dominates the process through which groups are instituted, that is to say, the process through which people associate in order to undertake historical and political action. The relation to God and the foundation of the city of salvation thus converge very early toward sainthood as an institution with a capacity for political existence. The construction, despite being repeatedly traversed by reevaluations, is not hindered from founding the associations of men and women in the city. It could even be said that from the moment when the issue of political foundation is defined, the master-disciple relationship that reaches other domains of the *socius* (relations of governance, labor, education, and so forth) tends to become more absolute and to be coupled to physical violence. The competition for the monopoly over the instruments of coercion, most visibly embodied in the army and the bureaucracy, is now under way.

This process thus comprises contradictions and conflicts that are not completely erased when power is instituted over entire nations and imposes the necessity of mediation. At this stage, we witness the effort toward theoretical uniformity and the enactment of rituals of submission—efforts that aim for "the high" but that are unable to eliminate the diversity of "the low." Indeed, it is somewhat extreme to assume, as Sharabi does, that authority and superstition prevail at all levels and that reason and egalitarian discourse are notably lacking.[6] Among young people in the workplace, for example, the debate is rigorous and rational, and equality is a given; the same applies to village meetings, where a gerontocracy accommodates divergent opinions and accepts arbitration. And finally, persuasion and attachments among women are more often than not averse to coercion. There are therefore spheres of equality that envelope rigid hierarchizations (those which govern the man/woman relationship being the most notorious). Of decisive importance here is that the more the center ("the high") is reinforced, the more these spheres of competition and equality ("the low") are menaced and penetrated. The colonial and postcolonial state, a political novelty imposed by a chieftaincy of technocrats, has been striving for at least a century to reduce these spaces of competition and equality. But in so doing, it also seems to have been destroying the hierarchical scaffolding that ensures its functioning. Are these the beginnings of a radical individualization that could provide the future with the foundations of a civil society? If that is the case, we should avail ourselves of this potential antidote to the impotence of individuals who live under the yoke of current authoritarianisms.

N   O   T   E   S

Introduction

1. This concept has been popularized by several well-known authors; see in particular the work of Gunder Frank and, for Arab countries, S. Amin.

2. M. Foucault, *Surveiller et punir: Naissance de la prison* (Paris: Gallimard, 1975), 207–8, and *Volonté de savoir* (Paris: Gallimard, 1976), 122. On the notion of *diagramme*, see *Surveiller et punir*, 207, and G. Deleuze, *Foucault* (Paris: Minuit, 1986), 42ff. On the notion of the "soil" on which power relations function and the conditions that make this functioning possible, see Foucault, *Power/Knowledge: Selected Interviews and Other Writings*, ed. Colin Gordon (New York: Pantheon, 1980), 187.

Chapter One

1. *Alawist* is not to be confused with *Alawite*. While the latter term designates all those who claim to be descendants of Ali (the Prophet's cousin and son-in-law), the former refers to a particular theory of Alawite monarchy found under the signature of Ahmed Alaoui and others. See, for example, Alaoui's statement in *Le Matin du Sahara et du Maghreb*, 1 June 1977: "To us independents, the king is the symbol of the nation's identification and of the primacy of royal power; it is the people's identity, since the king will always remain the representative of national unanimity as different political majorities succeed one another."

2. G. W. F. Hegel, *Principes de la philosophie du droit* (Paris: Gallimard, 1940), 76–77.

3. It is beyond the scope of this book to discuss—from the point of view of Muslim law in its various interpretations—the validity of the form of oath defended by Moroccan monarchists. It has been established that this particular form of oath stems from a practice (established very early in Sunni Islam) of recognizing the pretender who knew how to play up his qualities, especially his social and military strength. For this particular point, see R. P. Mottahedeh, *Loyalty and Leadership in Early Islamic Society* (Princeton: Princeton University Press, 1980), 50–51. For nineteenth-century Morocco, see A. Laroui, *Les origines*

sociales et culturelles du nationalisme marocain, 1830–1912 (Paris: Maspero, 1977), esp. 74–75, 77–78.

4. The first independent Muslim dynasty was founded (on the soil of what used to be Tingitane Mauretania) by Idriss, a descendant of the Prophet, in the year 788 (A.H. 172).

5. This point of view has been developed in particular in the monarchist press since the mid-1970s. See for example A. Alaoui's editorials of 3 March 1990 and 3 March 1991 in *Le Matin du Sahara et du Maghreb*. The concept of a pact between the king and his subjects also appears regularly in this particular newspaper; see, for example, Alaoui's editorial of 23 July 1991. See also G. Vedel et al., *Hassan II, fondateur d'un état moderne* (Paris: A. Michel, 1986), for information on allegiance and legitimacy, as well as the relationship between these two notions and modernization.

6. The year 1894 marks the death of Sultan Moulay Hassan, who was the last to preserve Moroccan sovereignty through forceful politics and constant campaigns. See J. Brignon, B. Boutaleb, et al., *Histoire du Maroc* (Paris: Hatier, 1967); Clifford Geertz, *Local Knowledge* (New York: Basic Books, 1983), 134–42; W. Harris, *Morocco that Was* (Boston, 1921).

7. Edmund Burke III, *Prelude to Protectorate in Morocco: Pre-Colonial Protest and Resistance, 1860–1912* (Chicago: University of Chicago Press, 1977), esp. chaps. 4, 7, 8. For the decline of sharifian prestige and the emergence of autonomous resistance movements, see also Laroui, *Les origines sociales et culturelles,* for example, 384–85, 407f.; Ross Dunn, *Resistance in the Desert: Moroccan Responses to French Imperialism, 1881–1912* (Madison: University of Wisconsin Press, 1977); A. Hammoudi, "Aspects de la mobilisation à la campagne, vus à travers la biographie d'un mahdi mort en 1919," in E. Gellner and J. C. Vatin, eds., *Islam et politique au Maghreb* (Paris: Editions du CNRS, 1981), 47–53.

8. J. Berque, *Le Maghreb entre deux guerres* (Paris: Seuil, 1962), 173–74; G. Ayache, "Les implications internationales de la guerre du Rif," in *Etudes d'histoire marocaine* (Rabat: SMER, 1979). For a picture of sharifian spiritual power against Abdelkrim, see R. Bidwell, *Morocco under Colonial Rule: French Administration of Tribal Areas 1912–1956* (London: F. Cass, 1973), 67; Charles-André Julien, *L'Afrique du Nord en Marche: Nationalisme musulman et souveraineté française* (Paris: Julliard, 1972); Roger Le Tourneau, *L'évolution politique de l'Afrique du Nord musulmane 1920–1961* (Paris, 1961).

9. J. Halstead, "The Changing Character of Moroccan Reformism," *Journal of African Society* 5, no. 3 (1964); Laroui, *Les origines sociales et culturelles,* 334 and chap. 9; Burke, *Prelude to Protectorate in Morocco,* chaps. 6, 7; C. Geertz, *Islam Observed* (New Haven: Yale University Press, 1968), 75.

10. Berque, *Le Maghreb entre deux guerres,* 227–30; Bidwell, *Morocco under Colonial Rule,* 54, 57, 69f.; E. Hermassi, *Etat et société au Maghreb; Etude comparative* (Paris: Anthropos, 1975), 111.

11. Berque, *Le Maghreb entre deux guerres,* 79.

12. In particular the appearance of his effigy in the moon.

13. Brick Oussaid, *Les coquelicots de l'Oriental: chronique d'une famille berbère marocaine* (Paris: La Découverte, 1984), 47, 52–53. On the role played by the nationalists in the reestablishment of the monarch as a symbol and leader of the nation, see in particular Geertz, *Islam Observed*, 75f.

14. The process of liquidating or controlling political organizations and unions has been described in detail by many scholars. See in particular I. W. Zartman, *Destiny of a Dynasty: The Search for Institutions in Morocco's Developing Society* (Columbia: University of South Carolina Press, 1964), 23, 61–63, 68, 83; I. W. Zartman, *Morocco: Problems of New Power* (New York: Atherton Press, 1964), for example, 66, 70–74, 98, 99f., on controlling the administration and the army. See also Hermassi, *Etat et société*, 121; D. Ashford, "Politics and Violence in Morocco," *Middle East Journal*, winter 1959, esp. 18–19, 24; J. Waterbury, *The Commander of the Faithful: The Moroccan Political Elite—A Study of Segmented Politics* (London: Weidenfeld and Nicholson, 1970), esp. chaps. 13, 14; R. Leveau, *Le fellah marocain, défenseur du Trône* (1976; Paris: Presses de la Fondation Nationale des Sciences Politiques, 1985), 3, 36–37, 41, 236–40. Leveau's book focuses on the palace's recapture of the crucial political mechanisms—local administration, communal organization, the control of reforms (especially regarding landholdings), etc.—in order to dominate the rural elites and through them the political system. We will later examine the works of Waterbury and Leveau.

15. Geertz, *Islam Observed*, 74–78; Hermassi, *Etat et société*, 52–53.

16. Brignon et al., *Histoire du Maroc*, 324–25; Burke, *Prelude to Protectorate*, 114–17; Laroui, *Les origines sociales et culturelles*, 393f.; J. Robert, *La monarchie marocaine* (Paris, 1963).

17. Brignon et al., *Histoire du Maroc*, 324–25; Burke, *Prelude to Protectorate*, 116. Laroui remarks that Kettani was "lending a deaf ear" to the pleas of Hafidians while opposing the ruling sultan. It is also noted that Kettani dominated the discussion and was able to impose the conditional bayʿa. However, Laroui does not go as far as suggesting that the Kettaniyine attempted to seize power. See Laroui, *Les origines sociales et culturelles*, 393–96.

18. Burke, *Prelude to Protectorate*, 129, 133–35; Laroui, *Les origines sociales et culturelles*, 400, 402, 403f.

19. Burke, *Prelude to Protectorate*, 133–35; Laroui, *Les origines sociales et culturelles*, 402, 405–6. On the penetration of Salafism, see Jamil Abu Nasr, "The Salafiya Movement in Morocco: The Religious Base of the Moroccan Nationalist Movement," *St. Anthony's Paper* (Oxford: Oxford University Press, 1963), 16, 96–98; Allal al Fasi, *Hadith al Maghrib fi al Machriq* (Cairo, 1956), 10. See also Paquignon, "Un livre de Moulay Abd al Hafid," *Revue du Monde Musulman* 7 (1909): 125–28; J. Berque, "Çà et là dans les débats du réformisme religieux au Maghreb," *Etudes d'Orientalisme dédiées à la mémoire de Levi-Provencal* (Paris: Maisonneuve et Larose, 1961), 480f.

20. Bidwell, *Morocco under Colonial Rule*, 135–37, 147, 149.

21. This decree was blocked by the protectorate authorities. See Bidwell,

Morocco under Colonial Rule, 151. For a summary of these struggles, see chapter 8 of the same book.

22. See Bidwell, *Morocco under Colonial Rule,* 151.

23. Bidwell, *Morocco under Colonial Rule,* esp. 149–51; see also Berque, *Le Maghreb entre deux guerres,* 105, 396–97. Bidwell reports on a virulent campaign by the newspaper of the Istiqlal party against the moussems in August 1954. The brotherhoods and their festivals were vigorously attacked by the Istiqlal leader Allal al Fasi in *al Harakat al-Istiqlaliya fi al Maghribi al-'Arabi* (Marrakech, 1956).

24. Geertz did not fail to note this focusing effort: "There is probably no other liberated colony in which the struggle for independence so centered around the capture, revival and renovation of a traditional institution" (*Islam Observed,* 78).

25. Germain Ayache, *Etudes d'histoire marocaine* (Rabat: SMER, 1979), 159f.

26. These services, attached to the royal cabinet, represent a modern form of the ancient institution of the *mazalim,* which every Muslim ruler had to make available to his subjects.

27. This was accomplished through the creation of a competing party that was loyal to the palace, namely M. Aherdane's Popular Movement, which was founded in 1957 and recruited its followers primarily from rural (particularly Berber speaking) areas. On the rural upheavals in the early days of independence, see E. Gellner, *Muslim Society* (Cambridge: Cambridge University Press, 1981), 194–206; see also Zartman, *Destiny of a Dynasty* and *Morocco,* Leveau, *Le fellah marocain.*

28. The country's third constitution, following that of 1962 and the still-born constitution of 1970, was adopted in 1972.

29. Technically speaking, the state of emergency occurred between 1965 and 1971. In practice, however, it continued until 1974–1975. The period included a number of events: rioting and repression in Casablanca (1965), putsches in 1971 and 1972, repression in public schools, and the very harsh trials to which various radical groups—Ila al Amam and 23 mars among others—were subjected.

30. The concept of sovereignty for the king is clearly expressed in the 1972 constitution. Analyses of these constitutions can be found in a number of studies. For the 1962 constitution, see O. Bendourou, *Le pouvoir exécutif au Maroc depuis l'indépendance* (Aix-en-Provence: Publisud 1986), 90f.; Octave Marais, "L'election à la Chambre des Représentants au Maroc," *Annuaire de l'Afrique du Nord* (1963). For an analysis of the 1970 and 1972 constitutions, see Bendourou, *Le pouvoir exécutif,* 198–206, 232–34, 248–49.

31. See Leveau, *Le fellah marocain,* 78; Bendourou, *Le pouvoir exécutif,* 122.

32. The year 1972 saw the appearance of so-called independent candidates who in fact were supported by the Ministry of the Interior. Their group played a part in the 1976 elections that followed the adoption of the 1972 constitution. In 1978 they founded a party called RNI (National Union of Indepen-

dents), the ideology and program of which were outlined by Ahmed Alaoui in the press (essentially *Le Matin du Sahara et du Maghreb*). See Bendourou, *Le pouvoir exécutif*, 246–48.

33. The palace's desire to distance itself from the monarchist party created in 1962 is reflected in the choice of a name for the party. The label Front for the Defense of Constitutional Institutions was chosen over the one suggested by Guedira, its founder, which was Monarchist Constitutional Front. See Leveau, *Le fellah marocain*, 78.

34. Press conference of 13 December 1963.

35. The king expressed Morocco's determination to recover the Western Sahara in his speech of 8 July 1974; the Green March was initiated on 6 November 1975.

36. Bendourou, *Le pouvoir exécutif*, 239–40, 245, leans toward the hypothesis of a deal with the Istiqlal leaders to the detriment of the USFP (Socialist Union of Popular Forces). Several majority parliamentarians privately recognized that there were electoral irregularities and deals. At least one Member who had announced his defeat in an official statement was (unbeknownst to him) miraculously elected a few days later. The constitution states, on the monarch's initiative, that 88 of the 264 representatives are to be indirectly elected by local, occupational, and union colleges. Given the determining influence of the authorities on these electoral colleges, no one was surprised by the outcome of the elections. For the 1976 and 1977 parliamentary elections, see M. Sehimi, "Les elections legislatives marocaines," and J. C. Santucci, "Les elections legislatives marocaines de juin 1977," *Annuaire de l'Afrique du Nord* (1977); Bendourou, *Le pouvoir exécutif*, 240–43. A new reform was put to referendum and is being implemented since October 1996. Indirect election of representatives is suppressed and a second chamber, elected at the regional level, is created.

37. This third round aroused much hope for a "clean" election process in which the administration of the Ministry of the Interior would remain neutral. Many observers as well as the allocation leaders insist that these hopes were disappointed.

38. After the 1981 riots union leaders within the CDT and some USFP leaders were arrested and the parties' newspapers suspended. As a result of expressing their divergent opinion on the handling of the Sahara issue at the Organization of African Unity's second Nairobi conference (1982), the leadership of the USFP was arrested and its newspaper headquarters searched. The press is automatically subjected to prior restraint by the services of the Ministry of the Interior, and during the years 1988–1989 two important magazines, *Lamalif* and *Kalima*, ceased publication due to decisions made by the Ministry of the Interior. *Kalima* was destroyed by repeated instances of censorship.

39. Clashes with government forces in Agadir, Kenitra, Tangier, and especially Fez claimed several hundred victims (*Le Monde*, 17 December 1990). *Le Monde* does not mention the incidents and unrest that took place elsewhere,

in Beni Mellal, Ouezzane, and Meknes in particular. These events were the subject of a communique by the government which appeared in the Saturday, 5 December 1990, issue of *Le Matin du Sahara et du Maghreb.* The disturbances themselves occurred on Friday, 14 December.

40. So-called private colonization land consisted of landholdings that had been directly acquired by settlers through private transactions. Official colonization land, landholdings originally given to settlers by the protectorate authorities, had been recovered much earlier. For the recovery of colonization land, see N. Bouderbala, M. Chraibi, and P. Pascon, *La question agraire au Maroc* (Rabat: BESM, 1974), 405f., 411–12.

41. Bouderbala, Chraibi, and Pascon estimate that three hundred thousand of the one million hectares of land recovered were acquired illegally (*La question agraire,* 441). Other scholars estimate that such acquisitions amounted to 410,000 hectares; Will D. Swearingen, *Moroccan Mirages, Agrarian Dreams and Deceptions, 1912–1986* (Princeton: Princeton University Press, 1987), 180. One of the incidents was the Ouled Khalifa case, which occurred in the Gharb plain in 1975; government troops fired on peasants occupying a plot of former colonization land to which they laid claim, killing some of them.

42. In 1971 a total of 94,372 hectares had been distributed and the plan was to reach 185,000 hectares by 1972; see Bouderbala, Chraibi, and Pascon, *La question agraire,* 409. The total was 187,000 hectares in 1973, at the end of the period of recovery of colonization land; see Swearingen, *Moroccan Mirages,* 177. As of 1990 it was estimated that approximately 1,258,000 hectares are irrigated, 431,650 of them by modern large-scale hydraulic systems and the remainder by small- and medium-scale hydraulic systems; ANAFID, *L'irrigation au Maroc* (Rabat, 1990), 17. Swearingen (*Moroccan Mirages,* 179) gives the figure for all land under modern irrigation in 1986 as 625,000 hectares.

43. N. Bouderbala, M. Chraibi, P. Pascon, and A. Hammoudi, "Commentaires sur les programmes agraires des partis politiques," in Bouderbala, Chraibi, and Pascon, *La question agraire,* vol. 2 (Rabat: BESM, 1977). Evidence for concern on the part of organizations can be found for example in the work of K. Griffin, *Distribution de la terre et inégalité des revenus au Maroc* (Geneva: International Labor Organization, 1978).

44. See proceedings of the colloquium (Rabat: Ministère de l'Equipement, 1988).

45. See the 1972 constitution, articles 19 and 22–35, regarding royal prerogatives.

46. Clifford Geertz has shown in another context that in Morocco the ruler's charisma is symbolized by will and forceful action, which are seen as signs of grace; see Geertz, *Islam Observed.*

47. Moroccan officials estimated that there were thousands of demonstrators. The figures given by domestic and foreign radio stations ranged from 350,000 to 600,000.

48. Zartman, *Morocco,* 66, 99–100.

49. See A. Coram, "Note on the Role of the Berbers in the Early Days of Moroccan Independence," in E. Gellner and C. Micaud, eds., *Arabs and Berbers* (London: Duckworth, 1973), 271.

50. Zartman, *Morocco,* 112.

51. Zartman, *Morocco,* 75.

52. Particularly in the Addi ou Bihi case. On these uprisings, see E. Gellner, "Patterns of Rural Rebellion in Morocco: Tribes and Minorities," *Archives Européennes de Sociologie* 3 (1962); Gellner and Micaud, *Arabs and Berbers.*

53. The Mouvement Populaire, founded by Mahjoubi Aherdane in early 1957, was first banned, then authorized in late 1958 following the publication of a law on civil liberties (legal recognition, Feb. 1959; constitutive congress, Nov. 1959) (Zartman, *Morocco,* 21).

54. Morocco had inherited its borders from the colonial era but had not accepted them and maintained claims on Mauritania and the Western Sahara.

55. J. Waterbury, "The Coup Manqué," in Gellner and Micaud, *Arabs and Berbers,* 400, 413–14.

56. See the list of ministers of the interior in Gellner and Micaud, *Arabs and Berbers,* 263. The ministry of defense was sometimes given to men close to the palace: in 1966 to Haddu Chiguer; in 1967 to M. Aherdane, leader of the Popular Movement, who gave proof of his loyalty in the very early years of independence; and later, between 1971 and 1972, to General Oufkir. After 1972 it was phased out, and the sovereign assumed direct leadership of the armed forces. See Waterbury, "Coup manqué."

57. Abdaslam Ben Kaddour, "The Neo-makhzan and the Berbers," in Gellner and Micaud, *Arabs and Berbers,* 262–65. See also Zartman, *Morocco;* Leveau, *Le fellah marocain,* 28; Coram, "Note on the Role of the Berbers"; Waterbury, "Coup Manqué."

58. R. Rézette notes in *Les partis politiques marocains* (Paris: A. Colin, 1955), 295–309, that in 1944 eight of the thirteen Istiqlal leaders came from Qarawyin. See also Hermassi, *Etat et société,* 114, and D. Ashford, *Political Change in Morocco* (Princeton: Princeton University Press, 1961), 57.

59. The split occurred in January 1958, but the newly formed party did not appear under the name UNFP till 26 September 1959.

60. The new cabinet was formed on 27 May 1960.

61. Zartman, *Morocco,* 128–29. The Moroccan Union of Agriculture was created in July 1958. "Two months later, the king inaugurated the UMA in a grand *mousem* [harvest festival] at Souq at-Tleta in the Gharb. It was to be one of Morocco's most effective modern pressure groups." For information on the group's founder, Mansour Nejjay, see Jean Lacouture and Simonne Lacouture, *Le Maroc à l'épreuve* (Paris: Seuil, 1958), 189.

62. Zartman, *Morocco,* 151.

63. P. Pascon gives the figure 18,422 ("Statistiques et sources," in Bouderbala, Chraibi, and Pascon, *La question agraire;* see graph and table, 409).

64. Hassan Zemmouri in the Ministry of the Interior killed the agrarian

reform projects of the A. Ibrahim cabinet with support from the Palace. After the downfall of the Ibrahim cabinet Zemmouri obtained the Ministry of Agriculture in 1960. Zartman, *Morocco*, 139f.; on these points see in particular Leveau, *Le fellah marocain.*

65. Dahir of November 1959.

66. Zartman, *Morocco*, 138; Leveau, *Le fellah marocain*, 28, 41.

67. A total of 23 percent, which accounts for the more than 2 percent increase in number of rural households between 1965 and 1973. On this point see Pascon, "Statistiques et sources," 411, graph and table on p. 409.

68. Leveau, *Le fellah marocain*, 41–53, 85, 88–89.

69. Leveau, *Le fellah marocain*, 125–26, 163, 170–71, 180–82, 193, 226–29.

70. Leveau, *Le fellah marocain*, 232; Marais, "L'élection de la Chambre des Représentants"; Bendourou, *Le pouvoir exécutif*, 141f.

71. On corruption and the distribution of favors, see Waterbury, *Commander of the Faithful*, 275f., and "Coup Manqué," 399–400.

72. Waterbury, *Commander of the Faithful*, chaps. 7, 14, and "Coup Manqué."

73. Waterbury, *Commander of the Faithful*, 6, 74, 88–89, 117.

74. Which took place in 1970.

75. An expression he borrowed from Henry Moore; see Leveau, *Le fellah marocain*, 238–42. Moore uses the notion of "stability group" in his discussion of North African political systems in *Politics in North Africa: Algeria, Morocco and Tunisia* (Boston: Little Brown, 1970), 237f.

76. Leveau, *Le fellah marocain*, 198, 180–82, 242.

77. The Rabat branch split from the UNFP in 1972 and formed the Socialist Union of Popular Forces (USFP) in 1974.

78. Leveau, *Le fellah marocain.*

79. Larbi Ibaaqil, "Discours scolaire et ideologie au Maroc," *La malif* 95 (March 1979): 32 and 43. See also his *L'Ecole Marocaine et la compétition Sociale* (Rabat: Babel, 1996).

80. Juan Linz defines authoritarian regimes as "political systems with limited, not responsible, political pluralism: without elaborate and guiding ideology (but with distinctive mentalities); without intensive nor extensive political mobilization (except at some points in their development); and in which a leader (or occasionally a small group) exercises power within formally ill-defined limits but actually quite predictable ones." J. Linz, "An Authoritarian Regime: Spain," in Eric Allardt and Ytjo Littunen, eds., *Cleavages, Ideologies and Party Systems* (Helsinki: Westermack Society, 1964); reprinted in Eric Allardt and Stein Rokkan, eds., *Mass Politics: Studies in Political Sociology* (New York: Free Press, 1970), 255.

81. J. Linz, "Totalitarianism and Authoritarian Regimes," in Fred I. Greenstein and Nelson W. Polsky, eds., *Handbook of Political Science*, vol. 3, *Macropolitical Theory* (Reading, Mass.: Addison-Wesley, 1975), 255, 259; Hermassi, *Etat et société*, 78–79, 112.

82. We cannot elaborate here on the economic power of the royal house,

which deserves full treatment in a monograph. The control of key sectors in the economy is handled by a large firm, called Omnium Nord Africain (ONA). See Saadi Mohamed ben Saïd, *Concentration financière et formation des groupes economiques privés marocains,* doctoral thesis (Paris, Dauphines, 1984), 266–69, regarding the ONA. See *Le Monde,* 22 December 1988.

83. Saïd, *Concentration financière,* 197, speaks of "feudalisms" in the public sector.

84. Capitalist enterprise accounts for only 9 percent to 15 percent of sales of agricultural products. Statistics of the Ministry of Agriculture, Rabat, 1987.

85. According to the local understanding of these commandments.

86. Robert Montagne, *Les Berbères et le makhzen dans le sud du Maroc: Essai sur la transformation politique des Berbères sédentaires (group Chleuh)* (Paris: Alcan, 1930), vol. 3, chaps. 1, 4; J. Berque, *Structures sociales du Haut Atlas* (1955; Paris: Presses Universitaires de France, 1978), 89f.; P. Pascon, *Le Haouz de Marrakech* (Tanger: Editions Marocaines et Internationales, 1977), vol. 1, pt. 2, chap. 3.

87. D. Seddon, *Moroccan Peasants: A Century of Change in the Eastern Rif, 1870–1970* (Folkestone: Dawson, 1981), 45–47, 143–45, 181–82, 221–22.

88. Burke, *Prelude to Protectorate.*

89. Especially in the media. See in particular the editorials of *Le Matin du Sahara et du Maghreb* and *Maroc Soir.* Radio and television, which were until very recently directed by a governor, constantly engage in this kind of exegesis. The Ministry of Information was for many years in the hands of the Ministry of the Interior, which is part of the restricted circle of disciples.

Chapter Two

1. Examples of the use of *dār-al-mulk* and *dār-al-sultān* can be found in Ibn Zaydan, *Ithāfi a'lāmi annāfi bi jamāli akhbāri ḥabirati maknās,* vol. 4 (1952), p. 393 and vol. 3 (1931), pp. 154–55; also Nāṣirī, *alistiqsā li akhbār duwali al-maghribi alaqsā* (Casablanca, 1956), part 3, vol. 9, pp. 79 and 124. *Duwiriya*—diminutive of *dar,* "house"—signifies a house adjacent to the main (i.e., male) house, which can generally be entered only through the main house. It houses the closest members of the family of the master of the house, in particular his wife (or wives) and children.

2. The reform of the state bureaucracy and the army and the creation of new institutions was in no small measure a reaction to the growing encroachment of Europe after the conquest of Algiers (1830). For information on the reforms, see Brignon et al., *Histoire du Maroc,* 314–20; Burke, *Prelude to Protectorate,* 31–38; J. L. Miège, *Le Maroc et l'Europe* (Paris: P.U.F., 1961–63), 3:224–34 (on military reforms), 4:106f.; Mohammed Lahbabi, *Le gouvernement marocain à l'aube du XXe siècle* (Rabat: Editions Technique, Nord Africaine, 1958); Laroui, *Les origines sociales et culturelles;* Wilfrid Rollman, "The 'New Order' in a Precolonial Muslim Society: Military Reforms in Morocco 1844–1904," doctoral dissertation, 2 vols., University of Michigan, 1983; Touria Berrada, "The Mo-

roccan Army and Its Evolution in the Nineteenth Century" (in Arabic), thesis, University of Rabat, 1984; Mohammed Kenbib, *Juifs et Musulmans au Maroc, 1859–1948* (Rabat: Faculté des Lettres et des sciences humaine, 1994); Bahija Smimou, *Les reformes militaires au Maroc de 1844 à 1912* (Rabat: Faculté des Lettres, 1995); Muhammad al-Monounī, *Madhahir Yaqḍat al Maghribi al Ḥadīth* (Beyrouth: Maṭbaʿat l-Gharb al ʾIslāmī, 1985).

3. The treatment of rebellious princes, as compared to that of military leaders and other notables, is very significant. For illustrations of these two cases under Hassan I, see Ibn Zaydan, *Ithaf aʿlām annās bijamāli akhbār ḥaḍirati maknās* (henceforth Ibn Zaydan), vol. 2 (Rabat, 1930), biography of Hassan I, 155ff. Anthropological studies have not paid sufficient attention to the fact that the maternal lineage, while not relevant in tracing descent, plays a role in daily life: first, it carries its own line of inheritance; second, and most important, it can mobilize important loyalties. Nineteenth-century sovereigns often married relatives—cousins were a first choice—according to an ancestral norm they shared with their subjects. But these wives also belonged to powerful tribes. The maternal "uncles" thus acquired by each generation counterbalanced in some way those on the paternal side. These individuals were often given military functions, and in important large-scale military campaigns the army was headed by an uncle, brother, or son of the sultan rather than the sultan himself. Operational command was often in the hands of these maternal uncles. See, for example, Ibn Zaydan, 2:230, where Sultan Hassan I addresses the Chragas' caid as "our maternal uncles" (*khālunā*); earlier, when Moulay Abderrahman seeks help, during the famous rebellion of the Oudaya, from the men of a Gharb tribe to which he is related through marriage, he calls them "our uncle." See letter in Ibn Zaydan, 5:28.

4. On the Moroccan elite in the nineteenth century, see Mustapha al-Chabbi, *Annukhba al Maghribiya fī Maghribi al Qarni altāciʿ ʿAchar* (Rabat: Publications de la Faculté des Lettres, 1995).

5. One rushes to visit the sultan every time the opportunity arises. There is real competition between dignitaries, as each wants to be the first to arrive for ceremonies, particularly the Mouloud ceremony. The first to arrive is the first to be received, which constitutes a great honor (Ibn Zaydan 2:525). The quest for closeness to the person of the sultan goes beyond political competition and brings about religious competition. Whenever there are festivities the notables come in contact with the prince, who blesses each of them and his tribe. And whenever they are granted the opportunity, the prince's subjects are anxious to touch him and apply to their hands and faces some part of his clothing. Extreme closeness indicates ascendancy, as clearly illustrated by the case of Ahmad ben Moussa (Ba Hmad); as soon as the other ministers become aware of it, they rush to ally with the chosen person against his enemies (Ibn Zaydan, 1 [1929]: 374).

6. The reforms attempted by nineteenth-century sultans did include granting wages for some government organizations. When Moulay Abderrah-

man revived the long-neglected Black Guard, he set up wages for the cavalry and foot soldiers, as well as pensions for those too old or too young to fight (Ibn Zaydan, 5:17). Such reforms in favor of the "Boukhari slaves" were innovative in more ways than one: the status of slave itself was modified by these reforms. But did they become wage earners? Not exactly; the system of regular wages had spread to the army, but it was combined with the "gift of closeness" (sila). Ibn Zaydan makes the following statement on the basis of a well-known source: "He recruited people from the Sous living in Marrakech, Chraga, and Oulad Jāma, people from Fez and slaves from Boukhari. This army was to be given clothing every six months, and a sila equal to the monthly pay already given out every second month. . . . This sila had to be distributed according to the same modalities as the wages" (Ibn Zaydan, 5:18).

7. Burke, Prelude to Protectorate, 15. Many studies highlight the economic and commercial offensive of the imperialist powers and their disastrous consequences for the Moroccan economy. Miege, Le Maroc et l'Europe, vol. 3; Burke, Prelude to Protectorate, chap. 2; G. Ayache, "Aspects de la crise financière au Maroc aprés l'expédition espagnole de 1860," Revue Historique 220 (1958): 271–310.

8. Ibn Zaydan 5 (1933): 180f. My views on this point and on confiscation of property converge with those of M. Kenbib in his Les protégés: Contribution à l'histoire contemporain de Maroc (Rabat, 1996), pt. 1, chapter 2.

9. E. Michaux-Bellaire, "Les impôts marocains," Archives Marocaines 1 (1904); E. Michaux-Bellaire, "L'organisation des finances au Maroc," Archives Marocaines 11 (1908); E. Aubin, Le Maroc d'aujourd'hui (Paris: Armand Colin, 1904).

10. Burke, Prelude to Protectorate, 35–36; Michaux-Bellaire, "Les impôts marocains"; G. Salmon, "Le Tertib," Archives Marocaines 2:154–58.

11. This whole section on gift exchange obviously owes a great deal to the famous works of Marcel Mauss on gift and sacrifice.

12. On slavery and black-white relationships, see N. Ennaji, L'esclavage au Maroc (Casablanca: EDDIF, 1991). On Muslim-Jewish relations in Morocco, see L. Rosen, "Muslim-Jewish Relations in a Moroccan City," International Journal of Middle East Studies, no. 4 (1972): 435–49.

13. As we know, genealogies are manipulated and one way to move upward socially is through acquired sharifism. However, although this path is used, it is not respected; hence a great deal of energy is spent proving the validity of "forged" genealogies. On the other hand a religious man's effort is recognized and respected by everyone; L. Valerosi, "La Tour de Babel: Groupes et relations ethniques au Moyen Orient et en Afrique du Nord," Annales, Economies, Societés Civilisations (1986): 817–38. A detailed study in the history of Moroccan Judaism and Jewish-Muslim relations in Morocco was recently published by Kenbib, Juifs et Musulmans au Maroc.

14. E. Gellner does this in "Patterns of Rebellion in Morocco during the Early Years of Independence," in Gellner and Micaud, Arabs and Berbers,

363–74. A. Laroui follows more or less the same line in *Les origines sociales et culturelles,* 121, 187; see also his section on the zaouia, 150f.

15. For information on the harka, see D. Nordman, "Les expéditions de Moulay Hassan," *Hesperis-Tamuda* 19 (1980–1981): 123–52; M. Afif, "Les harka hassaniennes d'aprés l'oeuvre d'A. Ibn Zaydan," *Hesperis-Tamuda* 19 (1980–1981): 153–68; Geertz, *Local Knowledge,* 138f.; Abderrahyan El-Moudden. "Etat et Société Rurale à Travers la Harka au Maroc du XIXᵉ siècle," *Maghreb Review* 8, nos. 5–6 (1983): 141–45.

16. Ibn Zaydan 3:480; my translations.

17. Ahmad ben Khālid al-Nāṣirī, *Al Istiqsā Li'Akhbar al Maghribi al Aqsā* (Casablanca: Dar-al Kitab, 1954–1956), 9:142–43.

18. Ibn Zaydan 1:390; my translation.

19. Ibn Zaydan 1:411–12, and the photograph on 410; Eduard Maldonado, *El Roqui* (Tetouan, 1949), photographs on 480 and 492, drawings on 496.

20. Foucault, *Surveiller et punir,* chap. 1.

21. See the text of this bay'a, dated 1 dhu-Lḥijja 1325 A.H., in Ibn Zaydan, 1:449–52; see also E. Michaux-Bellaire, "La souveraineté et le califat," *Revue du Monde Musulman* 59 (1925): 117ff.

22. Laroui, *Les origines sociales et culturelles,* 72.

23. Mottahedeh, *Loyalty and Leadership,* 181f.

24. Ibn Zaydan, biography of Hassan I, esp. 520ff.; see also p. 509 on other aspects of life and rituals in dar-al-mulk.

25. Ibn Zaydan, biography of Sultan Mohammed ben Abderrahman.

26. The painting and related sketches are in the museum of Toulouse.

27. Edmondo de Amicis, *Morocco, Its People and Places,* trans. C. Rollin-Tilton (London: Cassell, Petter, Galpin and Co., 1879), 261–62.

28. Edmund Burke III, "The Image of the Moroccan State in French Ethnological Literature: A New Look at the Origins of Lyautey's Berber Policy," in Gellner and Micaud, *Arabs and Berbers,* 181–88; Ayache, *Etudes d'histoire marocaine,* 159f. (see also, in the same volume, "Le sentiment national dans le Maroc du XIXe siècle" and "Société rifaine et pouvoir central marocain"); Laroui, *Les origines sociales et culturelles,* 121–24, 171–87, 189.

29. The kasbah is a large, fortified dwelling belonging to a strong lineage wielding political influence—at the tribal level—under the leadership of a notable. The term also designates the fortified seat of government in the provinces and in the cities.

30. On the first two points, see in particular J. Berque, *Structures sociales du Haut Atlas* (1955; Paris: P.U.F., 1978); E. Gellner, *Saints of the Atlas* (London: Weidenfeld and Nicholson, 1959).

31. Montagne, *Les Berbéres et le makhzen;* Berque, *Structures sociales.*

Chapter Three

1. Berque, *Structures sociales,* pt. 4, 475f. Berque considers the phenomena of holiness and brotherhood in the same book, pt. 3, chaps. 1, 2, and 3, and con-

tinuously maintains this interest in the rest of his work. Gellner stresses Montagne's neglect of the zaouia; see Gellner, *Saints of the Atlas.*

2. Gellner gives Montagne credit for being the first to state that the Ahansal in the Central Atlas constituted some kind of maraboutic state and for acknowledging that such a system was a notable exception to his theory, according to which the instability of the leffs and republics is due to an "oscillation" between republic and tyranny. However, Gellner states that this phenomenon still needs to be further described and interpreted—a task he then takes up. Moreover, since the theory of the leff contains notable exceptions—Seksawa according to Berque, and the Central High Atlas according to Gellner—and cannot account for the maintenance of order at lower segmentary levels, Gellner expands on Montagne's work by pointing out that two principles underlying the maintenance of peace among the Berbers are always the segmentary principle and the nonegalitarian "maraboutic state" (the sacred lineages). On these points, see Gellner, *Saints of the Atlas,* 64–68. See my own comments on these points in A. Hammoudi, "Segmentarity, Social Stratification, Political Power and Sainthood: Reflections on Gellner's Theses," *Economy and Society* 9, no. 3 (1980): 279–303; first published in *Hesperis Tamuda,* no. 16 (Rabat, 1974).

3. Geertz, *Islam Observed.* For an overview (since the eighteenth century) see A. Hammoudi, "The Path to Sainthood: Structure and Danger," Princeton Papers in Near Eastern Studies, 1995.

4. G. Drague, *Esquisse d'histoire religieuse du Maroc* (Paris: J. Peyronnet, 1951), 267 (for a description of this brotherhood, 251f.); J. Berque, *L'intérieur du Maghreb (XVe–XIXe siècles),* 273–75; J. C. Michon, *L'autobiographie (Fahrasa) du soufi marocain: Ahmad Ibn 'Ajiba* (Milano: Arché 1982), 12f. The biography of al-Haj 'Ali will be analyzed here on the basis of the account of his son, Mukhtar al Soussi, in two works: *Al Tiryāq al mudāwī fī akhbār al-shaykh sidi al hāj 'Ali al-Sousi al Darqāwi* (Tetouan, 1960) and *Al Ma'sūl* (Rabat, 1960–1963); henceforth *Tiryāq* and *Ma'sūl.*

5. *Tiryāq,* 22–23; *Ma'sūl* 1:222f. For a discussion of the concept of qarāba, see Dale F. Eickelman, *Moroccan Islam: Tradition and Society in a Pilgrimage Center* (Austin: University of Texas Press, 1976), 95–105, 183–210.

6. *Tiryāq,* 105 and esp. 219; *Ma'sūl,* 1:265–66, 280, and 3:41. For information on this caid, see *Ma'sūl* 5: 150–51, 152f., 159–60, 200f. This opposition is not surprising since the *tarīqa nāṣiriya* spread in the south under the influence of the founder of Tamgrout and his successor (1674–1729). Following the appointment of Sidi Mohammad ben Abdallah as vice-king in Marrakech (1759–1790) the Nāṣiriya obtained the favor of the makhzen and spread everywhere, including the higher levels of bureaucracy and the powerful circles of the central makhzen. The ascendancy gained by the Darqawiya among the populace in the nineteenth century could not be overlooked by either the makhzen or the Nāṣiriya. On the beginning and expansion of the Nāṣiriya, see A. Hammoudi, "Sainteté, pouvoir, et société, Tamgrout, XVIIe et XVIIIe siècles," *Annales E.S.C.,* May/August 1980.

7. *Tiryāq*, 212–13; *Ma'sūl* 3:41f.

8. For reasons which have not yet been elucidated. But one can already see the beginning of a "positivistic" orientation which considers the zāwiya as an institution in need of description. Mukhtar al Sousi devoted his energies to the description of this and other institutions he knew would disappear or change due to what he called the new (French) order.

9. *Tiryāq*, 35, 42, 56, 93, 96.

10. *Tiryāq*, 93; *Ma'sūl* 1:208.

11. For this episode, see *Tiryāq*, 6–7, 12–13; *Ma'sūl* 1:222, 227.

12. *Tiryāq*, 22–24, 60–63, 218f.; *Ma'sūl* 1:222, 227.

13. *Tiryāq*, 6–7. Regarding the gaze, see *Tiryāq*, 96; *Ma'sūl*, 1:189. See also 'Ali's 1877 epistle *'Iqd al-jumān Limurīdi al'irfān* (Rabat: Maṭba'at al-Sahil, 1984), 17; henceforth *'Iqd*.

14. *Tiryāq*, 7; *'Iqd*, 29 (my translation).

15. J. Berque, *Ulémas, fondateurs, insurgés du Maghreb, XVIIe siècle* (Paris: Sindbad, 1982), 68.

16. Berque, *L'intérieur du Maghreb*, 247–49, 260f.; and *Ulémas, fondateurs, insurgés*, chap. 2; A. Hammoudi, "Sainteté, pouvoir et société," *Annales E.S.C.*, esp. 617–18; Hammoudi, "Aspects de la mobilisation populaire," 47f.

17. "The initiate, for his part, leaves behind territorial allegiance as well as genealogies," according to Berque, *L'intérieur du Maghreb*, 262.

18. There are many examples in the hagiographic literature; see, for example, the cases of Ibn Nāṣir in Hammoudi, *Annales;* Al Yousi in J. Berque, *'Al Yousi: Problèmes de la culture marocaine au XVIIe siècle* (The Hague: Mouton, 1958), chap. 3, 13f.; and recently, Ibn 'Ajiba in Michon, *L'autobiographie.* For a case closer to al Haj 'Ali, see the manuscript biography of Ma'al 'Aynayn, "Qurrat al'-Aynayn fi karāmāt al Shaykh Ma'al-'Aynayn" (Rabat: Bibliotheque Generale), for example, 60f. See also the life of Shaykh Ahmad al Alaoui in Martin Lings, *A Sufi Saint of the Twentieth Century* (London: Allen and Unwin, 1971), chap. 3. Finally, there is the testimony of several murids of the present master of the Boutchishiya, who lives in the Oujda area and whose relations with his disciples do not differ much from the classical model, although success in life is represented by new signs and criteria (militancy, diffusion of the *da'wa*, moral reform corresponding to the new context in Morocco). Boutchishiya circles are widespread all over Morocco, particularly in large cities.

19. *Tiryāq*, 115, 13–15, 91; *Ma'sūl* 1:202f.

20. There were exceptions, the most notable being Al Ḥarraq, great 'alem and founder of the Ḥarraqīya in Tetouan. It seems that Moulay Larbi was accused by his disciples of having given him the secret without submitting him to the same conditions as other disciples, that is, to the murid life, which takes many years. See M. Dawud, *Tārīkh Tiṭwān* (Tiṭwān [Tetouan]: al maṭba'a al mahdiya, 1970), 6:202–5. on Al Ḥarraq's initiation.

21. See *Tiryāq* and especially *Ma'sūl*, 205–7, regarding these events.

22. *Tiryāq*, 6–7, 9–11, 89.

23. *Ma'sūl*, 1:266, 273–74, 3:44f.; *Tiryāq*, 8, 105.

24. Hammoudi, "Sainteté, pouvoir et société." The founder of the Naṣiriya prohibited music and dance during the *dikr*. *Tiryāq*, 105, reports that there was general hostility between Sidi 'Ali's Darqawa and the Tijaniya, except for the head Tijani of Ifrane. On Darqawiya and Tijaniya, see also Berque, *L'intérieur du Maghreb*, 274.

25. Michon, *L'autobiographie*. On al Majdub and the malamatiya, see L. de Premare, *Sidi Abd-Er-hanan El Majdub* (Rabat/Paris: CNSR/SMER, 1985), chap. 4, esp. 93f.; on Moulay Larbi's and the Darqawa's initiation chains, see Drague, *Esquisse d'histoire religieuse*, 265 and appendices, table 5.

26. *Tiryāq*, 87, 88, 92, 114.

27. *Tiryāq*, 12.

28. From 1879–1880 to 1884; he started building his own zaouia on 15 July 1884. *Tiryāq*, 24.

29. The rule was formulated by Moulay Larbi al-Darqāwi, following his own master, Moulay 'Ali ben Abderrahman al Amrani al Fāssī (also referred to as al-Jawal); Drague, *Esquisse d'histoire religieuse*, 263–64 (see 264 on al Jamal's commandments, quoted from Rinn, *Marabouts et Khouans: Etude sur L'Islam en Algerie* (Algier: Jourdan, 1884), 233.

30. *Tiryāq*, 12. On the conditions cited, quite usual among the Darqawa, see *tiryāq*, 86, 114–15; *Ma'sūl*, 1: 193. See also Michon, *L'autobiographie*, 32–74, 80–83, 96–98 (the biography of Ibn 'Ajiba, in northern Morocco in the late eighteenth and early nineteenth centuries), regarding the conditions, or *chourout*, for entering the path.

31. The epistle, *'Iqd al-jumān limurīdi al 'irfan*, was published by 'Ali's grandson Matba'at al-Sahil (Rabat, 1984), with a comment by Mukhtar al Soussi on "the meaning of *wali* according to the Shari'a." For the date at which the epistle was written, see p. 34.

32. *'Iqd*, 11, 12. The emphasis on food deprivation in a region as austere as the Sous reminds us of the monks' struggles with their stomachs in the Egyptian desert in late antiquity; for a suggestive description of this, see P. Brown, *The Body and Society: Men, Women and Sexual Renunciation in Early Christianity* (New York: Columbia University Press, 1988), 218f.

33. *Ma'sūl* 1:114, 193, 210; *Tiryāq* 107; *'Iqd*, 20–22, 30.

34. *'Iqd*, 22.

35. *Tiryāq*, 25. 'Ali's first marriage took place on 10 ka'da 1302 A.H. (21 August 1884). On his marriages, see *Tiryāq*, 25, 47, 210–11, 218–20; *Ma'sūl* 1:273–74, 3:41f.

36. The biographer says little about the few women renouncers (*munqati'at*). Women are "present" whenever the shaykh and his disciples meet, but they are separated by a wall built without mortar, so that they can hear everything that is said on the other side. On this point, see *Tiryāq*, 73.

37. *Tiryāq*, 86.

38. It was on the occasion of a construction project that the shaykh

"read" a death wish directed at him in the heart of an exhausted disciple; see *Tiryāq*, 46.

39. *Tiryāq*, 68, 68. Also *Ma'sūl* 1:261;

40. See *Tiryāq*, 62–65, regarding this prosperity.

41. There exist some standard arrangements which traditionally determine how much of the crop or flock each of the partners is entitled to (for instance, one-fifth of the crop [*khamessat*], one-fourth of the growth of the stock, and so on). But these proportions are not spelled out in specific contracts. There is only verbal agreement. Such "agreements" are often reformulated as a result of negotiations. Their guarantee lies in the *soḥba*, which constitutes the foundation of permanent relations, as much as it does in consensus.

42. This is the case not only for al Haj 'Ali's disciples and for the abovementioned disciples of al-Majdub. Regarding M'hammad Ibn Naṣir, *Durar*, see Hammoudi, "Sainteté, pouvoir et société," 619f. For Sidi Ali ben Ḥamdouch and Sidi Ahmed Dghoughi, see V. Crapanzano, *The Hamadsha: A study in Moroccan Ethnopsychiatry* (Berkeley: University of California Press, 1973), 23, 32; J. Jean Herber, "Les Hmadcha et les Dghoughyine," *Hespéris* 3 (1923): 217–35. In earlier times Abou Ya'za, a well-known figure, is reported to have dressed as a woman to wait on a disciple and his wife. For more information on this tradition, see A. at Tadili, *at-Taschawuf 'ila rijali at-tasawuf*, edited and annotated by A. Toufiq (Rabat, 1984), 218–19; E. Dermenghem, *Le culte des saints dans l'Islam maghrébin* (Paris: Gallimard, 1972), 62; Ahmad at Tadili as sawma'i, "Kitab al mo'aza fi manqib abi ya'za'," trans. Ben Cheneb, *Revue Africaine*, 1908, 11–114; Victorien Loubignac, "Un Saint Berbère: Moulry Bou 'Azza. Histoire et Légende," *Hesperis*, fascicule unique (1944), 15–34.

Chapter Four

1. In French, *chefferie et technocratie*. It is not easy to define technocracy, a competency (attributed to bodies of technicians) in the management of resources and people (themselves conceived as resources). Technocrats are agents who run teams of technicians; G. Brun, *Technocrates et technocraties en France, 1914–1945* (Paris, 1985, pp. 8–9). Technocrats tend to view their action as being based on "objective" criteria removed from political influence; hence a tendency toward the absolutization of these criteria. Like P. Rabinow, I believe that the technocratic elite, under Lyautey, produced a specific Morocco based on cleavage, difference, hierarchy, and so on; Rabinow, *French Modern Norms and Forms of the Social Environment* (Cambridge: MIT Press, 1989), 15–16, chap. 9. Indeed, Lyautey and his team were pursuing the creation of "social forms" independent from the moral creeds and characters of those who would be invested with the power to manage them (Rabinow, 124). In his book, Rabinow pursues the elaboration of the modernist power-knowledge "coagulation" as it obtained in the colonies and its transfer to the metropole. He clearly states that "responses to pacification are not the object of this book anymore than the

efficacy of the pacification strategies described" (Rabinow, 145). The present chapter is about the response to "pacification." What I call "proliferation of discourse" (and reappropriation) introduces, from the point of view of the response to the "pacifier" and colonization, some doubts about modernity conceived as an all-encompassing and controlling coagulation of power-knowledge.

2. Personal communication with G. S. Colin, 1969. On G. S. Colin and his works, see "Hommage à Georges S. Colin (1893–1977)," *Hesperis Tamuda* 17 (1976–1977): 5–45.

3. The caid's commentary, however, was doubtless not typical. Officers and native chiefs maintained close relationships which often turned into long-lasting friendships. In several conversations with me, General Spillmann and others confirmed this point (Paris, 1970). Spillmann was himself an officer in the Department of Indigenous Affairs and played an important role in what used to be called "the pacification" of the High Atlas—Azilal and Ahansal, then the Pre-Sahara, and especially the Saghro and the Dra Valley. He was named chief officer of the Indigenous Affairs post in Zagora in 1927. See Georges Spillmann, *Les Ait Atta du Sahara et la pacification du Haut Dra* (Rabat: F. Moncho, 1936) and *Souvenirs d'un colonialiste* (Paris: Presses de la Cité, 1968). On the French "officers," see Vincent Monteuil, *Les Officiers* (Paris: Seuil, 1958).

4. *Maʿsūl*, 1:265–66, 5:152f., 159–60. On the Nāṣiriya, see Hammoudi, "Sainteté, pouvoir et société."

5. *Fraction* is a word that French ethnography in North Africa consecrated to designate a tribal segment.

6. On the caids and the marabouts under the protectorate, see Bidwell, *Morocco under Colonial Rule*.

7. On the development of commerce with Europe and its consequences, see Miége, *Le Maroc et l'Europe*, vol. 3, chap. 3, and vol. 4, 374f.; Daniel J. Schroeter, *Merchants of Essaouira: Urban Society and Imperialism in Southwestern Morocco, 1844–1886* (Cambridge: Cambridge University Press, 1988). Commercial development depended on the power of the Moroccan notables. In remote regions of the country, for example, officers were treated like hosts and somewhat removed from the world of business; see D. Rivet, *Lyautey et l'institution du Protectorat au Maroc, 1912–1925* (Paris: l'Harmattan, 1988). The topic of the changing historical trajectories of family wealth dispersion is treated by A. Taoufiq in his monograph on the Inultan tribe of the Demnat region; see *Al-mujtamaʿ al-maghribī fi al qarn al-tāsiʿ ʿashar, Inultan, 1850–1912* (Casablanca, 1980), vol. 2, chaps. 11, 12, 18. Numerous families benefited from the modernization of the state at the end of the nineteenth century and under the protectorate regime, insofar as they were able to consolidate their symbolic and material wealth and to hold onto both through successive generations—the Nāṣiriyine, the Cherqawa, the Tamesloht, and the Ouezzane. Among the

notables' and tribal chiefs' lineages which benefited were the Glaoui, the Goundafi, the Mtougui, and the Ayadi, as well as others in the Gharb and Ghaouia regions and in the east. On the Tamesloht, Glaoui, and Goundafi lineages, see Paul Pascon, *Le Haouz de Marrakech* (Rabat: Tanger, 1977), 1:293f.; Montagne, *Les Berbères et le makhzen*, pt. 2, bk. 3, 393f. On the Cherqawa, see D. F. Eickelman, *Moroccan Islam*; A. Boukari, *Al Zawiya al Charqawiya, zawiyat abi-al Jaʿd*. (Dar al-Bida: Maṭbaʿat al Najaḥ, 1984), 2:63f. and pt. 5. On the Ouezzane, see H. El Boudrari, "Quand les saints font les villes," *Annales E.S.C.* 3 (May/June 1985): 489–508. On the course and shape of such transformations in eastern Morocco, see Seddon, *Moroccan Peasants*.

8. Berque, *Le Maghreb entre deux guerres*, 43f. and pt. 3, chap. 2; Pascon, *Le Haouz de Marrakech*, 2:446; J. Le Coz, *Le Rharb, Fellahs et Colons* (Rabat, 1964), 1:440 and pt. 2, chaps. 3, 4.

9. Rivet, *Lyautey et l'institution du Protectorat*.

10. On the birth of the *bidonville*, see Berque, *Le Maghreb entre deux guerres*, 45.

11. A. Adam, *Casablanca* (Paris: C.N.R.S., 1972).

12. *Ad-dar* connotes "house" in English; distinct from *duwiriya*, a diminutive derived from the same root, but one that implies more than just a reduction in size.

13. Berque, *Le Maghreb entre deux guerres*, pt. 1, chap. 1, esp. 142, 143; Rivet, *Lyautey et l'institution du Protectorat*.

14. Berque, *Le Maghreb entre deux guerres*, 43–44; Pascon, *Le Haouz de Marrakech*, vol. 1, pts. 2, 3. At the end of the protectorate, the unequal distribution of agricultural land continued along much the same course, leaving colonists and wealthy Moroccan landowners with the best land. See especially P. Pascon, N. Bouderbala, and M. Chraibi, *La question agraire au Maroc*, Bulletin economique et social du Maroc, no. speciale 2 (Rabat, 1976), and no. speciale 1 (Rabat, 1974).

15. Bidwell, *Morocco under Colonial Rule*.

16. A number of caids and other politico-religious authorities joined independence movements—Bekkai, Mansouri, ʿAyadi, and Liyoussi, among others.

17. Although not many in number, what few mixed marriages there were proved to be highly visible.

18. There was, for example, tension between Glaoui and Captain Spillmann over the mines in the Ouarzazate region. According to Spillmann, who was appointed chief officer in Zagora in 1927, the Glaoui was trying to control the mining industry in the region (interview with General Spillmann, Paris, 1970).

19. A sizable number of Jews took French citizenship or lived in the *ville nouvelle*. However, the majority of the Jews, like the Muslims, remained attached to their traditional way of life.

20. Such was the case in Turkey and Iran.

21. Villes et tribus du Maroc was the name of a famous collection of

monographs published between 1915 and 1932 by Mission Scientifique du Maroc (Tangiers, 1904, and later in Rabat, until 1920) and the Sociology Section of the Department of Indigenous Affairs; the two institutions merged in 1920. On the Mission Scientifique, see E. Burke III, *La mission scientifique au Maroc*, Bulletin Economique et Social du Maroc, nos. 138–139 (Rabat, 1979), 37–56.

22. In theory, because in the mountains and outside of *le Maroc utile*, a certain fluidity of boundaries and displacements still persists.

23. On Marshall Lyautey and the first phases of the French protectorate, see the penetrating analysis of Rivet, *Lyautey et l'Institution du Protectorat*, vol. 1.

24. E. Said, *Orientalism* (New York: Pantheon, 1979), 42, 273.

25. Said, *Orientalism*, 7 (emphasis in original); see also 243, 273.

26. Said cites and praises these orientalists. He is careful to depart from the deterministic position often associated with the concept of discourse. However, both the reaction of the "orientalized" and the tensions within the colonial discourse remain to be considered.

27. Michel Foucault, *Histoire de la sexualité*, vol. 1, *La volonté du savoir* (Paris: Gallimard, 1976), 123, chap. 4; Foucault, *Surveiller et punir*, chap. 4. For writing theory, J. Derrida, *Of Grammatology* (1967; Baltimore: Johns Hopkins University Press, 1974).

28. L. Justinard, *A Great Berber Chief: The Caid Goundafi* (Casablanca: Librairie Farrere, 1951). *La Rihla du Marabout de Tasaft* (Paris; Geuthner, 1940) is a translation of the eighteenth-century *Rihla al Haj Ibrahim al Zarhuni*. The work on mysticism is the *Al fawa' id al jamma bi-'isnad 'ulum al 'Umma* by al Tamanarti (Chartres, 1953). Justinard also published many other works on the history and ethnography of the Sous region.

29. As used here, *latifs* are prayers recited at mosques in reaction to a misfortune that has befallen the community. The *dahīr* stipulated that Berber customary law be the sole officially implemented law in Berber areas, at the expense of the shari'a. At the same time, it decreed that the high sharifian court would no longer have the authority to hear criminal appeals, and vested criminal appellate authority in a French high court. Such divisions and displacements, needless to say, were made in a country where linguistic and other cultural differences entailed no clear-cut social or political differences. Thus, a tempest of protests throughout Morocco resulted in reaction to the dahir. See K. Brown, *People of Sale* (Manchester: Manchester University Press, 1976), 198–200; Charles-Andre Julien, *Le Maroc face aux imperialisme, 1915–1956* (Paris: Editions Jeune Afrique, 1978), 160–63.

30. Such apparitions are discussed in Brignon et al., *Histoire du Maroc*.

31. Jerome Tharaud and Jean Tharaud, *Marrakech ou les seigneurs de l'Atlas* (Paris, 1918).

32. Justinard, *Great Berber Chief*, 52f., 56.

33. A number of authors have devoted pioneering critical studies to the colonial discourse; see especially Abdallah Laroui, *L'histoire du Maghreb* (Paris: F. Maspero, 1975) and *Les origines sociales et culturelles*. See also A. Khatibi, *Bilan*

de la sociologies au Maroc (Rabat: A.S.H., 1967). On the anthropology of "Berber religion" by colonial authors, see A. Hammoudi, *The Victim and Its Masks* (Paris: Seuil, 1988; Chicago: University of Chicago Press, 1993), chap. 1.

34. Justinard, *Great Berber Chief*, 16.

35. Justinard, *Great Berber Chief*, 24.

36. Justinard, *Great Berber Chief*, 35. On Islamic education and the Nāṣirī brotherhood, see 34, 49; Justinard discusses the knight's life and the character of the warrior on 41–42, 46, 51, 59–60.

37. These were times of (food) rationing, *"Sinin al bun, 'am al bun."* Goods were made available for commercial distribution and sale, with the colonial State fixing quotas.

38. On enframing, see Timothy Mitchell, *Colonizing Egypt* (Berkeley: University of California Press, 1988), chap. 2.

39. Justinard, *Great Berber Chief*, 156.

40. Berque, *Le Maghreb entre deux guerres*, 70f., 85, 379–80, 396f.

41. Rivet, *Lyautey et l'institution du Protectorat*, 1:194–96; on the Al Hiba movement, see 136f. and following. E. Burke III provides the most cogent and detailed analysis of the French imperial action in Morocco that resulted in the Protectorate Treaty (1912) and the prior beginnings of military conquest; on the jihad of Al Hiba, see Burke, *Prelude to Protectorate*, chap. 8.

42. Michel Foucault, *Raymond Roussel* (Paris: Gallimard, 1980).

43. Michel de Certeau, *La culture au pluriel* (Paris: Seuil, 1993), chap. 3. See also M. de Certeau, D. Julia, and J. Revel, "La Beauté du Mort," *Politique Aujourd'hui*, December 1970.

44. Rivet, *Lyautey et l'institution du Protectorat*, vol. 2, pt. 3, chap. 19: "Indigenous" society encircled the colonial apparatus and threatened it; see 1:216, citing Lyautey on the centrality of indigenous society in his own discourse. Among the best-known ethnographic works (one is wont to use the term *investigation* here, since the ethnographer's job was to gather information for the protectorate's needs) are those of E. Michaux-Bellaire, R. Montagne, and E. Laoust. In 1926, Massignon published the account of his survey on trade and craft organizations. See L. Massignon, "Enquête sur les corporations Musulmanes d'artisans et de commerçants au Maroc," *Revue du Monde Musulman* 58 (1924): 140–48. Soon after, in the 1930s, Berque began to publish his innovative works.

45. M. Merleau-Ponty, *Phenomenologie de la perception* (Paris: Gallimard, 1948).

46. Justinard, *Great Berber Chief*, 190–201; Agadir became a prime locus of French military power in 1920, and Taroudant became the seat of an office of the Department of Indigenous Affairs (p. 181). On the acquisition of farmland and water by colonists in other regions, see Pascon, *Le Haouz de Marrakech*, 2:446; Berque, *Le Maghreb entre deux guerres*, 42–45; Le Coz, *Le Rharb*.

47. Lyautey, cited in Pascon, *Le Haouz de Marrakech*, 1:341 and nn. 126, 127. Between 1894 and 1903 Hubert Lyautey served as a young army officer

under Gallieni in the Tonkin, the Gulf of Siam, and briefly Madagascar. In 1903 he was appointed commander in chief in the region south of Oran (Algeria) with headquarters at Ain Sefra. From there he implemented his policy of "pacific penetration," inspired by the so-called Galiéni doctrine: (a) the military occupation of a space, (b) the establishment of a territorial administrative apparatus run by French officers with the help and support of a network of native notables and chiefs, and (c) a relentless effort directed to spreading the colonial government's influence through intimidation, shows of military might, the granting of favors, and the encouragement and protection of commerce (in rural Morocco the souk, or weekly market, became a major focus of colonial presence). Under Lyautey's command French colonial troops crossed the Moroccan borders and occupied the city of Oujda in 1907. Lyautey was appointed the first Resident General in Morocco in 1912, a position he held until 1925. See Rivet, Lyautey et l'institution du Protectorat, chap. 7.

48. The relation, in colonial Morocco and throughout the Maghreb and the Arab world, between domination and the production of knowledge, especially ethnoscientific knowledge, has been investigated in an abundant literature. See Khatibi, Bilan de la sociologies; Laroui, L'histoire de Maghreb; A. Khatibi, "Berque ou la saveur Orientale," Les Temps Modernes 31, no. 359 (1975): 2158–81; M. Sahli, Decoloniser l'histoire (Paris: Maspero, 1965). See also "Le mal de voir," Cahiers Jussieu, no. 2, coll. 10–18 (Paris, 1976); Philippe Lucas and Jean-Claude Vatin, L'Algerie des anthropologues (Paris: Maspero, 1975); Burke, "Image of the Moroccan State," 175, 179; "The First Crisis of Orientalism," in J.-C. Vatin, ed., Connaissances du Maghreb: Sciences sociales et colonisation, conference proceedings (Paris: C.N.R.S., 1984), 213–26. For works whose focus extends beyond North Africa, see A. Abdelmalek, "The End of Orientalism," Diogenes 44 (1963): 103–40; Said, Orientalism. On geography's role in affixing social categories to social spaces, see M. Naciri, "Geographie coloniale: Une science appliquée a la colonisation," in Vatin, Connaissances du Maghreb, 309–43.

49. Mukhtar al-Soussi, "Lamma tala'a 'alayna, al-isti'maru bi nidamihi al-'ajib"; see Ma'sūl, vol. 1, Introduction, p. j.

50. Al-Soussi's investigation began in 1937 after he was kicked out of Marrakech by al-Haj Thami Glaoui and exiled to the Sous; see Berque, Le Maghreb entre deux guerres, 287. His forced sojourn in that region resulted in many works: Min afwahi al-rijali, completed in 1938 and published in 1962 (see 3:141); Tiryāq, which I have already commented on, completed in 1945 and published in 1961 (see p. 237); Ma'sūl, based on an investigation that began in 1937–1938, the draft written in 1941–1942 and the first edition published in 1960–1963 (see 20:270, 285); and numerous others. These are works of an 'alem and militant nationalist opposing attempts to weaken Arabic language and Islamic culture; his was part of a concerted effort by a circle of nationalist ulema with a salafi persuasion.

51. The publication of Mohammed Hassan al Ouazzani's works by the foundation that bears his name is one instance in the diversification of narra-

tives. In addition, other (alternative) accounts are in the making. Still, the debate is not yet entirely open.

52. See Rivet, *Lyautey et l'institution du Protectorat*, 1:194–200, for a discussion of the failure of the political projects of the "great caids" of the Middle Atlas, and the elaboration of a "Berber politic"; see also 1:30 n. 66. And see Brignon et al., *Histoire du Maroc*, 392, for discussions of the reactions to the Berber Dahir and the birth of the nationalist movement.

53. Adam, *Casablanca*; R. Montagne, *Naissance du proletariat marocain: Enquete collective 1948–1950* (Paris: Peyronnet, 1951); Albert Ayache, *Le Maroc: Bilan d'une colonisation* (Paris, 1956); L. Cerych, *Européens et Marocains, 1930–1956: Sociologies d'une decolonisation* (Bruges: College d'Europe, 1964). We see the expression of the same civil society in Fez in the municipal debates and the development of trade unionism and trade and artisanal organizations; See Berque, *Le Maghreb entre deux guerres*, 180–82, 187.

54. *Glass:* the parcel adjacent to the house. Where land ownership was collective, the *glass,* privately owned, was excluded from periodic division.

55. The scene dates to the years immediately following World War II. This shaykh ruled with an iron foot rather than an iron hand, for his foot had been amputated during the war and replaced with a heavy metal prosthesis. Demobilized from the army, he assumed the functions of a shaykh as his father's successor, thus playing a second-generation role in a network of caids, shaykhs, moqaddems, and jãrrays. The man who reported this incident said it took place after the war (*ura lguira dial lalman*).

56. Frantz Fanon, *Wretched of the Earth* (New York: Grove-Weidenfeld, 1988).

57. Justinard, *Great Berber Chief*, preface, 10.

58. M. Foucault et al., *Moi, Pierre Riviere, j'ai égorgé ma mère, ma soeur et mon frère: Un cas de patricide au XIXe siècle* (Paris, 1973).

59. I do not wish to suggest that I take these men as fetishes; rather, my use of "fetish" is intended to designate an extreme form of reification, which like other (minor or major) reifications, remains unacceptable to me.

60. On the concept of habitus, see Pierre Bourdieu, *Outline of a Theory of Practice* (Cambridge: Cambridge University Press, 1977), 78ff.; *Le sens pratique* (Paris: Editions de Minuit, 1980), bk. 1, chap. 3.

61. Allal al-fasi, *Al-naqd al dātī* (Cairo, 1952).

62. Driss Chraibi, *Le passé simple* (Paris: Denoel, 1989).

63. Abdallah Laroui, *La crise des intellectuels arabes* (Paris: Maspero, 1978), 53.

Chapter Five

1. It is well known that some former colonial French civil servants played a role in the establishment of the new Moroccan administration; see Leveau, *Le fellah marocain.*

2. Hermassi, *Etat et société*, 121, 160.

3. C. Geertz, "Holy Man, Strong Man," in *Islam Observed*, 8, 53, 116; Geertz, *Local Knowledge*, 134f.

4. Waterbury, "Coup Manqué," 397–420.

5. Such is the case for the shrine of M'ḥammad Ibn Nāṣir in the Dra and that of Sidi Rahal, fifty kilometers west of Marrakech at the foot of the High Atlas on the right bank of the Oued Rdat. Moulay Ali Chrif (Tafilalt) enjoys special favors as the ancestor who founded the Alawite dynasty.

6. It should be noted that the yearly moussems around Hadi Ben Aissa's shrine in Meknes and Sidi Ali Ben Hamduch's shrine in the Zerhoun, during which ecstasy takes highly dramatized and often violent forms (sacrifice through dismemberment with consumption of the raw flesh, scarification of the heads), are tolerated but tightly controlled. The Aissaoua and Hmadcha are recruited mostly among artisans and poor peasants and the state does not want to identify with the orgiastic scenes of their cults. There is a "refined" branch (*raqiya*) of the Aissaoua made up of Fez and Meknes townsfolk, but it is not the one that draws the large crowds. On the Aissaoua, see René Brunel, *Essai sur la confrèrie religieuse des Aissaoua au Maroc* (Paris: Librairie Oientale P. Gerthner, 1926); on the Hmadcha, Crapanzano, *Hamadsha*, and J. Herber, "Les Hamadcha et les Dghoughyine."

7. Berque, *Le Maghreb entre deux guerres*, 397: "Modernism in the 1930's was headed by young people who belonged to the old families abundantly represented in the hagiological armorial of Morocco. For individuals like 'Allāl al Fāsī, Bel Ḥasan al-Wazzānī, Brāhīm Kittānī, Mekki Nāṣirī, and Rachīd Derqāwī, this change in orientation was experienced in a personal way" (author's translation).

8. M. al Soussi, "Le wali selon la loi" (in Arabic, *Ma'na al-waliy fi al-char'*), a text included in the pamphlet containing al Haj 'Ali's *'Iqd*.

9. Robert Rezette remarks that in cities, while the structure of the party substitutes for that of the brotherhood and the (Muslim) community, it reproduces the same conceptualization of commitment to ideals and of the leader who must direct the party and militants; Rézette, *Les partis politiques*, 249, 316–22.

10. This phenomenon was noted by a journalist in the (Arabic language) weekly *al-Kashkul* (Rabat), 24 April 1991. See the front-page article dealing with the struggle for leadership within the parties.

11. This age-old influence was (briefly) described in the early part of the century by Massignon in "Enquête sur les corporations."

12. A sharp controversy arose in the fifteenth century regarding the need for a master, in a context marked by concerns about the new mystical schools, in particular Ibn Arabi and Ibn Sab'in. On this point, see Ibn Khaldoun, *La voie et la loi ou le maître et le juriste, chifa' al Sā'il li-tahdhit al Masail*, translated and annotated by René Perez (Paris: Sinbad, 1991), Introduction. On the same topic see, for example, M'ḥammad Ibn Nāṣir, *Ajwiba*, lithograph (Fez, n.d.). On

the need for a master in Ibn Ajiba, see Michon, *L'autobiographie,* chap. 9, 71–72, and esp. chap. 13, 91f.; J. L. Michon, *Le soufi marocain Ahmad Ibn Ajiba et son Mi'raj* (Paris: Vrin, 1973), 25, 121. Finally, closer to us, see al Haj 'Ali's *'Iqd* and al Soussi, "Le wali selon la loi."

13. For information on typical breaks, see for instance the biography of M'ḥammad Ibn Nāṣir in Muḥammad al Makki Ibn Nāṣir, *ad-Durar al Murassa'a fī a'yani Dra,* MS (Rabat: BG); A. Hammoudi, "Une zaouia marocaine," *Annales Economies Sociétés Civilisations* (1980): 619f. On Larbi al-Darqāwī's initiation, see his letters in *Lettres d'un maître soufi,* trans. Titus Burckhardt (Milano: Arché, 1978). Other examples of biography can be found in Michon, *L'autobiographie,* and the *Tiryāq.*

14. The violation of ordinary rules in Fez during the sixteenth century is reported by J. Léon L'Africain in *Description de l'Afrique,* trans. Epaulard (Paris: Maissoneuve, 1956), 1:220–24.

15. This current, or "emanation" (*effluve* in French), as Berque calls it, is well known by adepts of present-day brotherhoods, including new ones such as the Boutchichiya. For other periods, see *Tiryāq; 'Iqd;* Berque, *Ulémas, fondateurs, insurgés,* 50 (see also Berque's remarks on saintliness as disorder and violation of ordinary rules); Léon l'Africain, *Description de l'Afrique,* 1:222; A. L. de Prémarre, *Sidi Abd-er-rahman el-Mejdūb* (Paris/Rabat: CNRS/SMER, 1985), 79–81. For the twentieth century, see Crapanzano, *Hamadsha,* 49.

16. This is the famous anecdote about Al Yusi and his master Mhammad ben Nasser. The master consecrates his disciple with this invocation: "You will be the mainspring from which both the East and the West will Drink!" (*ad-Durar*); see also Geertz, *Islam Observed,* 32–37. See Crapanzano, *Hamadsha,* 35, for the swallowing of the master's vomit. For the master's placing of his tongue in his disciple's mouth, see Lings, *Sufi Saint,* 72.

17. Edward, A. Westermarck, *Ritual and Belief in Morocco* (London: Macmillan, 1926), 1:198.

18. Hammoudi, "Aspects de la mobilisation populaire." See also *Ma'sūl,* 16:263–314.

19. Crapanzano, *Hamadsha,* 49, 50–51, 226–29.

20. This relationship within the domain of *'ilm* is discussed in D. Eickelman, *Knowledge and Power: The Education of a Twentieth-Century Notable* (Princeton: Princeton University Press, 1985). Such authority is associated with the emphasis on memorization of a text which has an authoritative quality and is transmitted by the master; on this point see Eickelman, "The Art of Memory: Islamic Education and Its Social Reproduction," *Comparative Studies in Society and History* 20 (1978): 485–516.

21. For a more detailed description and interpretation, see Hammoudi, *The Victim and Its Masks;* for earlier descriptions, see chap. 1.

22. Max Weber, *The Sociology of Religion,* trans. E. Fischoff (Boston: Beacon Press, 1964), 52.

Chapter Six

1. This contradiction and others are the heart of the many changes and radical transformations occurring in Arab societies. Recent works have highlighted these transformations: see, for example, Mounia Bennani-Chraibi, *Soumis et rebelles: Les jeunes au Maroc* (Paris: CNRS, 1994); one of this author's conclusions is that, in spite of everything, young people seem to be still hesitant about what to do to change their current predicament.

2. On this point, see T. Leca, "Clientelisme et patrimonialisme dans le Monde Arabe," *International Political Science Review*, no. 4 (1983), 10.

3. Hisham Sharabi, *Neopatriarchy: A Theory of Distorted Change in Arab Society* (New York: Oxford University Press, 1988), esp. 4-6, 18, 20-21, 63-65, 118-20.

4. The literature on "radical Islam" is enormous. For Egypt see G. Kepel, *Muslim Extremism in Egypt: The Prophet and the Pharaoh* (Berkeley: University of California Press, 1986); on the Islamic threat, see John Esposito, *The Islamic Threat, Myth or Reality?* (New York: Oxford University Press, 1992).

5. P. J. Luizard, "Le soufisme egyptien contemporain," *Egypte-Monde Arabe*, vol. 2 (Cairo: CEDEJ, 1990); on the figure of six million adepts, see 51. This article summarizes the institutionalization within the brotherhoods since the nineteenth century and provides a good description of their current strengths and revival. There is a good bibliography in this issue on the Egyptian brotherhoods, including E. Lane, *An Account of the Manners and Customs of the Modern Egyptians* (London, 1836); Spencer Trimingham, *The Sufi Orders in Islam* (London: Oxford University Press, 1972); M. Gilsenan, *Saint and Sufi in Modern Egypt* (Oxford: Clarendon, 1973). For a detailed study of the reorganization of the Egyptian brotherhoods since the nineteenth century, see Fred de Jong, *Turuq and Turuq-linked Institutions in Nineteenth-Century Egypt* (Leiden: Brill, 1978), and "Les confrèries musulmanes au Machreke arabe," in A. Popovic and G. Veinstein, *Les ordres mystiques dans l'Islam* (Paris: EHESS, 1986), 205-43.

6. Sharabi, *Neopatriarchy*, 41-45, 94.